PRAISE FOR

"*Burning Butch* is a necessary and important memoir. A wonderful addition to underrepresented voices. Honest, insightful and moving."

—Angie Cruz, author of *Dominicana*

"This book snuck into my heart like a song I'd never heard but always wanted to, and now I can't stop humming it. *Burning Butch* is an urgent reminder that in any community where people read the same stories, sing the same songs, and pray the same prayers, there are stunning souls buzzing with contradiction, pain, beauty and desire, voices which create gorgeous polyphony rather than discord. With generosity and disarming honesty, R/B Mertz has written a book to help all of us survive being alive, being alive, being alive."

—Will Arbery, author of the Pulitzer Prize-finalist *Heroes of the Fourth Turning*

"This is a tale of resilience and hope penned by a writer whose singular artistic voice is like no other. *Burning Butch* is an account of a life lived bravely, honestly, and above all else, proudly."

—Alex Espinoza, author of *Cruising: An Intimate History of a Radical Pastime*

"*Burning Butch* by R/B Mertz howls against the dogged mouth of the past as much as illuminates the present, evoking the legendary Leslie Feinberg and their struggle for selfhood in the classic memoir, *Stone Butch Blues*. Mertz's extraordinary and stunning debut memoir extends and deepens the tradition begun by Feinberg for 'butch' life, butch recognition, gender non-conformity, and queerness by writing the catastrophic and world-shattering repressions that radical Christianity can inflict on children, adults, and communities. In this gorgeously written, powerful and moving literary accomplishment, Mertz reminds us of the sheer miracle that any of us queer kids are alive. *Burning Butch* is sure to be a new classic. It will lead us into a brighter future."

—Dawn Lundy Martin, author of *Good Stock Strange Blood* and Director of the Center for African American Poetry and Poetics, University of Pittsburgh

BURNING BUTCH

a memoir

R/B MERTZ

The Unnamed Press
Los Angeles, CA

"God is in the details."

—Stephen Sondheim

Overture/Disclaimer

In an effort to tell the truth and protect the privacy of everyone whose stories intertwined with mine, I made a genuine effort to obscure identifying traits without altering the narrative. If I was going to lie, I would've gotten laid a lot more.

For the big kids & the little kids

& for Mom & for Bob

I found that life was beautiful

only because I found that your life was beautiful.

—Francesco (1991)

Love. It's a new style. On the other hand,

our old ways were once new.

—Fiddler on the Roof (1971)

BURNING BUTCH

1 Hurricane

2019. I sit on the table at the front of the room, waiting for my new students to arrive for our first eight o'clock class. It's fall, they're first-year students, and it's Monday at 8:00 A.M. I'll be their first college professor. The first thing they'll notice about me is my clothes, my hair, my gender—they've gotten into a semi-exclusive Catholic college, and they aren't expecting to find a queer in charge of them, at least not such a loud one. They won't know how to categorize me, and it'll scare them.

"Are you the teacher?" a student asks me, entering the room, looking a little excited. She has long blonde hair.

My mom always said my hair was strawberry-blonde, but as I get older it gets more auburn, like it's settled solidly in between two poles. Most of my head is shaved—queer right out of the proverbial gate, like a proud anti-Samson, giving God's power right back to him. There was a time I couldn't have imagined looking like this, when I was afraid to even cut my hair above my chin, when I had to imagine being stranded on a deserted island like the girl in *The Swiss Family Robinson* to be allowed to cut my hair as short as I wanted, *like a boy*.

Since I'm getting better and better at being broke, I'm as thin as I get, even muscly in some places, with a little feminist belly. I'm wearing tight jeans, a bright blue button-down shirt with a tie and a vest, and black nail polish on one hand, the one without LOVE tattooed across the knuckles. I look far less traditional than any of my students, but they'll never look conservative to me if they're not wearing t-shirts with the Virgin Mary on the front, tucked into long cotton prairie skirts, like the girls I grew up with. In a shirt like this one, with the sleeves rolled all the way up, they can see the tattoos on each of my biceps: an unfinished Howard Finster angel on my left, and the circle drawing from *Hedwig and the Angry Inch* on my right.

"Yeah," I say, chuckling, "I'm the teacher."

Those words ring a little in my ears, because to me, teachers were always special people, like actors or priests, up there performing one-person shows for everyone. Sometimes with music. I always had crushes on them, from kindergarten onward. I remember kicking my feet under the dining room table, chattering on and on about Ms. Souder; Mom looked at me like she was amused and scared at the same time, and I could tell she wasn't saying something that she was thinking. "What?" I'd asked. "Nothing," she'd said.

The twenty-two freshmen assembled before me look more or less the same. Almost everyone's skin is the same beige color, their hair the same shades of light brown and blonde. Nearly all the girls have long, straightened hair, and all the boys have short hair, even for boys. All but two or three are wearing something that says the name of their school across the front, in navy blue or blood red.

When I was their age, I had long hair, too. I remember not understanding how to choose clothing and not feeling good in any of it. I was the oldest of seven kids and paid for everything with student loans. I didn't have enough spending money for a hoodie that bore the name of my college or even a t-shirt, but I remember wishing I could have one, wishing I could look just like everyone else. Still, no matter what clothes I wore, I never seemed to look like them. For years, I only shopped in the girls' section, then the juniors' section, then the women's section, like I was supposed to.

I write my name on the board: *Mertz*. My bad dad's name, the name I didn't share with my mother, since she'd remarried and become a Tuttle. Every situation that required us to produce identification resulted in confusion because we had different last names. Was I really hers, or was I his? As soon as I'd started teaching, the summer after grad school, my students started calling me "Mertz" and nothing else, intuiting that the "Ms.," "Miss," and "Mrs." they'd relied on thus far wouldn't work for me—nor was I a "Dr." or a "Professor" or even, technically, an "Instructor." Eventually, I accepted what I had resisted for most of my childhood: I was just Mertz. Most people had been resisting the girl name I was born with since I was a kid, opting for the last name that had that satisfying *tz* sound at the end, not to mention recalling Fred and Ethel from *I Love Lucy*. But they were dead now, and so was my dad, not even in reruns anymore, because there are no reruns. Now it was my name. Now it meant me.

"Are you the teacher?" another one asks, baffled, as she enters late. I confirm it again. They'd all been told they were going to a conservative school, and there I was, one of their first professors I'm *like* a professor, the same way I'm *like* a girl, *like* a boy, *like* a Mertz, and not one at all, like daughter to my stepdad, like a parent to my siblings, like a sister to my mom, like a lover to so many women who didn't want to admit it, like, like, like—

"Adjunct" means "a thing added to something else as a supplementary rather than an essential part," and for a while now, I've realized I've always been *adjunct*—half daughter, half sibling, half boy, half girl, half Catholic, half Protestant, half Democrat, half Republican, half young, half old, half Mom, half Dad, split down the middle. My students will notice that my clothes aren't as nice as theirs, that I can't stay organized, that I lose track of things, that I'm not good at keeping deadlines, and that I smoke too many cigarettes. Most of the adjuncts I know are writers, many of them poets like me—one foot in the world and one foot out of it, teaching like airline pilots, because we love to fly, not because it'll get us anywhere.

"They don't say 'she's the most organized' in my evaluations," I always say on the first day, before I ask them to go around the room and say their names and their favorite things.

"Our favorite things, like *The Sound of Music*?" one girl, Blythe, asks enthusiastically.

"Oh, I love that movie!" another says, and several agree.

"You like musicals?" I ask them suspiciously, not really believing it.

A chorus of "Oh, yes!" floods the room. Not everyone is talking, but the vocal majority are enthusiastically swapping which musicals are their favorites and what they've seen or haven't, and I wonder what it would be like to be young, among them.

PTSD whispers to me every day that all the things that happened before will happen again, but my students remind me that I don't know everything. I'm not stuck in that old loop—I'm not a movie; I'm a live show, and I'm distracted by memories of my freshman year of college, and how different the whole world was, and how it was the same, too, like flicking a light switch on and off in a room over and over again. I'm supposed to teach them about the significance, the power, of stories, but mine is still confusing to me. I ask them absentmindedly if they have any questions for me.

"Where did you go to college?" one of them asks me.

I tell them.

"Wait," says one girl, Emily, who has a CHOOSE LIFE patch on her backpack. "Isn't that a religious school?"

I nod. I wait for a few seconds, to see if anyone will ask the obvious question. I straighten the tie beneath my vest so I can do something with my hands. But Emily doesn't ask the question I thought she would.

"Weren't you sad there?" she asks.

"Yeah!" I say, and I laugh, a little because it's awkward and a little because, thinking about being there, I could never have imagined surviving at a Catholic school completely out, never mind teaching there.

"How did you... you know... get... like you are?" a girl named Adrianna asks, knowing what she is asking but not how to ask it.

"A lot of therapy," I joke, and don't joke. "But really, go to therapy while you're in college and it's free! You'll save yourself a lot of time and money later!" I hoped the counselors here were better than the ones at my school, and knew they had to be.

One girl, Maddy, looks at me with her mouth dropped open a little.

"What?" I ask, forgetting for a second that we are teacher and student and just reacting to someone staring at me with her mouth wide open.

"Nothing," she says quickly. "But, really... My friend goes there. How did you get out of there? Did you always know you were...*L-G-B-T*?" She said the letters carefully, sure to get it right.

I laugh a little nervously now. Is this one of those times when I should say that that's too personal a question to answer? Or is this a time when I'm being overly sensitive about boundaries? There's that old man–shaped craw in the back of my throat, stuck between me and the truth about myself.

"I've always been this way, but I didn't always look this way," I say. "But that doesn't matter. Some people realize things about themselves early, others later; others shift from one way of being to another—the important thing, I think, is knowing that you can and that the world won't end." I laugh. "At least not because of that..."

They laugh, but they still want more answers.

"Look," I say. "Part of how I learned to be myself was reading and writing. And I think you'll know what I mean if I can give you my little 'First Day of Class' speech."

It's about Frederick Douglass and how, during slavery, it was illegal for enslaved people to learn to read or write—for one thing, enslaved people needed a pass to be off the plantation, so if they could write, they could make their own pass, and that's exactly how the Underground Railroad worked. People wrote their way into freedom, literally, literarily. Douglass taught himself to read and write, and his autobiography is one of the few testaments of what American slavery was like, written by someone who endured it. When people like Douglass went around giving speeches about their experiences of slavery, it *changed people's minds*. To the point that people went to war over what had become the grotesque backbone of their country's economy. People also went to war, I remind them, to defend richer white men's right to own Black people, mainly because they identified with that rich man because he was white—they could see themselves coming into this good fortune of owning people someday, too, so they signed up to die and sent their children to die for it, too, this possibility of conquering. But what could not be defeated even by the power of all those white American dreams was the voices of Black people like Douglass who had survived, like Douglass, the unbelievable. Douglass made people believe.

This is just one of countless examples, I tell them, of how writing can change the world, even writing from regular people like them and me. I remind them that Douglass wasn't writing a book about how he'd walked on the moon or won fifty medals at the Olympics; his book was about something that happened to millions of other people, too. His enslavement and even his daring escape were not singular; they were experiences that generations of people had lived through for hundreds of years, risking their lives to see their children, to be with their lovers, to end the torture of themselves and others, to escape toward the words they'd heard about other places that were different. Douglass was writing about something that was considered, especially by those not experiencing it, something "normal."

Then my fifty minutes are up, and I say goodbye to them, not knowing which ones will drop my class, never to return, and which will become familiar faces, maybe over years.

After class, Andrea, the girl with the long blonde hair, comes up to me and throws herself on the table at the head of the classroom, like she's swooning or falling.

"I'm a lesbian!" Andrea exclaims, followed by a deep sigh. She laughs, and I laugh.

"Congratulations!" I say, not sure if this is the first time she's said it out loud or not. I glance around at the back of the classroom, but no one's there yet for the next class.

"Sorry, is that too personal?" she asks, but continues before I can respond: "I just feel like it's so *straight* here, you know what I mean? I just, like, had to say it out loud. Sometimes I just feel like I'm surrounded by people who don't know *anything*, you know what I mean?"

I laugh a little nervously. This is the kind of conversation I imagine would be safer in an office, if I had one, and yet, I think of all the abuses committed behind closed doors, and I think there might be a benefit to having even personal conversations out in the open. Andrea doesn't seem self-conscious at all.

"Sorry, is that too personal?" she asks again.

"No, no," I say. "I mean, I can imagine it's hard here—it's a little conservative, right? Are many other students out?"

"Some are," she says, "but not as many as when I was in high school. In high school, we had an LGBT Alliance, and all my high school friends and I came out in, like, ninth grade. But we all went to different colleges."

"How'd you end up here?" I ask as we exit the classroom and she continues to follow me down the hall.

"Great music program, far enough away from home but not too far, cool campus..."

I thought about Bennington for a second, like a girl I couldn't forget.

"There's an LGBT Alliance here, too, isn't there?" I ask, embarrassed that I don't know more.

"Oh yeah," she says. "They're cool. There's not that many people in it, but it's good that they exist."

"You know what that means, right?"

She wrinkles her nose. "Are you gonna tell me to go to gay club?"

"Absolutely," I said, imitating an old man voice. "In my day, we had to walk barefoot to gay club, twenty miles, uphill, in the snow!" She laughed. "And when we got there, it wasn't really gay club, they just prayed over us." She laughed again. "I mean, I can't tell you what to do," I said, "but I think it would've made a difference to me, in college, to have had a queer community. Nothing's better than people who know what you're talking about when you're talking. It kinda makes up for the people who look at you like you're crazy."

"That's true." Andrea nodded, smiling big. "Thanks, Mertz! It's really nice, you know, just having an LGBT teacher up there. See you next week!"

As I leave the building where I teach, I put on my headphones and press "play" on Mama Cass's "Make Your Own Kind of Music." I don't care how corny it is. Once I'm off campus, and I'm nobody's teacher, I roll a cigarette and inhale the familiar smoke like a sacrament; I know I'll have to give up this ritual, but I'm still too attached to it. It was there for me when nothing else was, when God had left, and I was burning, and I couldn't pretend that I wasn't. I walk quickly, till I have to stop at a red crosswalk light. People in all kinds of clothes are walking by fast, talking in different accents and languages and codes, happy and angry and excited; silent people walk by, too, mysteriously turning their corners. Sometimes I get moved by everyone on the street, carrying their years, their loves, their aches; it mystifies me, the things we can all carry around with us, and how invisible or not they are to everyone else. There are days I'm still shocked to be alive, to have this life at all. The light turns green.

PART 1
KILL YOUR DARLINGS

When they reached the place God had told him about,
Abraham built an altar there and arranged the wood
on it. He bound his son Isaac and laid him on the altar,
on top of the wood.

—Genesis 22:9

2 Tradition

1986-1987. Mom was determined to get the dress on me. The more she struggled, the more the dress resisted me, and the more I screamed my resistance to the dress. It wasn't too small, and the opening at the neck wasn't too tight for my head to fit through. The neck was unzipped enough. I was too young to put my pain into words. It wasn't the dress that I objected to, not then, not yet. It was the pin hidden in the dress, the weapon my mother didn't even know was there.

She knelt on my bedroom floor beside me, while Dad stood in the doorway, looking down on us. Mom had gone the day before to the only place in town to get a dress for a little girl in the rural, one-video-store Pennsylvania town Dad refused to leave. Here, they still used pins to attach price tags to clothes. I don't remember what the dress looked like, just the piercing, persistent stab of the sharp stick-pin into my cheek.

Dresses were for making women accessible; women were for making babies; mothers were for putting dresses on their little girls; pins were for putting little, imperceptible holes in things; fathers were for making wounds, poking and interfering and saying you didn't know anything. I could never tell what Mom knew or didn't know.

Dad said something that sounded mean. Mom had an MA in economics, but one thing she didn't know yet was that there were men who could love her without saying things like that. The pin was twisting farther and farther into my cheek, and Mom couldn't tell that the harder she pushed, the deeper she was hurting me. She just wanted to get me ready for church without my dad berating her. Finally, I just stopped breathing.

I'd screamed so hard that I fainted. A few eerie seconds passed slowly, Mom yanked the dress away and was confronted with my red face, cemented in a wail, the pin sticking out of my bloody cheek. I awoke to her shaking me. As I gasped and whimpered, Mom pulled me close, squeezing me so tight I thought I might stop breathing again, and I beat my fist against her shoulder as I tried to bury my face into her. She wrapped her hand around my clenched fist, brought it to her mouth, and kissed it. From her arms I looked up and saw my dad peering down at us, shaking his head. His voice got mean, and I felt Mom's hand move to cover my ear.

A year or so later, I'm three, and he isn't even happy with us in paradise. In the Cayman Islands, where my grandparents had a beach house, I played happily in the sand while my parents fought in the air-conditioned background. My fifty-something grandmother, covered in tanning oil, with her floral bathing suit top undone so she wouldn't get any tan lines, told me not to listen to them.

"Build your little castle, my precious thing," she said to me.

I studied the structure I had made thus far, dissatisfied with myself, but determined to make something that looked like the image of a castle I had in my head. I glanced up at the house, where I could see a silhouette of my parents arguing. I looked down at what I'd built and threw up in the moat.

For the rest of the trip, I lay on the living room couch with a fever, vomiting into a bathroom trash can in front of the TV. The only "kids' movie" at the local video store was *Oliver!*, a Dickensian 1960s musical that mesmerized me with songs and dances and little boys who ran around London without any parents.

Dad refused to wear sunscreen and turned bright red. The skin on his face and shoulders was peeling off. He lay across from me on the other couch, grumbling about why anyone would ever come to a place like this.

"You just watch your movie and don't worry," Nanny said, putting a cold cloth on my head.

Mom was smoking a cigarette on the porch, pacing and talking to my grandfather, her father. Dad watched on grumpily, glowering alternately at my mother and then at the TV. He said something about how no one sang and danced in real life.

The kids on the screen were twirling umbrellas around a pretty lady, singing a song about how they loved her, and what love meant, and how they'd do anything for her. "Anything?" she kept asking them. "Yes," they said, "anything, anything."

Within the year, Mom packed up her car in Pennsylvania and brought me to Maryland. For a while we stayed in my grandparents' big brick house on the farm where Mom grew up, just outside of Washington, D.C., but far enough south in Maryland that the only things we could see from their house were trees and a two-lane road that could take you everywhere else. There Mom and I met Bob, who'd been invited to Christmas by my mom's brother because he was new in town and needed somewhere to go. While my dad watched football and ignored me, Bob read to me and talked to my mom. A few months later, under a big greening oak tree, he asked Mom to marry him, and then they both asked me if it would be alright. Nanny and Papa sectioned off a piece of the farm, and Mom and Bob built a house and started having babies. Bob never said mean things.

After that, I had to go back to Dad's little town by myself. He and Mom would meet in Breezewood and exchange me over the state line like a package. Sometimes Dad was late to pick me up by hours, and we'd sit in the car and wait and wait, and that was when I learned that you could die in a car and that you could forget about your kid. Dad never died, but I spent a good number of hours wondering if he had, only to find out that no, he had just forgotten to leave, forgotten to call, forgotten to remember me. Dad's face was a collage made of running shoes, records, Diet Pepsi, glass jars, and golf clubs. People said he was handsome and that we looked alike. People also said we were all made in God's image, but you could never actually see God, so what did that mean?

Buckled into Dad's car, I could hear Mom's car start to pull away, and it was as if part of my body were driving away, too. I remember the moment of being situated in my father's car, screaming for her. He snarled back at me that this was his time—why didn't I want to be with him? I was bad, he said.

My attire in those days was varied, trending in a masculine direction. I had a long pirate phase, which was good because lady pirates just dressed like boy pirates, so I wasn't necessarily cross-dressing unless you thought about it a little bit. "What are you wearing?" he inevitably asked.

"I'm a pirate," I snapped back. I could feel Mom smiling from afar at my statement. But I could feel his annoyance, his self-consciousness of his pirate daughter, wearing her big hat with a feather in it and a plastic hook over her hand, as we walked into the Breezewood McDonald's.

"There weren't any girl pirates," he said.

"Yes, there were," I corrected him, and he didn't like this.

"Well, none of them had hooks," he snapped.

He had me there. I had not read of any female pirates with hooks. I didn't care, though; I was pretending.

"I'm being a boy." I shrugged. I didn't know I'd said anything "wrong," but he was angry now, not just annoyed.

"Stop that!" he said, tugging the hand he was holding too hard, so my elbow hurt. We were at the register, the woman behind the counter waiting for our order.

"Stop what?" I asked, confused. I felt tears welling up in my eyes, now that everyone was looking at us.

"You want to be a boy? Boys don't cry."

My dad would repeat this throughout my life, every time I cried. After a while, he didn't have to say it anymore; he'd just smirk at me, making that same point over and over again.

When I was old enough to sit in the front seat on the drive home, he would keep his hand on my thigh for the whole four-hour trip, and if I said anything that he didn't like, he'd squeeze his big hand around my leg tight enough to cut off my circulation. When he liked what I was saying, he'd caress my leg and tell me how much he loved me, how great I was. If I said or did anything he really didn't like, he'd just stop talking to me or tell me I was bad.

That's when I learned how to perform, in his company: how to make the outside of me so different from the inside; that sometimes it was better to say nothing, and that sometimes you had to outright lie to keep your blood flowing.

3 You're Never Fully Dressed Without A Smile

1992. A ballet recital generally constituted a horrible day for everyone involved. The parking lot of the dance hall was filled with kids in sticky, shiny costumes that poked and jabbed in random places and frantic parents running around holding tutus and lipstick, and flowers. When I had a dance recital, Dad drove to Maryland to see it, and we'd drive back for the first two weeks of the summer. I'd hold my breath for a few days, knowing they'd all be in the same room, and then I'd be alone with him, in a blank space I could never piece together. I tried not to think about him and tried not to rip my costume.

Mom kissed me on the forehead, and I walked to the basement of the building, where I was supposed to sit with my dance class until it was our turn to perform. I loved dancing, but I hated getting dressed up in girl clothes. I glanced ruefully at the two boys in the school, who got to wear tuxedos and got treated with kid gloves so they wouldn't quit and leave the school with no boys at all. I kept saying I could be a boy, I could play a boy, I could look just like a boy—but people reacted like I was saying I could be a bird or a unicorn, with a hearty laugh, or a nervous side glance, or a mix of the two.

My class of eight- to ten-year-old girls was sitting in a circle on the concrete basement floor, stretching and talking, as I approached.

"Rebecca!" Chrissy exclaimed. "You've got makeup on and *everything*! I can't believe you're wearing a skirt! How does it feel?"

Our dance teacher walked by and squeezed me on the shoulder encouragingly. "You clean up good, Mertz," she said, smiling sympathetically with me but not at me. She was like a boy, too.

When she walked away, Chrissy looked right at me and said to everyone else, "Miss Jane is a *lesbian*." The other girls giggled, and some looked away shyly.

"What's a lesbian?" I asked.

"You are," Chrissy said, and I could tell by the way she said it that she was certain and that it was bad.

Still, at that moment I was more nervous about going out there in front of everyone and being a girl than I was about being a lesbian. I thought about Miss Jane and all the ways we were alike, and I felt like I knew what a lesbian was and I probably was one. I just wished I could dance in pants or without a tutu. In boy clothes, I felt like there was some possibility of people seeing me, but the girlier the clothes were, the more I became something else. Wearing frilly pink tule or sequined lace-up bodices up there in front of everyone felt about as wrong as if I'd been wearing a costume of genitals.

I focused on practicing the part of the routine that always threw me off, and Miss Kelly, another dance teacher, came over to see if I was okay.

"I have to go to my dad's today," I admitted. "I don't want to."

My hands were raised above my head, and I was trying to make them look like they were supposed to, like they were graceful.

"You've got to relax," Miss Kelly said, taking my hands in hers and standing right there in front of me. She was one of the teenagers who helped with our class, and she was always nice to me. She shook my hands a little and said, "Wow, you really don't want to go to your dad's, huh?"

"Yeah," I managed to say, because I knew better than to say anything else and because I couldn't think about that now. She was holding my hands, and her face was very close to mine.

"You've got to shake it out, okay? Can you shake for me?"

I shook out my arms and legs, and she smiled and said I still needed to relax. She put her hands on my hips, then my shoulders, and I straightened my back and felt all the muscles in my body get hard and alert.

"You're tense all over," she said. "Maybe it's more in your personality."

"I think so," I said, and she laughed again in a way that made me feel like it was okay to be whatever I was. I had no idea what she meant by "relax."

Moments later we were out on the stage together, poised and controlled and delicate looking. My mind locked into performance mode, and I forgot everything except my body and what I was supposed to do with it. I could see the shape of my dad in the audience, in the shadows, clapping proudly when we were done, and I stood there grinning, looking like I knew he wanted me to look.

On the wall of Mom and Bob's house in Maryland, there was a picture of me at nine or ten, wearing a purple ballet costume, a backwards baseball cap, and red Converse high-tops. I posed with my arms spread out wide and a big grin on my face. I was headed into a ballet recital, just before I quit ballet. At first people thought it was funny that I was wearing those sneakers with my ballet outfit, but as I got older, people thought it was funny that I was wearing a tutu, that I had done ballet at all.

In the car, I wore my t-shirt and bulky Bermuda shorts, my red high-tops, and my baseball hat, backwards. Dad let me roll the window down, and we listened to music loud, and he put his hand on my thigh, squeezed my leg, and told me how much he loved me. After a few hours of getting up my nerve, I decided to go ahead and ask what I'd been wondering all day.

"Dad, what's a lesbian?" I asked, and he immediately let go of my leg like it was on fire. I regretted it right away, wishing I'd had time to ask Mom first, wishing there was some way to find things out besides asking people. He frowned angrily, not knowing what to say.

"Where did you hear that word?"

I told him about Chrissy, except the part where she called me a lesbian. He frowned some more.

"A lesbian," he said reluctantly, "is a woman who spends time with other women instead of spending time with a man. Like, instead of marrying a man, she marries a woman."

"Can you do that?" I asked. The chipper child-hopefulness in my voice betrayed me without even telling me.

"No!" he said in that way that bruised me with no mark. "It's disgusting! And it's a sin! God says it's a sin in the Bible! Why would you hear that word? You'd never hear something like that at home, people just don't talk like that. You'll see when you're older how much better it is in a small town. You don't have to worry about things like lesbians or ballet recitals."

My throat burned with all the things I couldn't say, things I wanted to ask and didn't want to know his answers for. I missed Mom and wished she could be there when I went to bed that night.

"Do lesbians go to Hell?" I asked.

"Yes," he said. No hesitation now. "Weren't you listening to what I just said?"

He put his hand high up on my thigh, and when I tried to move my leg away, he squeezed hard, his big fingers telling me not to try moving again. It felt like he'd hit me, even though nothing hurt. I looked out the window and thought about Mom, and how she'd told me to listen to him and be good. Did she know what that meant?

I thought about Miss Kelly, too, and how she'd laughed at what I'd said, like I'd said something smart, but how Dad was always telling me I didn't know anything.

"What do you think Hell is like?" I asked.

"I guess everybody's burning or on fire or something," he said. "Everybody's hurting all the time."

"Mom says if God loves us, why would he send us to Hell? He's like a dad."

"You think God loves murderers and thieves and really bad people?" He smirked, like Mom and I were stupid.

I thought about this. "Yeah," I said. "Wouldn't you love me even if I was bad?"

"No," he said, "I love you because you're good. You're my good girl"—he smirked again—"except when you don't listen to me."

"Would you send me to Hell?" I asked.

"Well, yeah," he said, "if you were bad. That's what God would do. That's what the Bible says. That's why we have to be good."

"How do you know what's good?" I asked, a little afraid that admitting I didn't know would reveal that I was bad.

"God tells you, in the Bible," he said. "You gotta be good, 'cause you don't wanna end up in Hell and hurt all the time."

He said this like it was funny, and he pressed his fingers hard into me like that would make his words stick. It did. I thought he knew what good was, whatever he was doing. I didn't have words for everything he did to me yet. He moved his hand briefly from my leg to turn up the radio, and someone I didn't know and couldn't see was singing exactly what I needed to hear, about how there must be some way out of here. I closed my eyes, listened, and let my mind go far away.

I still didn't understand the point of Hell. My dad was already hurting me all the time. Even when he wasn't there,

I felt him like a bruise. I resolved then and there I was going to do whatever I had to do to get to that place where it didn't hurt anymore.

4 Ya Got Trouble

1997. "Obedience to the Church is where we find freedom,"
Mr. Bernard was saying across the dinner table to the other
parents. I was watching the little kids in the next room, listening to the grown-ups in the book club talk. "This life is
full of chaos, full of confusion. The Church helps us make
sense of all these choices we have, which none of us, as
individuals, could ever come to enough understanding
about to make the right choices."

He continued, impassioned: "Birth control is a total
inversion of God's plan! It's the result of feminism and the
source of all this sexual promiscuity in our culture, all this
unnatural sexual deviance: fornication, cohabitation before
marriage, even homosexuality! People are separating sex
from the creation of life. Now it's just about *pleasure*. I mean,
the liberals want everything to be ecological and natural,
right? What's natural about two men together? Their bodies
aren't meant to do that! Natural food, natural honey, natural
water—what about natural men and women?!"

I was thirteen. I'd heard a great song about being a
natural woman, and I loved the way it sounded so much,
I bought a CD, but I never understood what the words
meant—what was a *natural* woman? But even though I
wasn't sure, I knew somehow that when Aretha Franklin
was singing, she wasn't singing about what Mr. Bernard
was talking about. I thought about the God I'd heard
about, who loved everybody and who made a place where
there was no hurting. I didn't think that God cared so
much about two men or two women loving each other, but
I didn't know how to prove that to Mr. Bernard. He was
talking about Catholicism the way lawyers talked about
the law, citing documents and Scripture and the diaries of

medieval monks. I could only sit there and listen, scared and angry.

Our whole world had become God, saints, and babies. Mom and Bob had always been religious, fluidly Christian, experimenting with different churches every few years—but then they converted to Catholicism, which might've begun solely to legitimize having as many babies as they wanted. Mom got a whole series of books on tape and lectures by someone named Scott Hahn, who was a Presbyterian minister from the same region as my dad, who'd been a prominent sort of wiz-kid Protestant until he'd converted to Catholicism. Now he and his wife had an increasing number of children, whom they homeschooled while he taught at a little Catholic college in Steubenville, which he compared to Jerusalem, a place where God was real and everyone worked together based on acknowledging it. He was a powerful speaker and talked about the Bible and the symbolism and poetry of everything in it. He was doing literary analysis, but I thought it was theology.

Gradually, our nonreligious friends started treating Mom and Bob like they were crazy and sometimes telling them they were. Mom was making new friends, other home-schoolers who didn't think there was anything wrong with wanting so many kids. Soon, it became clear that it wasn't about how many babies anyone *wanted*. The Catholic Church, Jesus's voice on earth, taught that using any kind of artificial contraception was a grave sin. While estimates suggest that over 90 percent of Catholics do use artificial contraception, the homeschooling Catholics we knew were very vocal about how contraception was basically abortion lite (i.e., murderous). Suddenly all our friends were conservative Catholics with tons of kids, who homeschooled and didn't have TVs. They listened to Christian music and only did Christian things. Everybody thought it was more important to have babies than to keep their heads above water. Mom was pregnant most of the time, or nursing, or trying to lose weight from being pregnant, or freaking out about not getting pregnant, or freaking out about being pregnant.

"Colleges and even high schools are giving out birth control now," Mrs. Bernard was saying, while her kids did the dishes, "which is why we homeschool, of course, and why I'll be sending my kids to Franciscan University or Christendom College, where they teach *real* Catholic values."

Mom and Bob nodded thoughtfully. They were never extremists, but the more our lives became about following the Church's teachings on birth control, the more outrageous we seemed to everyone who wasn't involved in our little Catholic homeschooling subculture. Even as a child observing it, the "openness to new life" that the Church demanded was all-encompassing, and exhausting, and against the grain. Sometimes even strangers made comments to Mom, like, "You know, they know what causes that now," as if she were stupid. The homeschoolers insisted that having five or ten children was natural, but everyone's bodies and minds and hearts were extended beyond their capacities. I saw Mom's heart break a thousand times, every time she couldn't give one of us what she knew we needed.

Each time a new baby came, friends and family gathered around to admire the baby, and Mom's eyes filled with a combination of love and fear, and a gathering knowledge of the implausibility of creating so much life. Some days she cried for a long time in the laundry room, and I tried to keep the kids amused until Bob got home.

Bob worked in Virginia, just outside of D.C. and across the river from the Pentagon. There he programmed computers. When I asked about his job, he explained that he worked for people who worked for people who worked for the military, and that he made computers do what they needed to do to keep track of things. Not exciting things, he said, but my brother and I remained convinced he did more important work than he could speak of, that maybe he'd invented the internet. He drove a pink car to go to work with a bunch of military guys who gave him grief about it, but he didn't care. The car had been a good deal and they'd needed it fast.

"Men who care about pink and things like that are just insecure," he told me, as if to tell me not to worry about it, either.

When Bob got home from work, everybody raced out to his car to be the first to give him a hug and tell him what had happened that day. He'd arrive, briefcase in one hand and suit jacket draped over the other arm, with his tie loosened as much as he could in the car on the hour drive home, and as soon as he saw everyone, he'd drop his briefcase, squat, and throw his arms wide so he could embrace the two or three toddlers inevitably racing toward him, scoop them all up, and squeeze. Then he'd stand and give Mom a long kiss to a chorus of "eww!" When I heard parents on TV complain about their kids or spouses, I didn't get the jokes—our parents were besotted with us and each other.

The other homeschooling dads had jobs like Bob's, where they put on suits to go into offices in Washington, D.C., or any of the worldly, secular enclaves surrounding it. There they looked like anyone else; they just had a lot more kids than their coworkers, and, as far as we could tell, they didn't bother to talk about their religion. Their wives, our moms, usually looked older than them, more frazzled, less well dressed, less passable as "normal" people; it was harder to maintain that when your body was at the mercy of pregnancy and life giving.

I knew God was watching, and God wanted me to help Mom and be a good big sister. But in actual practice it seemed that what he wanted us children to do was render our mothers exhausted and pulled in a thousand directions, our mothers who created us. Eventually there were seven kids in my family: Marianne, five years younger than me, then Jimmy, Lily, Beatrice, Todd, and Evangeline. When we surpassed four children, then five, people on the street began offering visible reactions. Impressed. Concerned. Awestruck. Disgusted. Outraged. This bonded us all, the kids of big families. The homeschoolers always seemed happy at first, telling stories about how they converted to conservative Catholicism and how they were so full of joy ever since they really started believing. Then later, sometimes the moms would begin standing apart at the playground, whispering and maybe crying.

Jesus just had to die for us on the cross, but our mothers' personalities died for us in laundry rooms, kitchens, delivery rooms, backyards, stairwells, driveways, long after we kids had fallen asleep. Eventually Mom's eyes started to look different, more still than they used to be. Her face, and everything else about her, got harder and harder to recognize. She and the other homeschooling mothers were carving molds out of their own bodies, right in front of our eyes, that they hoped we'd fit into, too. It felt good to be who they wanted me to be instead of trying to be myself. Day after day, I slipped further into their sameness.

My two closest friends in high school were Theresa and Angie Bernard, the oldest two of an ever-increasing number of Bernard siblings. The mothers who had borne eight or more children, and especially those who had surpassed ten, like Mrs. Bernard, were like celebrity saints in our homeschooling world. "You've made so many souls for Heaven!" priests would say to Mrs. Bernard. "Your reward will be mighty!" I wasn't sure if Mom would be punished if I didn't get into Heaven. The homeschoolers talked a lot about the unnatural homosexuals and how they were trying to destroy families, and I bit my lips and nails absently until they bled.

Theresa and Angie's mom grinned a little like a zombie, flat and colorless. I never saw her without deep circles under her eyes. She, too, was continually pregnant or nursing, always with two or three forlorn toddlers following her around, asking for more than she had. The Bernards' house was always messy, bleary, and desperate. The kids were sticky and frantic for attention, mostly unsupervised or supervising each other. Angie and Theresa were usually put in charge while their father worked and their mother prayed. They hardly ever did any schoolwork, though they read constantly.

Mrs. Bernard and her children regularly prayed outside the abortion clinic in Annapolis. Their aunt was close friends with one of the men who, in the '90s, shot an abortion doctor to save the unborn.

"I don't know," Angie said when we talked about it. "But I guess he did God's work, if he really did it... My aunt said the FBI framed him."

The Bernard children's world consisted mainly of the insides of churches and the outsides of abortion clinics. Praying outside the clinic was considered important, appropriate spiritual work that the children could perform. Feminism had created an army of baby killers, Angie and Theresa told me, and it was our responsibility to stop them, with our prayers, our work, our bodies—what could be more important than protecting and saving children?

When Mrs. Bernard realized that my mom wasn't exactly on her page about shooting abortion doctors or even praying outside the clinics, she shook her head. Later, she patted me on the shoulder and told me that some kids were closer to God than their parents, that some kids could see the truth when their parents couldn't, and it was up to us to lead the way. Sometimes I didn't tell Mom everything that they'd said, because I knew she'd think it was crazy, and I didn't want to stop being allowed to go over. Angie and Theresa were strange, but that was part of what I loved about being friends with them. Mrs. Bernard told me that it was okay not to tell my mom everything, since she had so much to do and since she was so spiritually behind and all. The Bernards made spirituality and spiritual warfare urgent and mysterious, like we were in *Star Wars*, fighting the Empire. Mrs. Bernard smiled gratefully as I bounced her baby.

No one's mothers had enough time for them, and everyone's mothers needed help from the older kids to keep the younger kids fed, clothed, and somewhat organized. A lot of the older sisters weren't sure if we were mothers, too, or what we were. The important thing wasn't who we were but that we did what we were supposed to do, and our worlds were so busy—there were always so many needs to meet—that there was hardly time for much reflection.

By the time homeschoolers were young teenagers, we policed ourselves and each other. Watching or reading anything "questionable" was a shameful thing to do. During Bill Clinton's impeachment, most of my friends had no issue with being banned from reading the newspaper or watching the nightly news, under the pretext of maintaining sexual innocence.

Mom and I watched his testimony live on TV, and she made me leave the room for some parts. I didn't have context for any of it, but Mom was mad.

"I want you to read the newspaper," Mom said firmly. "But maybe not today," she added, the day they published the president's testimony.

Late at night on the family computer, I tried to figure out what a "blow job" was and how on earth the president's DNA could end up on someone's dress. I knew I didn't want to ask my mom because of the way everyone talked about it when it did come up.

"What do you expect?" the homeschoolers would say. "That's what happens when you don't have a strong Christian marriage, you support abortion, you support gays—"

"I don't care about his politics," Mom would say. "That girl was an intern. He shouldn't have been sleeping with an intern."

But all the artists and the movie stars and the feminists seemed to be saying it was okay that he did it, that it was none of our business. I didn't know anyone my age who didn't already think he was a baby killer. From our sheltered point of view, the world was jam-packed with people who were either being duped or were so deranged that they were on a conspiratorial mission to defeat God and to fill the world with evil and death. Right now we were safe, but we had to prepare ourselves for our inevitable futures among them. If *we* couldn't resist temptation, who would?

5 There's No Business Like Show Business

1999. The commercial kept intoning that same phrase, "*Annie Get Your Gun*, starring Bernadette Peters!" I didn't know what the show was about, but every time I saw Bernadette Peters's face I thought back to *Annie*, the kids' movie musical featuring those fifteen minutes or so of Bernadette's blonde curls and bared cleavage. Now she was a redhead in a cowboy outfit with guns in both hands. Her gaze jostled my memories of other times, before I learned to lie about what I wanted.

The commercial played over and over again, and before bed, I knelt down onto the stiff carpet and folded my hands like I'd read about the saints doing. I felt the hard concrete under the thin green sheet of Home Depot carpeting Bob had let me pick out for my room in the basement.

Please, God, I began, night after night and whenever I remembered during the day. *Please get me to that theater — please, please, God.*

I made promises, bargained, begged, until the words disappeared and there was nothing but what I wanted, and my heart beating with clarity of all the ways it could happen. The floor was so hard, I started losing feeling in my knees after a few minutes, but I knew God loved that kind of thing. The saints were always miserable, and Jesus saved the world by getting slowly executed, so maybe if my knees burned hard enough, it was okay that I wasn't praying for world peace or a solution to all the complexities of the universe—just for myself to get into the same theater as one star, once; just to see what the light was like in real life, if the light was real, if celebrities and TV were real. Praying for what I wanted meant I had a lot of practice putting it into words.

I had just turned fifteen, and Mom had just given birth to Todd—a tiny baby compared to how big the rest of us had been coming out—with a smile that already lit up the room. By then I was an expert at changing diapers and making three sets of waffles at a time for the big kids' breakfast while mom nursed the baby. I knew how to make a baby stop crying, the certain way to hold them tight and bounce them in what Bob called "the baby bounce." Every time I thought of asking to go to *Annie Get Your Gun*, I remembered how much there was to do all the time, how theater tickets were expensive. I hated asking for things that Mom couldn't provide due to things beyond her control. The more of us there were, the more impossible it became for her to give us everything we needed, much less the things we wanted, but something inside me kept insisting like the voice in the commercial, that I had to at least ask. I waited till all the kids were asleep.

"Mom," I said, "Do you think there's any way I could go to *Annie Get Your Gun* at the Kennedy Center? I know it's expensive, and maybe I could do some extra chores or something? Or maybe it could be my Christmas present or something?"

"How are you going to do *more* chores?" She laughed. Then she thought about it enough to know she couldn't do it.

"Why don't you ask Nanny to take you?" Mom said finally, with a generous smile that masked what might've been a feeling of missing out on something. I got that pang—whenever I was with someone, I wasn't with someone else.

"Bernadette Peters?" Nanny exclaimed when I asked her the next day. "From *The Jerk*? Oh yes, absolutely."

"What's *The Jerk*?" I asked.

"No way you're watching that," Mom said, but I didn't mind, because Nanny was calling for the tickets. Then I started praying again, praying that nothing would go wrong, praying as an answer to each anxiety. I was sure that Bernadette Peters would get sick, or a snowstorm would hit, or I'd get in trouble by saying exactly the worst thing at the worst time and I wouldn't be allowed to go. I dug my knees into the floor and I promised to be good, and I was good, and even in my imagination I tried to be good, to not think about Bernadette's body or eyes or hair.

I didn't even care that I had to dress up; I'd do anything and I wasn't quite sure why. Nanny took me to the mall, to the juniors' section. Everything seemed like miniature versions of the sexy things teenagers wore on TV. Nanny helped me find dress pants and a shirt that fit both our standards. When the day finally came, I prayed the whole forty-five-minute drive to D.C., as my grandfather cursed the traffic, and my grandmother checked her watch, and I tried not to choke on the smell of her hairspray and perfume.

"This is so nice, isn't it, darlin'?" She smiled into the visor mirror, applying her hot-pink lipstick. I nodded, preoccupied with my prayers. I prayed until the curtain opened, until she walked out onto the stage and the audience cheered; she was real, and we were all clapping and whooping for her realness. For two hours, my eyes clung to the stage, swept up in the music like it was waves washing over me in the surf. I knew I was exactly where I was supposed to be and that I had put myself there by praying, which meant that praying worked and praying was real.

At the end of the show, the lights went out all at once before they came on again, and the actors all stood together in a line that said it was over, that it had all been made up. That they had made it. Everybody cheered and the actors bowed, and people were laughing and crying. My palms hurt from clapping so hard, and I realized at the same time that I was in love with Bernadette Peters, that God was real, and that I was in real trouble.

6 Every Day A Little Death

1999. God and Jesus were watching me all the time, they said. Before I knew what reality was, back when Santa Claus and the Tooth Fairy were all roughly the same, God and Jesus were two among many characters viewing my actions from afar, like my own audience in a theater. When we became Catholic, this extended to the Blessed Virgin Mary and all the saints, who could, like an army of real Santa Clauses, ride a cosmic Mardi Gras float in circles around the globe, flinging out spiritual favors like bright plastic beads.

Catholicism was a musical; there were sets and props and costumes and songs and mysteries, and a beautiful androgynous man, who died because he broke the rules, and it turned out breaking the rules was the right thing to do. When they killed him, he came back to life, just like characters onstage do, to sing another song, to say one last thing, before the story concluded in his glorious ascension to Heaven, like a middle finger raised slowly and dramatically against all the ones who'd said he was no good. I liked it.

My dad hated Catholicism—mainly, he often proclaimed, because the Catholic Church didn't let non-Catholics receive Communion. For some reason, this particularly irked him, though he was the one who argued that Jewish people couldn't get into Heaven—a much more unwelcoming idea, I thought, than the Catholic policy on Communion. He also thought that all priests were gay and "abused little boys." I wasn't sure if he considered it abuse because it was done by Catholics or because it was done to boys. His self-righteous hatred of the Church made me love clinging to it.

In church, real people sang in real life, and somehow everyone knew what words to say, whether you were in Maryland, Pennsylvania, the Cayman Islands, or anywhere.

I liked the idea that wherever I was, the same God was watching me, and God always had the same rules. Dad might smack me for saying something like "that sucks," which was frowned upon but never met with violence at my mom's house. The slap hurt more because I never knew it was coming. It was only after the hand or cruel word hit me that I suddenly realized I'd said or done something bad.

When I was at my dad's, movies and TV were my refuge. They were the same no matter where you went, and movie stars and singers dotted the covers of the same magazines in Dad's little town as they did in Maryland, even though most of the food and people and clothes and ideas were worlds apart. I loved movie magazines, cutting out pictures of movie stars and taping them up in my bedroom to any surface flat enough.

"Don't tape any of that crap to my walls," my dad said, reminding me that his house wasn't my house.

Mom frowned and rolled her eyes when I got into Madonna because I'd seen *Evita* ("It's musical theater," I argued). But she didn't question me much. I spent hours on our bulky off-white desktop computer, surfing the internet, reading interviews with Madonna, printing out pictures of Madonna and pasting them all over the big white closet in my bedroom. Mom hardly had time to come in there anyway, or to police my reading or watching. Madonna cracked open the eggshell of my universe.

"She's stupid," my dad said authoritatively when I told him what I was listening to. Something burned under my skin, in my cheeks. I swallowed it.

Lying on my bed in my room, alone, I could look over and see my two closet doors covered in fuzzy, pixilated photos of all the different Madonnas: Young Madonna of the Early '80s, Hip Ballet Madonna, Hairspray Madonna, Blonde Bombshell Madonna, Pointy-Bra Madonna, Dominatrix Madonna, Madonna the Wife, Madonna the Whore, Baseball-Playing Madonna, Besuited Madonna, Madonna the Mother, holding up her hand painted in henna just the way Mary, Jesus's Madonna, held up her hand in all those paintings of her around the world, wearing different clothes and going by different names, yet somehow all the same, many beings in one person, one name.

Looking into those countless sets of Madonna eyes, staring back from my closet doors, I thought about where she was and what she was doing, since she could do whatever she wanted. Could she see me, too, like Mary and all the saints? I thought about what my life would look like to someone like her and if she could remember back to when her life was as ordinary as mine supposedly was. Nothing felt ordinary infused with God and the saints; it wasn't the fact of *them*, it was more about what was possible in the universe, a technology of being able to be anywhere you wanted whenever you wanted, and see everything, and hear a little kid in Maryland asking for what they wanted—and that someone was listening to the asking.

I couldn't quite tell the difference between Heaven and the places where celebrities lived, but I knew that whether it was Madonna or the Virgin Mary, people were capable of profound, wholly unpredictable transformations.

One evening I found myself at a gathering of a group of women who were coming through town to spread the word about their school for young girls. We met them in a side room of an old church, dimly lit through a must of haggard yellow lamps.

"Our friend Elizabeth goes to the school. It's in Rhode Island," Angie told me. "So we haven't seen her in a long time, because you can hardly ever come home. And you can't talk on the phone or anything. And if you write letters, they read them."

The visitors from Rhode Island were called "the consecrated women" because their lives were dedicated to Jesus, but they weren't nuns because their order was new, so it hadn't been fully approved by the Church yet. Two women led the meeting and a third sat by quietly, demure and silent.

Everyone sat on the floor. The women wore long skirts, cardigans, and brown penny loafers, and they sat like they were at the feet of Jesus in a painting. They spoke softly and evenly, like they were deeply considering each word as it formed inside their heads. Like everyone in our world, they were white, as if there were nothing else to be. Like all the conservatives I knew, they looked back (but not *too* far back) to a "less confusing" time, like the fifties, "when men were men and women were women," and those of us who weren't just disappeared. When they were finished telling us about their boarding school, they asked if anyone had questions, and I raised my hand.

"Do you have to wear skirts all the time?" I asked. That had always been a deal-breaker for me.

The consecrated woman caressed her skirt, smiled eerily, and said, "Well, we are married to Jesus. And I believe that a woman should dress to look beautiful for her husband, to please him. I just know that Jesus loves it when I wear skirts."

"How do you know he likes skirts?" I asked. She looked into my eyes, and I smiled, challenging her, because I had already had this argument a million times, and there was nothing in the Bible about skirts.

"Oh, I just know," the woman said, nodding and smiling patronizingly. She and the two other women exchanged knowing smiles and one even giggled.

"Now, we're going to do some crafts!" the leader said, signaling our exchange was over. "Here are some blank bumper stickers, and everyone can decorate one to support Pope John Paul II's message of the culture of life! You can write something about ending abortion, or preventing same-sex unions, or—"

"Ending war?" I asked. Angie and Theresa smiled at each other and looked at me.

"Yes," the consecrated woman said, her smile turning annoyed. "Yes, war, of course."

I started drawing thin blue lines across a blank bumper sticker, trying to think of what culture-of-life-affirming slogan to write on it. One girl wrote, STOP YOUTH IN ASIA! and held hers up to receive praise.

One of the women laughed. "Oh! Do you mean 'euthanasia'?" She explained the distinction, then said, "But I like this point! Most of the youth in Asia are not Christian, so this could also be saying that not being Christian is like killing yourself, which is basically true, since by not being Christian you're sentencing yourself to eternal damnation, right? And all over the world, 'youth' are the ones who are really at risk in the culture of death, so it's like our youth are 'enasia,' do you know what I mean?"

She grinned proudly. Everyone said they did.

Alone in my room at night, praying, I didn't ask to be changed, exactly; it was more like I was asking God to change his mind and let me know he'd changed his mind. I thought about another world, another life, where I didn't worry about what God thought. I saw myself on the other side of a screen, looking like a boy, playing the piano, singing about women, dancing like Bob Fosse dancers in the videos that Mom let me rent, even though she knew the other homeschooling moms wouldn't approve.

Mom and I would watch *Les Misérables* in concert, on a crackling VHS tape we'd made when the show aired on PBS. We watched it over and over, and every time the disappointed woman with yellow hair would sing the song about dreams never working out, about how men were all tigers and thieves, I'd hope she was wrong. But the song always made Mom cry.

According to the Church, people can persuade us to sin, like the snake in God's first garden. Whether you think the snake is Satan or just a misguided liberal, it doesn't change the fact that the snake wants you to betray God, and the snake wanting you to do something has some effect on you, and being near the snake makes it more likely you'll do what the snake does. It doesn't matter why you do it, or if you're mistaken, or if you have good intentions—ask Eve.

Still, it was without much hesitation that the homeschoolers had let me into their circle even though my family was new and different: I'd been to public school, and not only was my mother divorced and remarried, she had worked—all of which was known to have ruined people. Maybe that's why there always seemed to be something wrong in the back of my head—I was already tainted. But at least I had some friends who were willing to overlook it.

Everyone I knew before we were religious had fallen away; we were too weird to them now, and they were too wrong for us. The homeschoolers were my world, the part of my childhood that stuck. We were making a montage together, and it was the only one we were ever going to make, against a soundtrack of music nobody listens to anymore: learning to play songs on the piano; figuring out how to talk to girls and boys, how to talk to anyone, and when not to talk; standing in the sunset of a Friday afternoon, in a field, picking blackberries, and nothing will ever taste like them. We can't see anything except grass, trees, sky, and each other. We can't feel anything but the breeze. Somewhere in the distance is the sound of other children playing on the other side of something we can't see. We have no idea what happens past the end of the driveway, what really happens in the places we've only seen on TV, or never seen.

We can't really see anything.

Angie and I were buddies, but Theresa and I were something else. I had to turn my face away from her so no one would notice she made me smile for no reason, or how I watched her mouth move, or how I couldn't stop looking at her. The funny thing was that Theresa smiled back. Angie said we had a secret language. We were something with an unnamable thing in it.

Sometimes Theresa and Angie would sleep over, and all three of us slept in my bed. Once when Theresa slept in the middle, I woke up with her in my arms, and her arm wrapped around me, her face just centimeters away from mine. For a few seconds, I didn't know what to do. We hadn't done it on purpose, but we were in a lovers' shape. Her hair was tangled in her face, and the sound of her breathing was like a big wind through trees, inside headphones. I closed my eyes and tried to memorize the way it felt to have my hand where it was, in her dark hair, behind her head. I moved it slowly away, and we both opened our eyes at the same time. Theresa smiled and then looked worried. She never slept in the middle again. A few months later, she said she'd decided to go to the boarding school in Rhode Island and become a consecrated woman. After that, I stayed in my room whenever I could, and listened to sad songs, and wrote sad poems. Angie and I became better friends and started talking on the phone more, about how we hated that school and knew Theresa would realize how horrible it was and come back soon. She never came back.

At a cookout one evening, one of the homeschooling moms asked me about Rosie O'Donnell, whose show I watched every day, on the little TV Mom had for watching the news.

"You know," said the mom, "I heard that she's G-A-Y... Have you heard that?" She had to whisper and spell out the word, as though she didn't even want anyone to hear her saying it. I looked over at my mom's friend Mrs. Carver, who was one of the less extreme homeschooling moms— somehow, mysteriously, she had only two kids. She smiled knowingly at me, brushing a piece of hair behind her ear. She was the prettiest mom, but I never let myself think about it for too long.

I watched Jimmy and Marianne running around the swing set in a jubilant cloud of kids, collected in our backyard for the cookout. Marianne reached out her tiny hand to tag someone, and they both collapsed in the grass in laughter. Maybe the little weed of doubt growing under my heart was just me. All the other homeschooler kids seemed happy all the time, doing the best with what they had.

Mom told me that night that Mrs. Carver was going to start tutoring homeschoolers my age in math, once a week at the public library. Did I want to go?

"I definitely need help in math," I said, trying not to smile thinking about spending extra time with Mrs. Carver. I tried to look like I wasn't looking forward to it.

Angie came, too, and it turned out we were the only ones who could get rides to the library on Thursday afternoon. Mrs. Carver made a comment under her breath about the educational priorities of the homeschoolers.

"Jesus doesn't care if you can do algebra," I said.

Mrs. Carver looked up at me a little astonished. Then she laughed a big, surprised laugh.

"I guess it's because he wants you to give all your money away," I said, and she shook her head. Angie looked at me with a funny expression on her face, too, like she wasn't sure why I was saying things like that. What if we got a lecture?

"Becca," Mrs. Carver said, shaking her head at me a little, "of *course* Jesus cares if you can do algebra. Jesus *loves* algebra."

"I think Jesus *hates* algebra," Angie said passionately, and Mrs. Carver and I both laughed.

Every week I got better and better at math, and more and more distracted by Mrs. Carver, even when I wasn't at the library. Sometimes she'd call the house when Mom was napping or wasn't home, and we'd talk on the phone, on and on, like it was special. She liked musicals, too, and we swapped recommendations, and I learned enough about math to talk to her. I made such an improvement, and stopped complaining about math, that Mom didn't mind driving me to the library every week.

Mrs. Carver told us we might as well look around the library and find something we'd like to check out, since we were coming and going every week. She started giving us ten to fifteen minutes at the end of every lesson to roam around freely. Angie called this "the best part of math." I learned how to find books quickly, so I could talk to Mrs. Carver while everyone else roamed the shelves.

I discovered the drama section, where I could read plays—not just Shakespeare, but the plays that were being written *now*. Every week I checked out new plays and kept my eye out for additions to the library's small collection of musical theater soundtracks. This is how I discovered William Finn and got my hands on every score by Stephen Sondheim. I started writing my own plays and lyrics. Once I learned how the plays worked and how they were supposed to look, I couldn't stop writing, but inevitably I wrote about gay people and had no one to show my work to. Still, I discovered the pleasure of staying up all night, creating new worlds, being bleary the whole next day and not minding it.

Once a week or so the homeschooler teens would go out together to the movies, or walk around the Barnes & Noble or the Borders in the mall or the shopping center in Annapolis, but none of the girls could drive. There was no public transit from the farm. If I wanted to go anywhere, I had to get the homeschooler boys who lived nearby to drive me. Usually, they would only consent to this if we were going to the movies, which meant we had to continually appeal to their taste in films in addition to the moral parameters of everyone's parents—anything with an actual sex scene was out of consideration for sure, while any amount of violence was fine. If the sex scene was in the midst of a historical war movie, that was fine, too. That was the past. But no contemporary sex scenes were allowed.

The boys would drive too fast, stop too fast, and, with a nod of their heads, challenge a stranger to some kind of contest where we'd weave in and out of traffic ten or twenty or thirty miles over the speed limit. They never listened when we asked them to drive slower and laughed when we got scared.

Outside of seeing each other at the movies and events like math at the library, Angie and I wrote letters. I never wrote Theresa, knowing that the consecrated women might read any letter I sent. She was too busy with the convent-like schedule at the school to write anyone besides her family anyway. Angie and I were both lonely for her, and wrote letters to each other. It was the only way to have really private conversation, since our houses were full of little kids we were always taking care of, or trying to find privacy from.

Since I was bursting to tell someone how I felt about Mrs. Carver, I wrote it into a story. Eventually I gathered the courage to tell Angie about the story, in one of our letters. Naturally, it was easier to write this than to say it out loud, just like it was easier to talk about a character myself. In my letter, I explained what this character's struggles might look like and asked Angie if she thought it was wrong to write about a gay character. But I was really asking if she thought it was wrong to be gay. I held my breath waiting for her reply.

When Angie's letter finally came, I went to my room and shut the door. Bob had refinished the basement so that everyone over ten could have their own room, just for moments like this. I tore open the letter, hoping for a miracle, hoping Angie would say she didn't think it was that big of a deal to be gay, what's the fuss? Maybe she knew some obscure theological thing that I didn't know, maybe it wasn't as bad as I thought. My heart beat fast, and I skimmed the first paragraphs of the letter looking for the right combination of words.

It was "interesting," Angie noted, that I was writing about such a thing. Homosexuality was a "sad disorder" affecting people who were confused about how to be "real men and women." She suggested that the character realize that her attraction to the same sex was pubescent admiration, wanting to be like the person versus being in love with them. She also suggested that I could have a foil, a character who was "disordered, in the physical sense instead of the psychological sense." She said that, if you thought about it, it was better for someone to have a terminal illness than to be cursed with homosexuality, because at least a terminal illness only ended your mortal life and didn't hurt your soul.

When I ripped up the letter, I could still see most of that word, "disorder," staring up at me from one of the tiny fragments of torn stationery scattered on the floor. Suddenly, Mrs. Carver and the character she inspired were like something I was choking on, something I wanted to swallow and couldn't.

Every year, there was an opportunity to get out in the streets in the nation's capital, just twenty-six miles from our farm and worlds away. There we and countless others like us came together to protest for what we believed in—Life. Mom said she "wasn't much for marches," so I went with Angie and her family, who always rented a hotel room in D.C. to retreat to after the march, where we'd eat pizza and guzzle cans of Sprite, starving and thirsty and exhausted. The March for Life often fell on Dr. King's day and, like most of the events of my youth, included no African Americans; the only Black people I ever encountered in this crowd were visiting nuns and priests from Africa.

"Blacks don't get abortions," Angie's aunt told me once. "That's why they're not here."

Something rubbed me the wrong way, the way she said "Blacks," even though what she was saying about Black people should've been a compliment, coming from her. Shouldn't low rates of abortion in Black communities be a sign that Black people had some wisdom that white people didn't have? I felt something chip away at my trust in Angie's aunt, like when I found out that she hadn't condemned the man who shot the abortion doctor. Some part of a wall started to go up inside me, like a brick of my own understanding that said something around me was amiss. Something tensed in the back of my neck, trying to figure out what to say, trying to point out the obvious flaw with the statement that any color of people did anything the same. What would that mean for white people? I choked on this thought, trying to get all of it in my head at the same time and failing. I tried to formulate a question, but Angie's aunt had started bellowing out the Rosary. Angie handed me a rosary (she and her sisters always carried them, and I never did) and I followed along, saying what her aunt wanted me to say and forgetting what I'd been trying to ask about.

The march itself was a strange combination of all kinds of conservative people, a little like a family reunion, but with something apart from blood in common. The pro-life speakers talked about how precious life was, thanked us for "standing up for life," and reminded us that only the Republican Party really cared about the unborn babies, so we all had to remember to vote.

The people from Operation Rescue, one of the more extreme anti-abortion groups who have been accused of advocating violence against abortion doctors, held up big, graphic signs of aborted fetuses. Shouldn't I have wondered why they weren't holding up signs of children getting molested, or queer kids killing themselves in closets, or the kids dying in all the wars their "pro-life" candidates kept waging, and waging, and waging? No. None of that had even started scratching against the Teflon of my mind, and wouldn't for a while yet.

"I hate those pictures," Angie would say, crinkling her face and looking away from the bloody Operation Rescue posters.

I looked right at them and then across the street at the people protesting us.

Even though I was in a world where pregnancies decided so much, it wasn't clear to me why abortion was such a feminist issue. It didn't seem so hard to me to just not have sex with a man if you didn't want to get pregnant—why else *would* you have sex with a man? Still, I understood that the baby changed everything for the woman and potentially nothing for the man—but my sign said that abortion was murder, and I was carrying it because Angie had handed it to me, because it was the sign I understood.

I liked the feeling of standing up for what I believed in, but across the street there were women holding signs that said they'd had abortions; they didn't look that different from us, though they were more stylish and cooler looking than most of the people on our side of the street. They didn't look like murderers to me. If we were walking down the street at the same time, I wouldn't be afraid. I'd want to ask them what kind of music they listened to.

I looked around me at all these homeschoolers, and normal-looking people, too, and people who looked far more detached from the world than the homeschoolers— people in clothing from all periods of history, with long, complicated signs. One man with a lengthy beard had a body-length placard that explained why women wearing pants was where it had all gone wrong. I looked at Angie and we both laughed, but I knew he was right, too. The men who had been opposed to women wearing pants were scared of all of this, of girls like me growing up reading books and wanting to be things and thinking we had a right to. Was the inevitable endpoint of my liberation abortion? Wasn't that the one thing all the conservatives and the liberals agreed on?

Both sides kept saying "us, us, us," and I was never sure if they meant me or not. Everyone here was talking about women, and I kept waiting to grow up more, to get old enough that I was finally a woman and not a child, when I assumed I'd *feel* like a woman. My period came, my breasts came; I started shaving my legs and armpits and getting little knicks like cracks in my skin where I bled to make myself smoother, for what purposes I did not know.

I started telling people to call me "Becca," as if having a nickname would change something. Only my dad refused. He never got into bed with me anymore, but whenever he hugged me hello or goodbye, he'd wrap his arms around me, find my bra strap, and snap it against my spine, perpetually disappointed—not with me in particular as much as with something much larger than me, something I didn't even know my part in yet.

I kept my Discman and a little CD wallet of showtunes on me everywhere. I could always put on my headphones and let the big voices of theater singers fill my ears. I liked big, rich female voices, like Audra McDonald's. I'd seen her singing "Wheels of a Dream" on *The Rosie O'Donnell Show*. I couldn't get her voice out of my head until I figured out how to get to Tower Records three different times to buy each of her CDs. I wasn't sure how a human body could make a sound so beautiful as her voice inside my headphones, wrapping around me like water, like I could jump into a note she was singing and stay there as long as I wanted. I could turn the volume as high as it would go, and it was like no one could hear her but me. I never stopped being amazed at how vast a human voice could be, how stunning, how thunderous someone could make themselves.

Mom got me the good headphones, the ones that didn't let any sound in or out.

7 Giants in the Sky

2000-2002. I learned how to hide myself in my own world, and I read about other worlds on the internet. Bob bought me a laptop "so you can write wherever you want," he said.

With the laptop, I wrote most of a novel, until a computer glitch deleted it. I kept writing plays and listening to musicals. I committed Sondheim's lyrics to memory the way other kids my age were memorizing the lyrics of Lauryn Hill or Lil Wayne.

Then we got the internet at home. On the internet, I could be a teenager with a less complicated backstory. When I chatted with someone on instant messenger, I was just who I said I was, nothing else; I existed only through my own writing. No flesh, just the word.

I met my internet friends on websites dedicated to musical theater; many people were queer, but no one had faces. I loved a particular website dedicated to Sondheim, but I felt too shy to say anything on the message boards. Sometimes someone would say something the others disagreed with or found offensive—usually a conservative comment—and who knew what might come out of my mouth that was wrong, that I didn't know was wrong? People discussed the meaning of Sondheim songs, debated nuanced plot points, and told stories about various productions and how they interpreted the work. I learned to draw a line between what I could tell my friends on the internet and what I could say to my friends in real life.

On the Sondheim fan page, I met someone I'll call Alfred Hitchcock. The nickname sums up who he was to me: imposing, charming, talented, and larger than life. Since he was a real adult who worked on real movies and real TV and real theater, he was, to me, a Very Big Deal, and he actually was, in certain circles; but most people have never heard of him. Hitchcock worked mostly in theater—musical theater. He produced showtunes. He made them. And sometimes he posted long, hilarious, charming, and brilliant (to my four-teen-year-old mind) posts on the Sondheim message board. Through a little low-key Harriet the Spying, I figured out who he was "in real life." When he posted his AOL email address for something, I decided to send him an instant message. I waited, holding my breath, for him to reply. He did.

Hitchcock admired Nabokov as a writer. He recommend-ed I read *Lolita* (so I did), that I watch *Manhattan* (so I did), and that I watch most of Charlie Chaplin (so I did). Eventually it became part of our banter that he'd ask what kind of underwear I was wearing, but he would've considered this innocent conversation. We talked about *Lolita* a lot. I identified with Humbert Humbert because it had become very clear to me that I, too, was not allowed to want what I wanted—and, truth be told, I was also attracted to teenage girls more often than not. Hitchcock said this was a typical adolescent phase and I shouldn't worry too much about it.

"Teenage girls are the most beautiful creatures," he said. "Who wouldn't love you all?"

It never occurred to me that there was a difference between him and me, that my desire for another girl my age, or even Mrs. Carver, was anything other than perverse because it was homosexual. At least Hitchcock was a man, and whatever happened between us would be heterosexual. In medieval times, men his age married girls my age all the time. It was less weird than being gay, for sure, I thought. And my father had already taught me that there was nothing special about being an adult—it didn't make you smarter or wiser or better. In fact, Hitchcock's humanity toward me surprised me; all the adults I knew were too overwhelmed in their lives to listen to me the way he did, or to talk to me about the ins and outs of a rhyme scheme in a Sondheim lyric.

I'd been keeping secrets my whole life, though I wasn't always sure what they were or who I was keeping them from. My body held them, tight. I vigilantly guarded my siblings, though I was never sure what I was protecting them from exactly. But I watched how other people interacted with them like I was their Secret Service. When I was away at my dad's, I had dreams they were in danger. I'd always been on my own, traveling between two worlds like the kids in literature who'd gone on adventures no one else would believe. Who, on one side of the looking glass, could understand anything on the other side, or how it felt to move between two sides, besides Alice?

Hitchcock swore up and down that he wasn't interested in sex. In fact, he thought sex was gross, and in his fantasies, he claimed, everyone had their underwear on. Maybe that's why he always liked to know what kind of underwear I was wearing, although he always said he preferred plain cotton briefs to any other type of underwear and kissing to any other type of sexual activity. Doesn't it sound so innocent? And it was just online; it wasn't even real. And it's not like he was my first lover.

He was a minor celebrity in the musical theater world I so idolized. And he was my friend. My special friend. He reminded me of Woody Allen; he thought I was smart and funny and, what meant the most to me, a great writer. He was jealous of boys my age, he said, because they could have me in all the ways he couldn't. He said things like this that made his asking about the underwear feel different. He asked if I wanted to kiss him, and I said I did.

My father had never been so nice to me.

Hitchcock wanted to send me things in the mail, but I had promised Mom and Bob long ago that I wouldn't give anyone on the internet my address, especially not a man in his early fifties, needless to say. So I got a PO box that I could check on my way to and from the library. I also wasn't supposed to give anyone on the internet my last name, so I told him to address his correspondence to "Rebecca the Old." Most of the things he claimed he sent never actually arrived, and I never knew if he was really sending them or not. But a book came, which he wrote and inscribed to me, but blandly enough that anyone who saw it wouldn't suspect there was anything special between us. After a while, we laughed about my paranoia. "I'm not going to stalk you," he said. "You know I have too much work to do!"

I knew theater was a small world and a world where who you were friends with mattered, where being friends with someone could make or break you. But somewhere deep down, I also knew Hitchcock would never be able to be that kind of friend to me, a friend in public. Still, I asked. The response was as expected. What if, throughout his fifty-plus-year career in show business, he kept advancing the work of girls a third his age? No, he could not write me a recommendation letter to college—how would we explain how we knew each other? He wasn't even a friend of the family. "What would your mother think of me?" he asked, laughing at my mother a little, I imagined, as she slept, exhausted, upstairs. I hated and loved him for being so beyond her scope of understanding.

With him, I was playing the role of Dolores Haze, the only role available for me in the scenes between a teenage girl and Alfred Hitchcock, talking late into the night together about what kind of underwear they were wearing. He'd talk about romances between adults and "younger people" (I'm not sure what his threshold was) the way pedophile apologists do—as though they are beneficial to the youth, as though, without those adults there to teach them, the youth would never learn about the finer things—the literature of justifications.

Years later I would realize that what appealed to him about me was precisely that I wasn't myself yet, that I could play the role of Who He Wanted so well. He liked that there was so much I didn't know, so much empty space inside me that no one seemed to be paying attention to but him. My dad had lost his enthusiasm for me years before; his new wife had revised his life, like restarting a computer. Now we just performed the father-daughter scenes we were expected to play out, in front of friends and family and each other. I was sure he wasn't getting into bed with his new kids, with his wife there in the house, but more than that, I never imagined he would do anything to anyone besides me— who else had ruined his life so completely just by existing? Who else was such a constant disappointment to him?

Hitchcock was someone I never disappointed. Sometimes I called him "Hum," like Lolita called Humbert in the book. But I wasn't Lolita, I was Humbert, something inside me said. I was a pervert and a writer and an *adult*. She was an adult, too, I decided, because he wasn't mean to her. She was an adult in a child's body, and that's what I was, too. I had read all the love stories and poems, seen the movies, and sung along with every love song: the "I" was usually a boy, singing about a girl. I knew I was the boy, but when people looked at me, they just saw a girl. Everyone kept saying I would grow up into a woman, that childhood's gender was blurry and insignificant.

The songs and the movies made it clear what a girl was supposed to be and what a woman was. I knew how to act like a girl if it meant I got to talk to someone smart who wanted to talk about the same art I wanted to talk about, who would teach me and take it seriously—even if it did give him a special thrill that I was wearing white cotton bikini briefs and a t-shirt and nothing else while we did it. He'd never seen me, never seen how boyishly I held my body; in his mind, I could be a real girl, and maybe somehow that would make me a real girl in real life.

Alfred Hitchcock didn't understand Catholicism, of course. I didn't reveal much to him about my day-to-day life, other than that I was in "high school," which sounded like a completely foreign place, though technically the words "I'm in high school" were true enough. He didn't seem very interested in knowing the details of my life aside from what I looked like, my underwear, my sexuality, and my intellectual formation. He often made comments asking if I'd met any sweaty young boys who appealed to me. Of course, I had not.

He sent me a draft of his memoir and I read about his parents. He knew, like I did, how it felt to need to sit on your floor and listen to a whole musical theater soundtrack as loud as possible, imagining the entire production, just to get out of your own house for a while, even if it was inside your head.

Through the Sondheim website I found out about a weeklong playwriting camp in Manhattan called Young Playwrights, which was founded by Sondheim himself. Of course, Hitchcock couldn't help me get into that, either, but I got in on my own, and my grandparents paid for me to go. For one amazing week, I stayed in the dorms of Pratt Institute and took theater classes, went to plays, and tried to blend in with the other high school–aged students. I felt completely out of place, and I was, but most of the students were forgiving enough. I couldn't make friends with any of the girls, who all seemed to regard me as strange. I liked talking to the guys, who weren't as hung up about gender as the homeschooler boys I knew and who'd also been staying up late to read David Mamet by themselves.

One student made me feel like I wasn't so different: Marshall, who was Jewish and "getting into Orthodoxy," even though he'd grown up Reform. Marshall grinned easily and was the most performative person I had ever met, but his performance was himself. I don't think there was any difference between the inside and the outside of him. He was hilarious and beautiful. Marshall didn't think I was weird for having a religion, even if, as I'd realize later, my religion had tried to destroy his.

One night at dinner in an Italian restaurant in the city, Marshall tried to confront me about the sins of Catholicism, but it turned into an argument about Abraham.

"What kind of god would want anyone to *kill* their child?" he asked, horrified.

I had always been taught that Abraham's willingness to kill his own child was a sign of his devotion, the ultimate act of obedience to God. Marshall was outraged by it.

"No, no, no," he said. "Abraham failed that test! He should've taken care of the child! He was supposed to say no, even to God!"

There was no language for this in my religion. I was stunned out of the conversation, but Marshall just patted me on the back, like we'd played a round of tennis and he'd beaten me, but he liked my technique. I felt alive when we talked about theology and I wanted more. I loved literature and theater so much, but religion was a whole world of stories that people had been arguing about for thousands of years. It was literature, but true—or at least people acted like it was.

I tried to tell Hitchcock about it, but he hated religion and religious topics, except for *The Apple Tree*, he said, "because Barbara Harris is perfect." I felt sorry for him and a little jealous, too, that he didn't worry about his place in the cosmos. When I tried to explain why it mattered, he dismissed me. What mattered to me didn't matter to him; he liked me as a blank slate, not one with writing on it— especially not religious writing.

Hitchcock never touched me, could never touch me, because I never met him in person. In fact, I even resisted his attempts to talk on the phone, not wanting to have to respond to him "live." Still, we graduated to occasional sexual conversations and "underwear reports," as he called my descriptions of such garments and sometimes how my body felt underneath. This was exciting, but I didn't know why, exactly, and it all felt like acting in a play. There was pleasure, but it was unpredictable, never something I could count on. As far as I knew, sex was something that swept people up in a moment, particularly male people, and that in that upsweep, sexual expression was inevitable and went either beautifully, like a movie with a great score, or some degree of less than beautiful, from awkward to deadly. Rape involved the woman screaming and crying and everything happening through violence, with lots of physical scars that showed how criminal it had all been. Hitchcock and I only talked. If it was online, it was more or less unreal, and if it wasn't physical, it definitely wasn't sexual.

When I tried to tell Hitchcock about being attracted to girls, he said something belittling about "dykes" that made it clear that they were objects of pity and ridicule in his world, much as they were in mine. But Hitchcock made me feel like straightness had claimed me. If I were to become gay now, that meant that whatever had gone on between me and Hitchcock, or me and my dad, had been destructive and had made me an angry lesbian. It would be like a relapse into something that was a sign of a wound. I was learning how to erase myself. More than anything, I wanted to be good. I wasn't even sure why anymore.

At some point, my cousin Brad visited us for the weekend. He was only five years older than me, in his earliest twenties versus Hitchcock's early fifties. Brad's mom was Bob's most religious sister, and his family was ostentatiously Catholic but not conservative; Brad argued with me that women should be priests, and I argued the Church's position, that maybe God was working through this teaching somehow in a way that we didn't understand yet. Given that he came from Bob's side of the family, he was technically my step-cousin, which he emphasized in the letter he wrote me after his first visit. He liked arguing about Catholicism. He was real. He wrote me a letter and it got to me. He began showing up in my real life suddenly, attending extended family gatherings that he'd seldom attended previously.

Meanwhile, Hitchcock started getting harder and harder to pin down, and so did I. He faded into black, and I left the movie theater, walked back into my real life. I knew I belonged as much in one world as in the other and that neither world seemed to know what to do with me. The best part of me, I knew, was the part that was both, my heart beating as I held out both my arms as wide as I could so that each hand could touch the edge of the two poles I was always being pulled between. But how could I write like that? How could I live? I had to choose eventually.

Hitchcock sent CDs, a few that he had made, and I got a new CD player that let me play the same song over and over again if I held down two buttons at the exact same time and pressed another button right when the song started. I couldn't stop listening to the show tune sung by two women, one a middle-aged, veteran wife and the other a virgin, just married, and how they both felt the same way about men and love and how it was all just death in the end. I didn't know what it meant or how it could be true—how could women keep falling in love with men if they were all really so terrible? I loved the version of the song Hitchcock had made and how the women's voices sounded. There was a depth, a texture, to their voices that I knew could only be achieved by years of training, years of being able to raise your voice like that, in front of other people, doing it over and over until you got good at it. I could barely get myself to sing along in my room when I knew no one was home.

I read about the colleges my favorite writers had attended and made lists of little liberal arts schools in or in close proximity to New York City. Most of the homeschoolers I knew had to choose between Christendom College, in Virginia, and Franciscan University of Steubenville, in Ohio—schools where Catholic doctrine trumped intellectual rigor and liberal educational ideals. I was determined not to go to a religious school, and Mom said it was my decision.

I was certain that I wanted to go to a school in New York, or at least New England, and study theater. I got into Bennington College with a respectable financial aid package partly based on a play I sent them. They sent me a t-shirt and Vermont maple syrup, and someone called to tell me how impressed she was with the play. Everyone was proud of me for getting into such a good school, and as the spring turned into summer, everywhere I went turned into a going-away party.

One day just before I graduated high school, Mom grinned at me in the weird way she did whenever she had to tell us something we wouldn't want to hear. I braced myself. Evangeline looked up at me from the back seat and grinned, her three teeth gleaming, too little to understand the different ways of grinning and the things that could hide behind a smile.

"I have to tell you something," Mom said. "I just talked to Mrs. Carver today..."

My heart sped up. Had my crush been found out? I imagined Mrs. Carver calling, outraged and insulted, disgusted and violated, after somehow discovering my feelings.

"Sooooo," Mom said, leaning into the steering wheel like she didn't want to say what she was about to say, "Mrs. Carver told me that she had a friend who went to Bennington, and she said it's got a reputation as a lesbian school."

There was a pregnant moment of silence, more pregnant than my mother had ever been with a child. I felt my heart explode up into my throat. I couldn't move, and I let my fingers sink into the windowsill of the car, trying to pretend I wasn't gripping it like I was about to fall right down through the floor and into Hell where I belonged. My every instinct worked together to hide what was happening inside me: I knew how to do this, I knew how to keep secrets, I just had to play my role.

"Oh," I said, frowning. "Like, a lot of lesbians go there? What does that mean, 'lesbian school'?"

"I don't know," Mom said hurriedly. "And I don't think it means you shouldn't go there! I just... she told me, so I thought I should tell you, so you'd have all the information... I support you wherever you want to go, you know that," she added. "I mean, Slippery Rock, where I went... it was known as a gay school and there were a lot of lesbians there. You know how I walked in on my roommate that time. But it was just a little weird—it's not like they're gonna do anything to you. It just might be different than you're used to, that's all. And I wanted you to be fully informed! But who knows, she could be wrong! I mean, Mrs. Carver doesn't know everything, right?"

I wasn't sure if I was more heartbroken that I had to have this conversation at all or that it had been started by Mrs. Carver. Was she warning me against going to a lesbian school? Did that mean she knew what I was? And did that mean I *was* what I was? If I went there, would everyone know? Would they be able to tell? Would I explode? A chorus of confident male voices—Hitchcock, and Marshall, and Brad—was no help; just as I began to think differently, things became more and more limited.

Eventually Hitchcock had just faded away into the internet, into the infinite sea of things that happened when I was just surviving as a teenager. Years later I would ask if he remembered me, because I met him when I still couldn't remember huge swaths of my childhood and my brain was still developing, and I wasn't sure if possibly I had made it all up. "Mertz," he replied when I messaged him after all those years, "how could I forget one such as you?"

But I had been trained, cultivated, to forget myself.

Later that week, Mom and I went to a talk at the church by Scott Hahn, the dynamic theologian whose tapes had led us to the Church. He talked about how the Old Testament looked forward to Jesus, and how when Jesus quoted a line of the Old Testament, each line referred to whole passages, and how it all fit together so beautifully to tell this story of the world being redeemed, the resurrection of the dead, and the mystery of love and the unknowable.

A week later, I found out that Franciscan University of Steubenville, where Scott Hahn taught, had rolling admissions. This meant I could still apply for my freshman year, and I did. They accepted me before even receiving my application essay or my transcripts. I called Bennington, told them I wouldn't be able to make it.

When I called Franciscan to figure out the finances, a person on the telephone connected me to a woman who explained the loans available to me. There wasn't any financial aid, but she told me that private and public student loans were basically the same. She reminded me that a Christian education was priceless and how all the churches wanted to hire graduates from Franciscan. Student loans made sense, kind of like Heaven. If you worked hard enough, if you were *good*, you could translate the debt, and the years it would take to pay it back, into an idealistic after-loan-life, a retirement heaven.

After we figured out the paperwork, Mom looked at me, a little nervous.

"Now you just have to tell your dad," she said.

I went to Mom and Bob's room, where there was a phone that could be used privately. Their room was at the back of the house and always felt like a quiet, peaceful, orderly place compared to everywhere else. Closing their bedroom door created a cool, quiet place, where the strongest air conditioner and the lock on the door made certain no one else could interfere or overhear. The phone cord stretched across the big bedroom, where Mom kept her treasures. Here there were little figurines on delicate shelves, precious objects from my mom's life arranged atop dressers that I was only just tall enough to see the top of. I had gotten in trouble when I was little for trying to examine the contents of every drawer, which was how I'd discovered the lie of the Tooth Fairy, when I'd discovered a jewelry drawer of our old, tiny teeth.

Later, when I was older, Mom and I had looked at them again together: "Look how little they are, it's amazing. I grew those teeth in my body. I'm keeping as many of them as I want."

"How many do you have?" I asked.

"I just kept one from each of you," she said. "I'm not a serial killer."

In the precious quiet of Mom's room, I waited for my dad to pick up his phone for what seemed like forever. He had been supportive of Bennington because it was a "good" school, and he had no idea about the lesbian issue, so he would be able to brag about it and act like my going there was some kind of reflection on him. Franciscan was a "crazy Catholic" school, a title the place wore like a badge of honor, which would disgust him. Still, I knew that if I asked for what I needed in the right way, in the right order, I could also make him happy, and he wouldn't be mean to me about it.

"Hey," he said. "What's up?" It was like this when I contacted him on my own, like he was holding his breath, waiting for me to drop a shoe into his life. Later I realized I was the shoe, appearing in his life inconveniently unless he'd summoned me, which meant there was some use for me, a callback, a scene in his play in which he needed me to play my part to show he was a good guy. When I summoned him, he didn't know his lines.

"I wanted to tell you," I said, noticing that my voice had gotten higher all of a sudden, "I changed my mind about where to go to college."

"Oh," he said, poised for anger. "Well, what are you doing now?"

"Instead of going to Bennington, which is, like, nine hours away from everything, I'm gonna go to a school in Ohio, which is only two and a half hours from your house actually!" I paused and waited.

"What school?" he asked.

"Franciscan University of Steubenville," I said. "It's a Catholic school. Because I want to study theology more. Not just theology, I mean, I'm still going to major in English."

"You can't do that at the Vermont place?" I heard in his voice that he was angry.

"I want to study Catholic theology. They don't have that at Bennington."

He was fuming, I could hear it by how he was breathing. I was choosing a side, it looked like to him, and it wasn't his.

"You aren't going to be a nun, are you?" he asked angrily, in a way that made me desperately want to want to be a nun.

"No," I said, instinctively honest, though I knew being a nun would be the ultimate thing I could do for God, probably, the most radical kind of self-erasure I could think of—not to mention the ultimate thing that would piss off my dad.

"Good," he said. "Because that's just plain weird."

"Yeah," I said, automatically agreeing. "I guess."

"You guess? There's something wrong with those women. Why don't they want to get married and be with a man and have children? I think it's because there's something wrong with them."

I swallowed again that thing that made my throat and my chest heat up, made me shift my feet where I stood, like I was standing on something hot, inside something hot. All I needed to do to keep the peace with him was erase myself.

I kept thinking about what Marshall had said, his indignance in the face of me trying to defend a man slicing open his twelve-year-old child to prove a point to God, who was supposed to know everything anyway.

"If you're willing to kill your child, what does it matter what you're doing it *for*?" Marshall had asked.

Everyone else at playwriting camp who sat around the table looked from Marshall to me, trying to follow along.

"Are you guys, like, okay?" asked a guy named Jason. "What exactly is happening here?"

Marshall was standing, gesticulating wildly, talking about how God was love. But finally he collapsed in his chair, the sadistic tragedy of child sacrifice he had been rendering now transformed to comedy. "I mean, how do you think that made Isaac feel, huh? Can you imagine Abraham showing up at Little League games and things, like, 'I know I tried to kill you that time, but I'm sorry, it was actually between me and God and had nothing to do with you'? How's *that* supposed to make Isaac feel, huh? And he's like, 'Dad, you tried to kill me, don't come to my games!' Do you think Isaac had good instincts about people? I don't think so! He was like, 'Hi, at least you're not trying to kill me, that's better than my *dad*!' What kind of decisions do you think that child is gonna make? Healthy choices? I don't think so!"

PART 2
EAT YOUR HEART OUT

If your right eye causes you to stumble, gouge it out
and throw it away. It is better for you to lose one
part of your body than for your whole body to be
thrown into Hell.

—Matthew 5:29

8 Wicked Little Town

2010. I sat across from my new therapist, not sure where to start. She didn't look much older than me, and the woman who'd placed me with her told me she had only just recently been an intern. I was twenty-six, about to get married, and still suicidal. My graduate health insurance had ended, and I found myself in a community center in Pittsburgh, at an intake meeting where someone determined I was fucked up enough and poor enough for the city to cover my treatment.

"So, what brings you in here today?"

I shrugged, said I wasn't sure, and kept studying the things in her office. There was a clay sculpture of a person, a little sloppy but artful, and my eyes lingered on that.

"My little sister made that," she said.

I could feel my face light up. "I have a lot of little sisters," I said, "and brothers."

She smiled and asked me to tell her about that. I felt myself choke up.

"I don't see them as much... since I went to college. There's six of them. Two boys and four girls. I left for college. I haven't... you know, I haven't lived there since I was eighteen and I guess I'll never live there again. When I left, they were all little, and now they're big."

"How old are they? They're half siblings, right?" she asked.

"We don't say that," I said, cutting her off. I listed their names and ages and reminded her of my age. "There's no half or step- about it," I said, probably too forcefully.

"That's a lot of people to love," she said, smiling.

"Yeah." I laughed. "Maybe too many. It's hard to love so many people—I mean, they're easy to love, too, I mean... they're just... you know, when you take care of a baby, you see everything that changes them, how they learn new words and discover things—but then, if you have to go away, you miss it. And you miss it. And college—I just got so... I mean, I guess I was pretty depressed in college, too."

Outside I could see Penn Avenue, snowy and gray, and the afternoon light starting to come up over Pittsburgh.

"What happened in college?" the therapist asked.

I laughed.

"I dunno if we have time for that," I said.

9 Unworthy of Your Love

2002. Everything revolved around Jesus, like things in Disney World revolve around Mickey Mouse. Many people brought Jesus gear with them, and others purchased it at the bookstore on campus: t-shirts, hoodies, polos, neckties, necklaces with little images of saints hanging from them (some wore one, others wore ten), chains worn around the ankles and wrists to symbolize obedience to God, headscarves, bracelets, rings, rosaries, posters, statues, snow globes, office supplies with Bible verses painted on them—anything was possible. There was endless stuff.

In my dorm room, half-naked Jesus spread his arms wide in ecstasy upon the cross, a loincloth falling carefully over his vaguely bulging groin. This and other posters featuring the Risen Lord adorned the concrete walls of my dorm's hallway and most of the bedrooms of everyone I met that first day in Steubenville. Everyone wanted to be closer to him, or look like they did.

Since I had applied late, I'd been assigned a last-minute room with Amy, an RA who was supposed to have her own room. She had decorated every wall with pictures of Jesus and Mary, but mostly Jesus: Jesus in all kinds of positions and scenarios, with light surrounding him and shooting from his palms and his side and his feet, where the Romans had pierced him. Little shadows of blue sticky tack bled through some of the pictures like ghosts. Postcards of Jesus in various holy situations consumed the eye from every available wall or desk space; a banner in the window showed Jesus embracing a lamb, and several statues of Jesus ranging in size and style sat stiffly on the sill, from a souvenir Infant Jesus of Prague attended by several plastic fetuses I recognized from anti-abortion activism, to a handsome Jesus being crucified. A little blood was painted dripping down his stomach, collecting at his crotch's mysterious swell. His eyes looked imploringly toward Heaven—was he praying, or was he rolling them?

In the few hours I had been on campus, I'd met dozens of students, nearly all of whom were majoring in theology or religious education. There was a whole dorm set aside for the guys who were planning to be priests, the "pre-theologates" or "pre-thes." There were no coed dorms. Some of the girls said they "felt the call" to be nuns, and some wanted to meet "a righteous man" so they could start big Catholic families like the one I'd come from.

Amy browsed my books while I waited until it was time to go to the freshman orientation Mass. Whatever was different here, I could count on Mass being at least basically the same as it was at home.

"*Angels in America*, wow! Is this by that woman who has visions of angels, from Indiana?"

"No," I said, laughing nervously. "It's about AIDS..."

"Oh!" Amy cried, shocked, grabbing the book. She opened it hastily to a beginning page and her eyes got wide. She shut it quickly. "Why do you have that?" she asked. "And what does that have to do with angels?"

"The angels appear to the people who are dying of AIDS," I explained.

"The homosexuals?" She looked disgusted.

"They aren't all gay," I said, and she winced at that word. "You know, I always thought it was like Jesus loving the tax collector and the prostitute." By that point I was performing this show perfectly, the split of myself into one who was talking *about* the homosexuals and one who *was* a homosexual.

"Oh!" Amy said, as if mentioning Jesus changed everything. "Oh, well, that's great, I'm sure Jesus loves all the homosexuals, too, even though they've betrayed him and put their bodies at risk of that horrible disease. I mean, I don't know why people just don't control themselves! It's really a testament to how strong the sin of lust can be, that all these people just follow it to their deaths!"

I tried to straighten my body at the same time as it slumped a little, closing like an anemone when something swam too close to it. For most of my life, I'd thought AIDS was something you got from being gay. It wasn't until I was a teenager, and found *Angels in America* in the library, that I learned straight people could get AIDS, too. It wasn't until years later, when I finally went inside a Planned Parenthood for an STD test, that it was explained to me why gay men had a higher risk of infection than lesbians.

I tried to concentrate on unpacking my unisex-looking clothing, mostly t-shirts and the assortment of button-down shirts and sweaters I liked to wear over them.

"Oh, did I tell you about the water?" Amy asked suddenly. "There's something wrong with it. So don't drink the water. It gives a lot of girls"—she looked awkward—"irregular periods. And there's a high rate of miscarriages and birth irregularities in Steubenville, all to do with the water, I guess. Do you have a big family? I don't."

She seemed sad about this but lit up as I started talking.

"Yeah. There's seven of us: Marianne, Jimmy, Lily, Beatrice, Todd, and Evangeline." She wanted to hear more, so I continued. "Marianne likes to read, and Jimmy likes to keep things clean and play with swords—well, they all play with swords, I guess—and Lily draws all the time, since she was like, two, and Beatrice is obsessed with Disney movies, basically, and reading, and she's, like, a language genius, and Toddy is three, he likes to follow my stepdad, Bob, around, and Bob does a lot of woodwork, so Toddy has his own tool belt and little plastic tools and stuff, and he puts on his rain boots and follows Bob around. And Evangeline, she's just two, she basically likes to follow Todd and Beatrice around and try to do whatever they do. She's really into her blanky, which is named Blanky. And Blanky's sister, also named Blanky. She's into carrying those around."

"Wow, you must miss them so much," Amy was saying, but I was already feeling something inside me shatter into six pieces. I had been there since each of them were born and every day after that, except when I went to my dad's, and they cried and missed me and ran to me when I got home. When I was apart from them, I missed things, and I hated that. I had been integral to their childhoods, and now we were all racing into the future, their new words and favorite things changing every day, their lives racing past with me offstage.

I ached for them. I felt like I'd abandoned my mother and them. I told myself that somehow nothing would change, that they were fine without me, that I hadn't been that much help, that I was just homesick. When I talked about them, I'd often cry, so I stopped talking about them. When I thought of them, I swallowed the words down and let them wrap around the six pieces my heart had broken into. Later that semester, a friend of mine laughed out loud, shocked that I had any siblings, because I hadn't mentioned them to her at all. She couldn't imagine me around little kids, she said.

At an orientation meeting in our dorm before Mass, we learned about households, which were effectively sororities and fraternities, except they were groups of women and men "striving together toward Christ." They all had different themes or concentrations, some devoted to different Marys (Our Lady of Fátima, Madonna of the Streets, Virgin of Guadalupe) or Jesuses (Lamb of God Jesus, King of Kings

Jesus, Lion of Judah Jesus), and others affiliated with particular saints or types of devotion. Households got together
for prayer, service, sports, and, we were promised, weddings,
baptisms, and First Communions in years to come. Every
fall there was a household fair, where each household set up
a booth with information about itself and representatives to
talk to, promising instant community.

Whenever there was a household event, and I could see
the groups side by side, I'd be reminded of all the movies
I'd seen about high schools: the Brothers of the Eternal Song
were like football players, big and boisterous and somehow universally handsome, while the Knights of the Holy
Queen were sleek and stylish, their hair gelled and their
pants fitting just right, in button-down dress shirts and ties;
even their flip-flops were cool. The Lions of Judah were like
everyone's goofy little brothers, generally unimpressive
looking, with sloppy bodies, dirty jeans, and untrimmed
hair, but always friendly and always funny.

Many of the households had "brother-sister" affiliations:
the Lions of Judah were the brother household of Love of
the Lamb, a female household that called incoming members "sheep" and made them carry stuffed lambs around
campus during the initiation period, or as a punishment for
transgressing some rule or not living up to the household
"commitments"—a list of household and/or Church-related
rules and practices that members agreed to live by as long
as they were members of the household. The Love of the
Lamb girls all seemed fairly fun and carefree; they weren't
much concerned with style, either, and many of them were
majoring in religious education and planning to become
nuns. Some of the female households seemed to exclusively
welcome girls who had achieved advanced stages of personal grooming and style that had as yet alluded so many
of us.

"What I love about my household sisters," Amy said in that first orientation meeting, "is that if I'm about to go out or something and, like, my skirt is too short, or my shirt is too low cut, my household sisters will call me out on it and remind me that Jesus wouldn't want me to look immodest."

Everyone smiled. I sweated inside my t-shirt and jeans, not because I thought I'd ever get called out for being immodest, but because I wondered what else could they tell just by looking at you. I tried to think of something I could do to remind myself and everyone there that I was definitely a girl like them, a normal girl, so I started playing with my hair. It was too short for a ponytail but long enough to demonstrate I was a girl. Soon, we were asked to introduce ourselves. I explained that I had just decided to come here last month and that I didn't even know much about the school yet.

"The Lord just wanted you here," the girl across from me said softly, seriously; she was moved by my story, even though it wasn't moving.

"Our Lord obviously has a plan for Rebecca here in his fold!" Amy exclaimed. I was too overwhelmed to tell anyone to call me "Becca."

"All the religious education programs want to hire Steubenville graduates," another RA explained, "so think about religious education! Everyone knows that Franciscan is the only place where you can learn from faithful theologians—"

"*Mostly* faithful theologians," a mean-looking girl interjected. "Look out for a certain theology professor. She's practically a heretic—"

"Now, Maria, that's not necessary to go into right now," Amy said with a sigh. "But everyone might as well be aware that Professor Ritter Blake *is* a *feminist*. And of course, feminism is ultimately a very dangerous ideology. But the point of all this was just that God has a plan for Rebecca and everyone here! You never know what the Lord might be calling you to do!"

I imagined the Lord calling me on the phone and nagging at me. *I can't hear you right, Lord! Your beard is ruffling against the phone!* I looked over at the biggest Jesus, a lawn statue meant to be kept outdoors, which stood in the center of the room, like a featured guest at the meeting. In my imagination, he shook his head at me and sighed. I tried to pay attention to the rules about bathrooms and boys in the common room. Someone asked how long we were required to live on campus, mentioning that it was much cheaper to live off campus.

The RA frowned. "It might be less expensive monetarily, but living off campus, you definitely won't find the kind of culture and lifestyle that you'll find here on campus. Here, we have households, we have chapels, we have rules and regulations that will prevent you from doing anything you'll regret."

A few people giggled but stopped quickly when the RA shot them a look of reprehension.

"No amount of money is worth your virtue," she said solemnly. "And God wants what God wants. If he wants you to go to Franciscan, he probably wants you to live on campus. And like most of us, you just have to take out the loans and make it happen. Obviously if he wants it, he'll provide a job later to help you pay it off."

"Right, or it might be his desire for you to be poor," one of the girls said. "But the Lord will always provide."

"That's right," said someone else, nodding. "The Lord will provide."

That evening, at orientation Mass, the president of the university, Father Eugene, gave a homily about remaining steadfast to the will of God in the midst of a world that threw Jesus out with the bathwater. I imagined the Lord surfing out of a bathtub, long beard flying behind him like an infinite tail. Father Eugene reminded us of the cultural scourges of abortion, homosexuality, fornication, contraception, and euthanasia. He smiled broadly, reminding everyone to pray for peace in the Holy Land and to vote for life. His bald head, shined pink, reflected the bright fluorescent lighting that badgered us from overhead.

This was my introduction to the Charismatic Movement, and later people would be amazed that I'd come to Steubenville never having heard of it. At first, I just noticed that at certain parts of the Mass, people raised their hands, both hands, a little like the statues of saints I'd seen. I'd seen people do this in Catholic churches before, but never so many people at once. Some people were also swaying and closing their eyes, their faces raised toward the ceiling, a look of beatification about them.

I'd seen Black congregations on TV, people moving their bodies and raising their hands and saying "*Amen!*" in this joyful, dynamic, attractive, *charismatic* kind of way. While there was some similarity, it was odd to see white people, usually so uptight, suddenly using their bodies to "worship." When Catholic charismatics are saying "charismatic," they're talking about the "charisms of the Holy Spirit," which refers to the idea that they're not just moving their bodies and saying "*Amen!*"—it's God and/or the Holy Spirit infusing them with his presence. The theology is a little oblique and confusing.

Then I noticed people were also mumbling, some quite loudly. I later found out that these folks were supposedly "speaking in tongues," which is another confusing point, theologically speaking, but basically it means that they're infused with the Holy Spirit and God is talking through them in unknown languages, like the prophets and apostles in the Bible. Now they reminded me of news footage of creepy white people in the woods or in big barns, holding snakes and raising their hands wildly, never letting their kids go to the doctor.

The Charismatic Movement originated in the 1960s at a Catholic university in Pittsburgh, Pennsylvania, right across the river from Steubenville. A group of white Catholics had been interested in participating in the Civil Rights Movement and began holding nondenominational prayer services. This did not result in much activism, but rather a movement wherein mostly white Catholics adopted practices that are more commonly associated with Black Christianity and Evangelical Protestantism in general. Soon enough, the Catholic charismatic (and non–civil rights) movement spread throughout the United States and found one of its most powerful bases in Steubenville, Ohio. This was mainly credited to a trio of priests, Father Michael Scanlan, Father Sam Tiesi, and Father Gus Donegan, Franciscan TOR priests. When Scanlan became president of Franciscan, he "infused" the school with the Charismatic Movement. Charismatic Catholics spoke in tongues, prayed over each other dramatically, and were generally more "touchy-feely" than more orthodox, Latin Mass–type conservative Catholics. They were just as conservative, but with a less repressive style.

I couldn't imagine then becoming used to the "tongues" that sounded like animal or baby languages, or the gyrating and withering people did in the pews like accidental commedia dell'arte. Some worshippers even fainted, or were "slain in the Spirit," completely losing control of their bodies, all for Jesus. Usually this didn't happen at daily Mass, unless it was Sunday or a holy day; full-body displays were typically reserved for special events called Festivals of Praise. A Festival of Praise was a charismatic gathering where speakers and musicians would lead crowds in hours of worship, and everyone would ask the Holy Spirit to infuse them and let them speak in tongues or fall on the floor, too. I always wanted to know what would happen if someone got up and said something they'd all disagree with, like, "God doesn't care if you're gay or not." I imagined them all mauling me, their bodies a throng of white blood cells resisting differences in thinking like a disease.

I avoided the festivals, or FOPs, as they were called, for most of my tenure at Franciscan. Eventually the swaying and mumbling became normal parts of attending Mass on campus. That first day, I just wondered what they were saying, and I marveled at how many young people were here and how we didn't have to be self-conscious of how religious we were, or whether we were homeschooled, or how many kids were in our families. It had been a long time since I'd felt anything like normal, and I liked the feeling, even if I didn't trust it.

Since this Mass was in the school gym, the floor was hard school-grade linoleum. We weren't required to kneel if there weren't kneelers, so only the holiest did, casting disapproving looks at those who remained seated. When my knees couldn't take it anymore, I stood up. The longer you knelt, the more you loved Jesus. I couldn't tell how much I loved him.

I felt a tap on my shoulder. I turned, and there was Brad. I'd told him in a letter that I was coming to Steubenville, but I hadn't heard from him since then.

"Hey, kid," he said, shoving my shoulder playfully. "You say your prayers?"

10 Sixteen Going on Seventeen

2002. Brad was a little scandalized by Franciscan, even though he had grown up almost as religious as me, with a mother active in her church, friends with priests—but he'd also gone to a liberal arts college and studied art. His girlfriend was a ballerina, elegantly thin with long hair, much more graceful than I was. When I met him, his hair was long, past his shoulders, falling in his eyes like a girl's. When I'd told him I was going to Franciscan, he'd applied to the graduate program in theology without telling me. "Surprise!" he said, appearing at that orientation Mass out of nowhere. Just like that, something old and familiar had appeared on the landscape of my fresh new life.

"Wanna get outta here?" he asked. He had a car. It was either that or talk to a bunch of other really religious people I didn't know, people my age—my least favorite.

When we left campus, it felt as if we were crossing an invisible security system to get back into "the world." In one direction there was a river and a bridge that led to Pittsburgh, and in the other direction there was downtown Steubenville, a formerly thriving factory town, stretched out like a game of Monopoly plopped down in the middle of nature. I didn't care if it was beautiful or not. Brad's hair fell around his face like Jesus's. His features were fine and pretty, like italics.

"Have you heard we shouldn't drink the water?" I asked him.

"Yeah, I guess the city doesn't pay the fines on the bad pipes," he said. "They were talking about it at the grad orientation. I guess it's bad for girls and their periods, so watch out, Mertz."

I felt embarrassed and got quiet. The most beautiful part of town was the cemetery, which dated back to the Civil War.

The more recently constructed sprawl included a Walmart and a large, half-empty mall with a few lackluster occupants, including a video store. Everywhere we went, the dead businesses outnumbered the living, empty storefronts with broken windows and peeling painted letters, decayed out of their meaning.

Back on campus, the dead outnumbered the living, too: two thousand years of bishops and popes making laws about how to live, which, they said, was the same in 2002 as it was in 1950 or 1862 or 1545 or 325. The dead voices blared through living bodies like music through a set of old speakers, piercing and persuasive, eclipsing the sound of everything else.

One day Brad mentioned how his class had snapped at him for suggesting that homosexuality wasn't a sin. I looked into the distance, imagining Brad with a beard, like Jesus's, holding his hands up high, his body rising above the throngs of students on their way to class, his face lifted toward Heaven.

"I used to think I was gay," I said impulsively. I felt my chest tighten. I looked away, then at Brad, then away again. Brad was quiet for what seemed like a long time.

"Well, that's pretty normal," he said finally. "A lot of teenagers think they're gay for a while."

I wrinkled my nose. This seemed impossible. I looked away, red, wishing I could turn my face even farther away until it disappeared.

"Seriously, Mertz," Brad said, squeezing my hand, "everybody does. And you're not gay, okay? Trust me, I knew a lot of lesbians, from going to a liberal arts college, and you are no lesbian. You just thought you might be for a while, and that's totally normal."

When we got into his car that night to go for ice cream, he put his hand on my thigh for a second and accelerated on the highway. Against the backdrop of the music, I thought about my dad and how big his hands were compared with my knees, how small Brad's hands were compared with his. This is what men did when they loved you, they put their hands on you and told you you were wrong. Dad's face and hands were always clear in my mind, but his body was an empty space, like a page after somebody already poked a paper doll through, and I was the paper doll poked through, singular, with little rips at my edges.

Most nights I got back to my dorm room to find Amy on her knees, her rosary laced around her folded fingers, her eyes tightly shut, an urgent expression on her face, pointed Heaven-ward. I tried to come in quietly, but she'd always hear me. She'd turn and grin hello at me, then go back to mouthing her silent prayers, locked in place on her knees.

Sometimes I watched her: lips silently smacking against each other, robotic and rhythmic and imperative, like tiny footsteps racing up an infinite staircase toward an invisible destination. I didn't know what Amy prayed for, what secret struggle she struggled, right there in the same room as me, with her knees falling asleep against the cold, slippery floor. She had covered most of it with a pink rug from Walmart, but her knees pressed against the place between the edge of the rug and the bottom bunk. I knew that was the place it would hurt her knees most. She was making the choice to suffer more because that meant the currency of her suffering would go further.

I thought about an interview I read with John Irving, how he'd said he'd never write a pro-life character because nobody who was pro-life was interesting. I knew I was interesting, and so was Amy. I'd been so mad I'd left his books at home, even *A Prayer for Owen Meany*, which I'd loved so hard. I looked at the books on my shelf, knowing that great writers wrote their own experience, and that their experience mostly involved rejecting the big conventions of society, especially religion. They were all by men, all the books I'd brought with me. I kept trying to have the experiences I was supposed to have to write like them, but nothing I'd experienced fit into their blueprints for stories.

Anyway, who would believe my experience, and who would care? Who would ever believe Amy's hot-pink knees, the pink turning into blue-and-purple prayer bruises? I pictured her pale skin getting pinker, then red, filling with blood cells, swarming there like red bees inside her body's deep white monotony. I clenched my teeth stubbornly. Why did choosing one thing always mean losing another?

I thought about what was happening at Bennington right now. Somebody was taking the Sondheim class. I knew Jesus demanded sacrifices and that the biggest sacrifice you could make for him was yourself. Somewhere he'd said something about tearing out your eye if it caused you to sin. I wondered if I could tear my heart out.

2002. "Well, we're not *really* cousins," Brad would say when we were alone. Or he'd say, "You're not like a Tuttle at all," or "If you were a Tuttle, then..." like he was hammering nails, building a foundation, driving me a little further from Bob's side of the family, a little closer to him, and, without knowing it, a little closer to my dad, sticking me into a still place, behind a board that couldn't be pried away again.

A professor lived above Brad, alone. She was shy and masculine, and Brad joked that she must be a tortured, heartsick lesbian. He warned me of her fate, laughing about her isolation after we'd pass her outside or on campus. One night we fell asleep next to each other, almost in each other's arms. I woke up and we were moving, and everything was blurry, and I was blurry to myself.

"You're so beautiful," he was saying, holding me close, his long fingers reaching under my shirt. He pulled me on top of him, moving my hips back and forth like I had no weight of my own, until I was moving on my own, and my eyes were closed, and I was thinking, *This is that thing I've read about that I'm supposed to want...* until nothing else seemed real. Then something burst inside me, and I woke up from the blur, and I couldn't move.

"Why'd you stop?" he asked.

I felt waves of shame fill me till I could barely keep from vomiting. My mind flashed back to my dad's bedroom, his bathroom, his car, the prickly red hair on his legs, the smell of his hands.

"Do you think you had an orgasm?" Brad's voice was hard and distant, like a foghorn. "Did you feel a big release?" He moved away from me, looking angry. "Shit," he said, frustrated. "We have to go to confession."

I ran to the bathroom and washed my face with cold water. I couldn't look at myself in the mirror. Jesus was up on the cross, dying for our sins, and I was "giving in to temptation," which was the whole reason Jesus had to be up there, suffering and dying so majestically.

Suddenly it didn't just seem like a weird, beautiful story anymore, like an internet conversation—it was real. I could tell by how everything had changed, how my whole body and heart shifted from being distracted by the pleasure of someone wanting me to feeling ashamed and naked, like Adam and Eve in the garden.

Brad insisted we go to confession the next day, but that we couldn't go on campus or someone we knew might see us and *know*. He drove us to one of the many off-campus Catholic churches. In the car he could barely look at me, tapping his fingers on the steering wheel nervously. I couldn't stop crying and shaking and feeling like I'd hurt someone I couldn't see.

Saint Mark's was in downtown Steubenville, surrounded by old storefronts and restaurants that had last been full decades ago, full of people who were all dead now. Saint Mark's was a dark old church built for Latin Masses. Only on Sunday morning was it light inside, but we hardly ever went there then. We went only on Sundays when Brad felt confident, because that's where Scott Hahn went, and Brad thought it would be good for Scott Hahn to see him attending Mass.

"Next time we should walk," he said as we got out of the car. "You could stand to lose a few pounds."

Brad wasn't the only one who'd thought to go to confession off campus. I recognized a few student couples I'd seen around campus, standing hunched over toward each other, not meeting eyes, but silently mumbling in synchronization over worn-out rosaries. Shame-infused bodies looked like they'd inhaled too much of the same thick smoke, bent over, folding with the effort to be free of it.

When it was my turn, I knelt in the dark crawl space. Behind the filigree metal screen, I could see the old priest holding his rosary.

"Bless me, Father, for I have sinned," I said. "It's been a few months since my last confession..." I paused. I wasn't sure what to say next since we hadn't had sex—or had we? I knew we hadn't gone all the way, but it felt like something important had changed.

"Yes, well, what have you done?" the priest piped impatiently.

"I..." I tried to talk, but my throat was dry as a stone with shame. "I was... I mean, I have this cousin, my stepcousin, and he has a girlfriend, and..." I swallowed hard. "We were sexual together..."

"You mean you had sex?"

"No," I said.

"Well, what did you do?" he probed eagerly. "Kissing? No kissing? How about petting? Heavy petting?"

"I guess so," I said.

"You're not sure what you did?" He scoffed like I must be pulling his leg.

"I'm not sure what to call it."

"Well, you need to get outta there. Stop interfering between this boy and his girlfriend. No more dishonesty. No more of this shameful behavior. To give your body to a man who isn't your husband is to give away something that belongs to your husband, something you should be saving for him!"

After the priest absolved me, every part of my body felt lighter and easier to use. Brad kept apologizing to me, which made me feel like he'd done something to me I hadn't noticed. I thought, if he'd done that with me, it meant he must be in love with me. For some reason I remembered only the beginnings of all the movies, when the fun songs played and people were falling in love. When we went back to his house that night, and I asked him if he really loved his girlfriend, he turned and took me in his arms so tight I couldn't move. Soon he was kissing me, and the noodles he was cooking were limp, languishing in the lukewarm water, and my body was limp in his grip, and my mind was stuck, back in that familiar loop.

"Just don't tell anyone," he said. "Never. Tell. Anyone."

To somehow emphasize the importance of my silence, he touched my chin sensitively. Then he paused and looked closer.

"What's this?"

He'd noticed the little hairs that grew there, that I hoped no one else could see.

"Growing a beard, Mertz?"

"Shut up," I said, shoving his hand away from me, trying to recover from the sting of the mix of exhilaration from his tenderness and the shame of his tease.

He laughed. "Is that because you wanted to be a boy when you were a kid, Chub?" He was always calling me names related to my belly being too big.

Brad insisted that as long as we didn't have sex, we weren't doing anything wrong. The story became that we were trying to be friends. We just kept failing. He said we were practicing for marriage, for our future marriage partners. Whenever it was over, my brain snapped back into my body, and the meaning of what we did washed over me like a salty storm in my throat, and I choked on the name of every person we lied to—especially Brad's girlfriend. Her name flashed over and over in my mind, and words like "fornication" made my brain throb between my temples. The chorus inside me rang out that I was bad and my body twisted with shame, all the prettiness wrung out of me.

One night in Brad's bathroom, I found a pair of tweezers and started plucking the hairs from my chin, one by one. I'd already learned somewhere that if I shaved them off, they would just grow back thicker—good for a boy, maybe, but not so much for a girl. Each one stung worse than being kicked in the shin, like I had to stick a needle in my face for each hair I wanted to remove. My eyes were red, full of tears, not just from the physical pain, but from the shame of growing something where it didn't belong, of being weird and ugly, just like I felt inside.

"Why're you crying?" Brad asked when I got back into bed with him.

"It's just from pulling out the hairs," I said. "It hurts a lot, being a girl."

He had his arm around my waist and his fingers around my belly, squeezing it and making a face like he was being charming.

Confession was held twice a week at the university: anywhere from five to ten priests filled the chapel, sitting scattered among the pews in addition to the confessionals. We had our pick of priests and never had to go to the same one twice.

One week, the priest told us to pray at the abortion clinic in Pittsburgh for our penance. Every Saturday morning the campus Mass was offered for the souls of the unborn babies, and students assembled there before caravanning to Pittsburgh by the carful to stand outside the clinic and pray. There were doughnuts and little bottles of orange juice, and directions to the abortion clinic were printed out on half sheets of paper in piles near the doors of the chapel. Brad was eager, saying this was a revolutionary kind of penance, one that would force us to interact with "the world" and stand up for our beliefs. This would redeem us, he believed, and give us the strength to overcome future temptation.

Angie and Theresa always talked about all the dead babies and how their souls went to Hell because they weren't baptized. They knew someone who went to the dumpsters in the middle of the night to baptize the dead baby parts. I knew that all the women writers and artists I admired had fought for legal abortion, but I still didn't understand why feminists thought abortion was important, and I didn't understand why God would send unbaptized babies to Hell. I'd been protected from real poverty, the full extent of human cruelty, and the violence demanded by everybody's gods, even mine. I told Brad I didn't want to shame the women.

"It's not shaming," Brad said. "We're there to pray *for* the women. Maybe we can save them from a decision that they'll regret for the rest of their lives! And maybe we can save their babies. We have to pray as hard as we can today. People's lives depend on it."

Brad's friend Clark went to pray at the abortion clinic every Saturday morning. He was a "counselor," which meant that he and another student would approach women going into the clinic and try to talk them out of getting abortions. Clark told us how he'd been trained to talk to the women, their boyfriends, their fathers, their friends, their mothers, and how there were laws about how close any of us could get to the clinic. There were other people who volunteered to stand between the women and us until the women got to the door of the clinic, at which point they were beyond our reach. Clark said that sometimes the women would say they weren't there for an abortion. "But,

I mean, it's an abortion clinic," Clark said incredulously. "So it's kind of like saying you're in a McDonald's, but not for a burger... Yeah, right."

Clark explained that no one was allowed to be a counselor who didn't have the best interest of the women at heart, that if anyone said anything combative or judgmental, they were immediately corrected by the other counselors. I started to feel sick, and I blamed it on the doughnuts. Violent images of fetuses flashed through my head, the ones I'd seen all my life. Clark and Brad discussed the statistics often cited by pro-lifers, connecting abortion to breast cancer. I imagined getting pregnant, like the priest had said. If I got an abortion, I wouldn't have to tell anyone anything. Nobody would know that I'd had sex. My heart started pounding, and I insisted we put music on. Brad and Clark talked about the well-being of "the women."

Meanwhile, Brad and I were getting closer and closer to having sex and spending all our time together. Of course, we never bought condoms, and he told me that he knew a girl who got pregnant when her boyfriend's semen got on her thigh. I genuinely didn't know what could make me pregnant, and the second month had gone by without getting my period. When I confided this to him, Brad cried, cut his hair, and said we were never, ever going to do it again; but he said he was too embarrassed to buy me a pregnancy test—what if he saw someone at the store who knew us? I begged him to drive me, and he wouldn't, because if anyone saw me, they'd know I was sleeping with him. So I just waited to bleed.

"Of course, there's even debate in the Church about whether abortions are even forgivable at all," Clark was saying. "It's truly one of the most unnatural things a person could do, a mother killing her own child."

I knew enough to know that it wasn't all that unnatural, but when I tried to raise an objection, they didn't hear me over the sound of their own voices, and the car engine, and the music I had asked for because I had known this moment would come. I leaned back in the seat and tried to focus on the song stuttering out of the radio. The Verve was singing about how nobody could change their mode, or their mold—I was never sure.

At least we were going to Pittsburgh. We passed through a long white tunnel, which spit out onto a bridge. When the car emerged from the tunnel, the cold bright morning shocked my eyes, and the dawn-lit city became visible so quickly it was impossible to get a good look at it before the bridge split three or four ways, and we swooped onto a ramp that sloped and curved and spat vehicles into different parts of the city. Soon, we were rolling up a little hill into Oakland, the college neighborhood. There were a few people out on the sidewalks, but there were more people in cars, all kinds of people inside their own little traveling closets. We were in the world again, and this time it was called Pittsburgh.

In Pittsburgh, everything looked mostly gray: sidewalks and street ramps and endless buildings. As we got closer to the clinic, a McDonald's big arches cut the monochrome, sprouting up like a yellow dandelion from a crack in the sidewalk. At a bus stop, a man with jet-black hair, covered in tattoos, lit a cigarette next to an old woman wearing a plaid headscarf, hunching over like she was in a state of reverence. A few hard-looking teenagers slowed down at a red light on their bicycles. They met my eyes and I smiled, but they didn't smile back.

That morning, I realized there wasn't going to be a building with a sign out front that said ABORTION CLINIC. We pulled up to a nondescript parking lot, and Clark led us to a block of mostly unmarked buildings. We found a group of people standing and praying across the street from a set of glass doors. The sign said something about a clinic for women and children, but I couldn't read it all from across the street. I stood awkwardly for a few minutes, unsure of what to do with my body. Several people were kneeling, and Brad knelt immediately with them and bowed his head dramatically. I grew more and more convinced that I was pregnant, even if it was unlikely, even if it was impossible. Look at Mary.

A woman I didn't know handed me a packet of prayers and smiled at me like I was her very own hero, before turning to the FUS student behind me and doing the exact same thing. I backed up to the wall and leaned there, looking as holy as I could manage. It felt good to have something else hold me up. I opened the booklet to find a bizarre funeral ritual, a litany of prayers someone had composed for the purpose of praying at this "temple of genocide." At this point in my life, I heard the word "genocide" mostly in reference to abortion; the real genocides were called "history" and were considered somehow inevitable, accidental, even framed as natural. The abortion genocide was the clear result of feminism, clearly evil versus accidental, unnatural versus natural.

Some of the protesters weren't from Steubenville. One man held huge signs with apocalyptic paragraphs scrawled on them in red marker. The women wore long skirts, jean jackets or windbreakers, and bulky sneakers. Kids with prairie hair and jelly on their faces stood, barely visible, behind signs the same size as they were. Two little eyes peeked out from behind a sign that read ABORTION IS MURDER.

When the first woman walked up to the doors, protected by two pro-choice activists in yellow vests, I wanted to run up and tell her that I didn't really know what I was doing there. Brad nudged me and, pointing at the girl with his eyes, nodded toward my prayer book. I looked down and tried to focus on the page, but it was all about God sending people to Hell, and the blood of Jesus, and the blood of the unborn babies.

A woman was trying to get to the doors, but a swarm of Franciscan students was trying to get her attention, like the people in the Bible who just wanted to touch the hem of Jesus's clothes. The yellow-vested women yelled at the students, and the students backed off. I felt like they were swarming me, too, but I could choose to turn away from it if I wanted, and she couldn't. Finally, she got through. Turning back to the students, she flipped them off.

"Yinz can fuck off!" she said passionately, slamming the doors closed behind her. I bit my lip because I wanted to laugh and cry at the same time. The protesters all looked righteously wounded; it was their moment of taking a bullet for Jesus.

I looked at Brad to laugh with him, and he started to smile, but his face autocorrected to disapproval. He closed his eyes and started praying again. I imagined a baby with Brad's face and felt weak in the knees with dismay, like I was watching myself from above and didn't have any way to shake myself awake from this bizarre dream. I couldn't figure out how I'd landed on this side of the street, and the path from one side to the other was vast and invisible.

"Souls are falling like snowflakes into Hell!" the bearded man intoned at us. "Snowflakes into Hell!"

I thought about Mom getting pregnant with me as an unmarried college senior. Had she thought of getting rid of me? She must have, I knew now. Instead, she married him, even though, she'd told me, she hadn't wanted to, she just thought she *should*, for me, for him, for the sake of how it looked. I thought about how we both still got cut, split apart—when I was three and I had to go see him without her, and our bodies, hers and mine, felt the distance like needles puncturing us apart, point by point. Our bodies had to bear it, the punishment for making me before she was allowed to, and we "split it," and she got hurt in her way, and I got hurt in mine.

In that moment, I saw clearly that the women walking into the clinic weren't murderers; I recognized myself in each of them, and I recognized Brad's fear in the eyes of the men, if they were there at all, whose bodies bore no proof of their sins like ours could. The woman would lie on the surgeon's table to protect both of them, and that was how it had always been. Our bodies were built to pay a price, to be cut open just like all the fairy tales and Bible stories had warned us, of the inevitable crucifixion. We were supposed to be praying for these women like they needed it more than we did, but what did we know? I realized, looking around me, that the people in yellow vests were there to protect the women from *us*.

When we got back to Brad's apartment, I wanted to throw up, but there was nothing in my stomach since we'd been fasting all day, for the babies. Brad was talking about fornication and how we had to stop seeing each other, all the while pulling me closer. I kept seeing Jesus looking back at me, so disappointed. I was sure I was pregnant. That soon everyone would know. It would be written all over my body, everywhere, all the time, for the rest of my life.

"Let's just be glad that, you know, that you're still a virgin. Mary was a virgin when she had Jesus, because virginity is so special and holy... it's God's most precious gift to us, and it would be such a deep sin for me to take that from you."

Brad and Bill Clinton agreed on one thing: blow jobs weren't *really* sex. I started crying, and I couldn't stop. He said my face looked funny and started laughing. He got out his camera and took pictures of my sobbing face. He told me how silly I looked and said I'd laugh at myself later.

"If you loved me, you'd be with me," I said, storming out of his apartment and walking back to campus in the dark by myself. When I got back to my room, I was bleeding. Still, I knew I wasn't a virgin anymore, even if some particular part of me was still there. Later, when I wanted to laugh at myself, Brad confessed there hadn't been any film in the camera.

12 Sit Down You're Rockin' the Boat

2003. I sobbed quietly into my book bag inside a bathroom stall, emerging only when I was sure no one else was in the restroom. I had to get myself ready for the English department social hour, which I told my new friend Helen I'd attend. It was the spring semester of my freshman year now—almost summer, but the night air was still cold and wet.

I tried to get my hair in order. I didn't know where to get my hair cut or how to get off campus to do it without bothering Brad, so it was past my shoulders now. It hadn't been longer than my chin since I was young, in ballet. I'd kept it hovering around that short tomboy, flapper, woman-writer (like Jo March) length. Now that seemed too short. Long hair was an easy camouflage; for some reason it was a sign of being obedient to Jesus, a way of being classically feminine and somehow giving up vanity at the same time. If I went around with short hair *and* thought the things I thought, which one day I might accidentally say out loud, they'd definitely discover me.

I thought of the beautiful man in *Jesus Christ Superstar*—his hair billowing, and the women in love with him—who didn't know how to be. When I looked in the mirror, my breasts and hips were small enough that, in a sports bra, t-shirt, and baggy jeans, there wasn't much to identify me as a girl. I looked at myself from those angles, just to see what it was like. If I held my body in a certain way, I thought, maybe someone could still recognize me, even under my layers of disguise. Other times, I'd get scared and shift my shoulders in that way I knew made me look feminine, and cross my legs, and tilt my head like I was letting the thoughts pour out.

I came out of the stall to wash my face. It was red and salty. Just as I was starting to run the weird-smelling Steubenville water from the faucet, another girl walked into the bathroom. In a moment, she looked at my eyes, and we were locked in the shock of mutual recognition, of the pain and shame about where the pain comes from, when you'd wanted it to stay invisible.

She looked away and hurried into a stall without meeting my eyes again.

At the mixer, I found myself standing awkwardly with Helen, trying to make conversation. Suddenly her eyes got wide and she said, almost inaudibly, "There's Dr. Madison! She's so cool! And also a little annoying," Helen added, which made me like her instantly. "She's in the philosophy department, but she teaches lit sometimes, because I guess she can do *anything*."

I turned to see a pretty, petite woman, her face red from the cold, stride into the room, a bit awkward in an ill-fitting, expensive winter coat and bulky snow boots. She hung her coat neatly on the coatrack no one else had used. In a moment, she was surrounded by a swarm of puffed up and eager students.

"She'll probably never talk to us," Helen said with a sigh.

We talked about what books we liked, but I kept noticing that I was aware of where Dr. Madison was in the room, that I couldn't stop looking over at her. She'd noticed me, too, but I wasn't sure if it was just because I kept staring at her. I did that thing with my body, holding my shoulders out like wings, like I was a man.

"Bonjour, Helen!" said a cheerful voice, just as I was explaining why I liked Woody Allen movies.

Dr. Madison had sidled up to Helen. She and Helen spoke in French for a few minutes, but Dr. Madison's striking blue eyes kept making their way to mine. Her skin had gone from bright red to a faint peach, flushing light pink when she laughed. Her lips were red, but she wore no makeup. She wore a thick wool sweater and strangely straight-legged khaki pants. Her clothes didn't betray even the slightest hint of what her body might look like beneath them. She held herself with a sternness that reminded me of being alone.

"What are you going to do after college, Rebecca?" Dr. Madison asked pointedly, turning from Helen and switching from French to English without skipping a beat. I was flustered and said something unimpressive about how I wasn't sure, and she looked less interested.

"I want to be a writer," I said, and her whole attitude changed. Suddenly she was challenging me.

"What writers do you like?" she asked.

I strung together a list of famous names I'd heard in movies, Nabokov and Faulkner and Hemingway and Willa Cather, who'd written one of my favorite books in high school.

"Well, what do you have to say about Willa Cather that hasn't already been said?" Dr. Madison asked me. I was stunned by the scope of her question. I thought for a few seconds, wanting to come up with something that would impress her. I knew only two things about Willa Cather.

"I could write about how Willa Cather influenced David Mamet," I said, but Dr. Madison scoffed playfully, pushing me to try again. "Well," I fumbled, "I could write about how Willa Cather was a lesbian and her protagonist, Jim, in *My Ántonia*, is actually *her*, Willa Cather, and how she writes about what it's like to be a lesbian but using a male character." It was the smartest thing I could think of to say, but I hadn't considered the theological ramifications.

Dr. Madison's whole face changed. She seemed suddenly irritated, and her lips curled and pressed hard together.

"Willa Cather was *not* a lesbian," she said firmly, fire behind her eyes.

"Yeah," I asserted hesitantly, "I'm pretty sure she was a lesbian..." I thought for a moment and recalled: "She lived with two women. Successively. Like, one woman for seven years, and then the other woman for thirty years. And when the first one left her to get married, she had a breakdown."

"Two women living together doesn't make them lesbians," Dr. Madison snapped back immediately.

I raised my eyebrows at her and said, "I thought the breakdown part was more—"

"Oh, come on," she said weirdly. Her face was red now. "First of all, there weren't any lesbians back then, people just didn't think of things that way. Secondly, this is all speculation, there is no real evidence that Willa Cather had any inappropriate relationships with other women."

I felt like a balloon had just deflated inside me, and I tried to think of something else to say. The word "inappropriate" rang in my ears. I laughed to defuse the tension, made a joke and an excuse to leave. Dr. Madison forced a smile, still looking a little frazzled. I couldn't tell if she was disgusted or just shocked. I looked back at her as I left the room, pretending to tip an invisible hat. She laughed, surprised and relieved, like she was catching her breath.

13 | I Know Things Now

2003. At home for summer, I finally got my driver's license and borrowed the car as soon as I could, to go to confession with Father Tim, my childhood priest. I'd never been to confession to him—what had I had to confess before? But I had to go to confession before I could receive Communion again, because I'd almost had sex with Brad before leaving Steubenville for the break.

Father Tim recognized me through the screen and asked if I'd sit in a chair across from him, "just like a regular talk," he said. In a few minutes I had told him all about Brad. Immediately I felt relieved. Father Tim wasn't shocked at all, so I told him my other secret, that part of the reason I was so afraid of losing Brad was that I didn't know if I'd ever like another boy again—"Because," I said, "well, I mostly fall in love with girls."

I thought about Dr. Madison smiling back at me at the department party, and Mrs. Carver, and I knew I'd just been pretending with Brad, wishing I felt things that I didn't.

Father Tim looked at me patronizingly and said, "Well, there's a big difference between *lust* and *love*." He paused, looking at me curiously. "Did anything ever happen to you?" he asked.

"What do you mean?" I asked, genuinely confused.

"When you were a child, did anyone ever... touch you?"

I frowned my face into an expression I knew would look like disbelief and said, "What? What do you mean? Of course people touched me..."

"In a way that was inappropriate? I feel like... around eight or nine years old, maybe? Did something happen to you?"

I said I didn't remember, and he said that child abuse could warp people's sexualities and that he got the feeling someone close to me had abused me. I drove home in a fog, realizing how much of my childhood I didn't even remember and how, when I thought about my dad's house, the time blurred away like it had never existed. *Eight or nine years old,* I thought. *No, I was smaller than that.*

I drove and drove after that, and felt for a long time after like I was pulling with my whole body weight on the string of a curtain jerking open.

I was smaller than that, I kept thinking. *I was so much smaller than that.*

PART 3
IT'S NOT YOU, IT'S ME

Then Jesus said to Thomas, "Put your finger here
and look at my hands. Reach out your hand and
put it into my side. Stop doubting and believe."

—John 20:27

14 For Forever

2011. I was out of Catholic school for exactly four years, enough time to take a year off and get an MFA before I found myself back again, this time as a teacher. A month after getting my MFA, I was an adjunct professor of first-year writing at a university where a big crucifix looked down at everyone from a grassy green hilltop. Everyone who ever hired me for an adjunct job apologized about the pay and the working conditions, but I was so thrilled to be a teacher that for the first few years I barely thought about it. I got all my adjunct jobs at the last minute, because someone had disappeared, or dropped out, or gotten a better job, or finally given up teaching in a rage, and the department needed someone as desperate as they were.

When I started teaching, I struggled to get dressed. Being a butch grad student and poet among my cadre of University of Pittsburgh and leftist friends was different from being a butch teacher of first-year college students at a Catholic school. I didn't know how to dress *up*, and I didn't have enough money to buy new clothes; I had some vests and ties and button-down shirts I could wear, but then they'd definitely *know*. That would be a statement. Was that aggressive? And if I did buy new clothes, what would I buy? Since I'd come out, I'd been far too preachy about how queer and out everyone should be to take any steps back toward the closet. I tried to live up to my own drunken prescriptions not to care, not to think about it—but I held my breath before I went into every classroom.

One of my first classes at the Catholic university was mostly nursing students—maybe fifteen out of twenty-two majoring in nursing, all taking the same classes together—and, except for two snarky guys, all girls. They were mostly the kind of girls that I never got along with, who wore lots of makeup and jewelry, and coordinated all their clothes, and blow-dried their hair, which was never shorter than their shoulders. It was early enough that I still questioned my authority with them, and they didn't expect someone like me to be in charge. I didn't hide my politics, and since I taught rhetoric, politics came up a lot. They talked down to me, like we were on a playground. I didn't mention that I was engaged to a woman, and I didn't wear ties or vests; I wore the most masculine clothes in the women's section, scared for the first time in years to wear what I wanted. It felt like a pointless resistance, like I'd be pinning targets to myself. I let my hair get a little longer. I thought about buying a skirt.

On National Coming Out Day, I felt like I had an excuse to say the thing that I usually felt like I definitely shouldn't say, especially at a Catholic school—even if it was a university. There was a crucifix in every classroom. I'd look up at it when I came in the room and look away fast, like I'd seen an ex-girlfriend at the grocery store. Like she was in every class I taught, Jesus tilting his head away and pretending not to look at me, too.

I wrapped up the lesson in twenty-five minutes or so, leaving time enough to come out, answer a few questions, and end class early. If I was going to piss some of them off or make them uncomfortable, at least I could set them free earlier than they expected, and they'd appreciate that. As I always did when I was about to finish up, I asked them if they had any questions about their homework, and they looked confused because it wasn't time to go yet. No questions.

"So, today's National Coming Out Day," I said, and immediately the back row of conservative mean girls rolled their eyes nearly in unison, like they were doing the wave in a stadium. I gritted the teeth of my brain and closed my eyes for a second. When I opened them, I saw the front row of girls, the three or four of the twenty-two who seemed friendly—they were smiling, so I smiled back at them and kept going. "So," I said gingerly, "I'm gay... if that wasn't... already clear."

The back row looked horrified and annoyed, a little more than usual. A few girls looked like they might laugh. The two boys in the class did laugh a little, until I looked over at them. *Really?* I said with my face, smiling a little, like a challenge, and they stopped laughing and tried to look respectful.

"Well, so what?" the Regina George of the conservative girls said. "Isn't that, like, not a big deal anymore?"

I felt the blood rush to my face and tried to think of something to say. The girls in the front row gave Regina George the side-eye.

"I think some people still think it's a big deal," I said, smiling as easily as I could manage. I felt sweat trickling down my back, and I leaned against the podium, trying to look cool even though I felt like I might fall over. "That's the interesting thing about it, from an academic standpoint," I continued, "that some people think it's a *very* big deal and others don't. Which is maybe what makes something an 'issue.' But since it's National Coming Out Day, I thought I'd come out. And," I added, thinking of it off the top of my head for the first time, "what I'd like to do here is give you the next ten minutes to ask whatever you want." I said it like I'd done it a hundred times.

Some of them looked delighted, others dubious. For once, they were all paying attention at the same time. I felt like Saint Francis with no clothes on after handing them back. What did he do then, naked and standing in the middle of town in front of everyone? I waited, stood there in my metaphor for them to scrutinize, to decide what they wanted to do with me. None of them seemed indifferent, though several of them were noticeably trying to seem like they were. I realized how young they were, and however angry my blood got in response to the words they said, they were the same age as Marianne or Jimmy, maybe even younger.

Jesus still looked away.

"We can ask you anything?" Regina George asked.

"Yeah." I laughed. "Within reason."

"Well, when did you know you were gay?" she asked confidently. The girls next to her looked uncomfortable, like they were curious but shouldn't be.

"When I was five, maybe?" I said, recalling my kinder-garten teacher. "It took a while for me to come out, though. It was a pretty big deal when I was a kid. And I was raised pretty religious."

This surprised them, and one of the good-natured girls in the front, Lauren, asked cheerfully, "What religion are you?" She asked it with a smile, like it was an uncomplicated question that might even change the subject.

"Catholic," I said, and Lauren looked immediately sym-pathetic.

"Oh," she said.

Regina George looked annoyed now, and I recognized the disbelief in her eyes as the notion that maybe queer adults just weren't raised right.

"Don't they, like, care if you're gay here?" she asked. "'Cause this is, like, a Catholic school."

The other students looked surprised and impressed that she'd asked this, and a palpable tension filled the room. Lauren turned her whole body to give Regina George what I supposed was a dirty look.

"Well," I said, "no, they don't care that I'm gay—there are other gay teachers here. And there are a variety of views on homosexuality within Catholic theology."

"Well, not really," said Regina George with an air of authority. "I mean, the pope's been pretty clear on it."

I remembered being in college, reading everything that Ratzinger wrote about homosexuals and women, and now he was pope. I'd called Jenny from a pay phone in Europe when it was announced. I'd sent Matilda Ritter-Blake a cartoon of a priest holding up a baby-sized pope with the caption, "It's a boy!" All the Catholic theology rushed to the top of my brain.

"Well," I said, trying to breath and to remember that she was a little kid. That line of Jesus's about people not knowing what they were doing came to mind. "Yes, the hierarchy has been pretty clear about their position on homosexuality..."

"And aren't they *infallible*?" Regina asked. "Like, they're always right?" Her facial expression said that she thought she'd backed me into a corner. The other students were looking back and forth between us like they were watching a tennis match.

"Well, there are three infallible entities in the Church, and they all have to be in agreement for something to be considered infallible. The pope, the bishops, and the people—the members of the Church, the 'Body of Christ,' as the Church says. For example, the pope and the bishops have been fairly universally against contraception, but about ninety-eight percent of Catholics use contraception. So, is the *Church* against contraception? Part of it certainly is, and part of it certainly isn't."

A few of the girls now propped their chins up with their hands, watching me with that curiosity I recognized well: I was teaching them something. Now we were doing school. I recognized in some of their eyes that feeling of being vindicated. A few others looked troubled, sitting up straighter in their chairs like they weren't sure what to think.

"Well, that's not the same as being gay," one of them said abruptly, more forcefully than she meant to.

"That's an interesting point!" I said, knowing I sounded like a nerdy scholar. I walked out from behind the podium and sat on the table with my hands folded in my lap. "Which issues are theological deal-breakers? Certainly the Church is also against lying and stealing and breaking the law, in most cases—speeding, for example—so when does it become something the Church is against to the point of refusing people Communion or excommunicating people, et cetera. So if a gay person is in church and a heterosexual married couple is using contraception, what's the difference?"

"I'm pretty sure they say being gay is a bigger deal than using condoms," one of the boys said.

"Interestingly, the Church puts both homosexuality and contraception in this category of the 'culture of death,' of denying the real purpose of sexuality, which according to the Church is procreation. And they are being literal, talking about making babies. And of course there's disagreement on that point."

"Well, obviously they have a bigger problem with homo-sexuality than contraception, because they don't kick out the people who use contraception," Regina George asserted with a tone of superiority that reminded me I was on Jesus's turf now, that the powerful men who ran this institution were against people like me.

"Yes," I conceded, "although that might also have to do with what you can tell by looking at people... But the Church has actually changed its mind on a lot of things over the years, especially rules about moral behavior. There are lots of examples of this, especially slavery—"

"But that's what *you're* saying," Regina George said. "I mean, you're not a theologian, right? You don't really look like you know that much about Catholicism."

I heard a few breaths go in, like gasps. The girls in the front row looked as offended as I should've felt. Regina raised her eyebrows in return: *Just saying,* they said. I thought about Sara and wondered if she thought of me. I just smiled, knowing that Jesus could hear this conversation, even if he wasn't looking. It was time for class to be over.

"That's an interesting assumption," I said. "Let's talk about stereotyping next week. Everyone have a very good weekend!

As they packed up their things, I noticed a student named Angela was packing up slower, not standing up, lingering in that way I used to do after a teacher's class when I wanted to talk.

"Can I talk to you for a minute?" she asked me.

I always got nervous when students asked me this. I knew they were looking for something in me that wasn't really there; my job was to affirm the search, so they could figure out that what they were looking for was inside themselves. Yet they'd still look at me with the same expression years later: like I knew something they didn't, like they had faith in me. Angela was looking at me like that.

"Sure," I said. "Of course."

I sensed this might be a longer conversation, and I sat on one of the long laminate tables that stretched from one end of the classroom to the other. Angela hopped up next to me, a couple feet away, and I was sure we looked alike, like we were sitting on swings in a playground, our legs dangling unselfconsciously.

"I'm gay, too," she said, and I looked over at her and saw the relief flood her face. "I used to say I was bi, but... I'm gay. This is my girlfriend." She held up her phone and showed me a picture of another young person, one who looked like a regular girl, just like my student. Angela came to class in a military uniform sometimes, too, so I knew she was in ROTC.

"Wow, cool," I said, smiling, because I could tell she was already worlds ahead of where I was at eighteen. "Are you out to your family?"

"Just my mom," she said, and I smiled again, for the things I couldn't do that she could, and I knew it had nothing to do with who our mothers were but with our times, with the mother of culture that it took waves and waves of people to diminish. And the ones who'd come before me, they'd made the world a little more tender for me, beating against it with all their fists and firsts. And maybe I had done something, too—I couldn't imagine what it would've been like to have a teacher who looked like me when I was young.

"Is she all good with it?" I asked.

"Yeah, she's great. My dad is a little more closed-minded. But he's a good guy."

"Are you out in ROTC?" I asked hesitantly.

"Yeah, sort of," she said. "Can I ask you something else, though?" Before I could finish saying, "Of course," she interjected: "Are you trans?"

I opened my mouth and nothing came out.

"I don't know," I said finally. "I think so... You know, I didn't even know what trans meant when I was your age. At least, I didn't know there were people who transitioned from F to M."

She looked shocked. "What?!"

I was shocked that she was shocked, and for a minute all we had in common again was being surprised by each other. I laughed, because I was starting to feel old and I never thought that would happen.

"I think I am, too," Angela said. "So maybe I'm not gay? I don't know."

"Yeah, same," I said, and we both shrugged, and I hardly ever got to shrug with anyone about this. If it had been any other kind of person, I knew it would annoy me, even offend me or depress me, but Angela and I were the same somehow, and we both knew, and we both knew there was nothing to do about it today except to tell the truth and keep going.

"Do you... do you still get bummed out about it?" I could tell it was hard to ask the question.

"Here's what I know," I said. "I've been in therapy for a long time, and I've actually gotten better. The world got better, too, but even if it didn't... I had a lot to heal from, and the healing is a process, but it makes everything easier. Until maybe what the world thinks of you doesn't matter as much anymore."

Angela nodded and said, "I'm glad you're here now."

"I'm glad you're here, too," I said.

They nodded, satisfied, and looked at me in that way, like I'd changed something for them. When I thought of how easy it was to change things for them, it terrified me. Later that semester, when everyone was choosing their final paper topics, Angela kept procrastinating. One day toward the end of the semester, I announced in class that anyone who hadn't chosen a topic by the following class would receive a topic from me that they had to write about.

"Can you just give me one now?" Angela asked, whiny but good-natured. "I know I'm not gonna be able to decide."

I thought about it for a minute, looking down at Angela's tan uniform with all its bells and whistles. I always said they should write about things that mattered to them, real things in their lives. I couldn't stop looking at the little colorful things on Angela's uniform and how they'd gleam out there in the world, in danger somewhere far away, or inside the danger of a place where people cared more about protecting the institution than its members. I thought about it for a few more seconds and felt all their eyes on me, curious about what I'd say. "You can write about sexual assault in the military. There was just a documentary out about it, and if you're going to go into this institution, you should know about it."

A week later, Angela appeared in my office with a grin, a boy haircut, and their paper in hand.

"I'm dropping out of ROTC," they said.

"What?" I swallowed my coffee wrong and coughed. I didn't know what to say.

Angela laughed. "I was thinking about it before. And then I watched that documentary. And I was like, 'Fuck that!'" They started spouting off the statistics to me, like they had to convince me they shouldn't join up, like I was going to say otherwise. I felt a wave of relief; at least Angela would be a little safer.

By the time he graduated, he was starting to pass as a guy and going exclusively by Michael.

Whenever I looked at him, I felt like crying from joy. I didn't know how any of my teachers could've looked at me as anything else but a child who had only just started growing up. I understood that my students weren't children, but in reference to me, it was a metaphor that worked. Their orientation toward me was like a child facing someone who was supposed to lead them somewhere. I thought about Dr. Madison reading Wordsworth's daffodil poem to our poetry class; for years after we talked about the daffodils, and how Wordsworth had come upon them in a field and compared them to the stars.

My students were flowers I could pick and take home with me if I wanted—pause them forever just like I'd found them. I'd been picked young, pressed in a book I'd had to climb out of so I could be alive again and be myself. Now they were looking up at me, and I hated that anyone could want to stop them from becoming whatever it was they were going to become.

What was I supposed to tell them? Walking across campus, now an adult, I was always aware of the beneath-of-things, the way you never knew what might be happening behind people's eyes, behind the veneer of their lives, the way someone could have brand-new tennis shoes from Goodwill. I couldn't blame my students for what they couldn't tell just by looking at me, and I knew it was true of me and them, too, because I hadn't always looked this way.

I was almost the age Dr. Madison was then, nearing thirty, and they were eighteen, nineteen like I'd been when I'd taken those first classes with her, and we'd read all those young, idealistic Romantics, and she'd taught me how to read poetry.

"I don't understand how to read it," I'd said. "It never makes any sense."

She laughed and taught me that new language, her fingers traveling the length of each line as I read it out loud.

"Don't pause if it doesn't make sense," she'd said, and that had changed everything.

Later I was bringing her my own poetry to read, and she was calling me a poet.

I wished I could go back and ask Dr. Madison what she'd been thinking. I loved my students—they moved me, they challenged me, they made me feel like I was passing something on, like I was more than just myself. Still, I was never alone with any of them for more than fifteen minutes in the hallway or walking to the parking lot.

When I got home, I looked up the poem and laughed at my younger self, realizing it contained a line I probably thought of as a billboard confession. *Why couldn't she see it?* I always thought, when she could look at a page of words and see the long-dead man's daffodils waving through time, more beautiful, he said, than the ocean—and what *did* she see?

> A poet could not but be gay,
> In such a jocund company:
> I gazed—and gazed—but little thought
> What wealth the show to me had brought...

15 Willkommen

2004. During their sophomore or junior year, about two-thirds of Franciscan undergraduates spent the semester in Austria, in the town of Gaming (*GAH-ming*), near the blue of the Danube River (whose waltz some people know). There stands a Carthusian monastery called the Kartause (*CAR-tau-ze*). A Hapsburg duke built the Kartause in the fourteenth century just so he could die there. He left it to the Carthusian monks, who tended it until 1782, when the Protestant government suppressed the monastery, taking the land from the monks to sell. The property was neglected by various owners and occupants, culminating in a particularly destructive occupation by Russian troops in 1945, until the 1960s, when the Kartause was purchased by someone known in Gaming as "Architect von Hildebrand," who devoted himself to two things in life: practicing Catholicism and restoring the Kartause.

In the 1970s, persuaded that Franciscan University bore the gifts and good intentions necessary to bring about a massive Catholic renaissance in America, Hildebrand decided to let FUS students use it as a home for their study abroad program. The free, majestic location birthed a study abroad program that attracted even non-Franciscan students (some of whom left midsemester to get away from the unexpectedly evangelical culture). Nevertheless, the program became the jewel in Franciscan University's crown. It was rated highly in *U.S. News & World Report* and won international awards. The program was centered on travel, with classes just three or four days a week so that students could visit all the (holy) sites of Europe.

I signed up to go as early as I could, to get away from Brad, to clear my head. It was the spring semester of my sophomore year. Our attempts to stay away from each other that fall had worked about as well as the previous year, and it all just made me feel worse, and worse.

Dr. Raymond Ragucci, a Rush Limbaugh–style conservative Texan, had run the study abroad program in Gaming for as long as anyone I knew could remember. The Kartause also housed another program, the Language & Catechetical Institute, which brought students from the former Soviet Union to study Catholicism, in English, among Americans, from Franciscan. So, young conservatives from the former Communist Bloc met with the young conservatives from the capitalist United States of America. There were protests all over Europe against the American wars, but students at my school were talking about John Paul II's *Theology of the Body* and the evils of communism and socialism, suspicious of Islam and eager to support any Republican agenda.

Ragucci had an MBA and a Texas accent similar to George W. Bush's. Sometimes the world just seemed to be an intricate patriarchal matrix so big and small it was immune to any amount of logic or feminism, with George Bushes in charge at every level. Ragucci believed in monarchy and theorized that the French king killed in the revolution might've been the descendant of David, of David and Goliath, as though God worked in easy equations and bloodlines and absolute power. The program in Gaming was his tiny kingdom. Every semester, three or four buses arrived from the Vienna International Airport with a crop of fresh subjects.

When I called home, Mom passed around the phone. Marianne and Jimmy sounded like moody teenagers, not so interested in talking, but the little kids asked all kinds of questions. I described the Kartause, the fresh bread, the sparkling water, the mountains. Beatrice wanted to know what I could see from my window—just part of a tree, and the walls were so thick and ancient you couldn't lean out to see more. Evangeline was turning four soon, and she told me she missed me and loved me, and asked when I was coming home. My chest tightened. I felt like I might never get home again. The closer I got to myself, the farther away I got from them.

"I can't come home until summer," I said.

"How long till summer?" she asked.

I didn't know how to explain it to her. Grief surged through my lungs and my heart, and I bit my lip so I wouldn't cry.

"A long time," I said.

One day at lunch, someone tapped me rapidly on the back, like it was urgent. I turned around to see a pretty woman smiling at me. She was my age or so, with her hair cut short like the girls who were going to be nuns. Like them, she wore a long denim skirt, a simple cardigan over a plain t-shirt, and no makeup, though I thought I could see a trace of eyeliner or mascara.

"Are you Rebecca Mertz?" she asked. I got worried, but she continued. "You wrote those pro-Muslim articles in the newspaper last year, right? My name's Leslie. I loved those articles."

She held her hand out, and I shook it, blushing a little that she'd come up to me because she liked my writing. She invited me to sit with her, and we made introductions as I followed her to the far back of the cafeteria.

Leslie was a theology major who had recently left a convent in Los Angeles to complete college before committing to becoming a full-fledged nun. She led me to a table where another girl, a striking girl with an impressive mop of curly hair, was sitting in jeans and a t-shirt and reading a history book over a plate of half-eaten food. Something about her was nerdy but sophisticated, too, and I felt a little intimidated.

"I was in a convent right out of high school, but I left to get my degree," Leslie was saying, as the other girl introduced herself to me as Heather, a philosophy major. They peppered me with questions and liked my answers so much that it got easier and easier to talk to them, until the whole cafeteria was empty and the servers were asking us in German to clear out.

"Well," said Heather, "we have that *huge* thing of Nutella in our room, but we need pretzels. And if we're getting pretzels, we might as well get some vodka."

"What's Nutella?" I asked.

"*What?*" Heather and Leslie were both shocked, and it was settled. They led me to the tiny village of Gaming to find pretzels before I tried something I'd never had before.

Soon, we were unloading a paper grocery bag in their bedroom, which happened to be just down the hall from mine. The three of us sat in a circle on the floor, dipping pretzel sticks into Nutella and drinking the vodka straight. Heather asked if I liked any boys, and Leslie jumped right in. For the first time with my new friends, I felt that sting of not belonging.

They didn't know each other well, either, and were roommates only because they were both members of the same household, the Love of the Lamb, or the Lambs for short. They talked about boys they thought were cute, and I wondered if this was the end of my feeling that we three were somehow the same. I realized I'd barely noticed the names of the other boys on our trip. The more vodka I drank, and the more comfortable I felt in this half-lit room so far away from everything I'd ever known, watching and listening to these smart women, the more it rung in my ears that I wouldn't want a boy or a man again, not anymore, not if I was being honest, which we were, there in that little circle.

"She's getting away from something, but she won't tell me what," Leslie said to me, playfully eyeing Heather.

Heather sat up straight and pointed her forefinger into the air as if she were a politician about to make an important moralistic point. "I do have a problem!" she said. "But it's a secret!"

My heart was beating fast: Did Heather have any of the same secrets as me?

Leslie crinkled her face, disappointed. She pushed further: "Something is making you cry randomly and go all up and down and all over the place whenever you get an email or don't get an email, and I'm not thinking that it's the desire to improve your German."

"My desire to improve my German is *not* a problem," Heather said haughtily, "because I am very good at German."

"I think Dr. Tenerfort's pretty cute," Leslie said.

"Me, too," I said, which wasn't so untrue. Then, on an impulse of honesty, and vodka and chocolate and friendship, I confessed, "But I always fall in love with my teachers."

"What?! You do?" Heather exclaimed in a way that I knew meant she liked a teacher. They grilled me about teachers, wanting to know about me with a kind of enthusiasm that I'd seen in movies about teenage best friends in groups I never thought I'd find myself a part of.

"So, do you go... like... go to Dr. Tenerfort's office hours every time he has office hours?" Heather asked expectantly.

"No." I laughed, since I didn't really have a crush on him at all. "Do you... go to someone's office hours?"

Heather shut her eyes, grinned, and pulled her knees to her chest. "No!" she shouted into her lap. "That would be ridiculous!"

"Alright, Heather, out with it!" I teased. "Whose office hours *do* you go to all the time?"

Heather straightened up and said with full dignity, "Dr. Frank Blake."

"He is *married*," Leslie said, leaning her head back in shock. "And his wife is ahh-mazing."

Heather's expression changed immediately to one of scorn. "Supposedly," she said.

Leslie balked. "She *is* amazing. Have you seen her? She is gorgeous, *and* she is, like, a genius."

"Who's his wife?" I asked.

"Matilda Ritter *Blake*," Leslie said. "She's, like, six feet tall and has amazing curly hair and cool glasses, and her clothes are so cool. Plus, some people hate her because she's a hard-core feminist."

I recognized the name, mostly from hearing the whispers about Ritter Blake, that she was a feminist and maybe even a *liberal*. I watched Heather's face grow indignant. She peered down at Leslie with an expression of condescension exaggerated by their difference in height. Heather's curly hair was pulled back in a ponytail, and she was defiantly tall, with glasses. I could see that maybe Dr. Blake had a type.

"How many classes have you had with him?" I asked.

"Three," she said shyly. "Two last semester."

"And now you're here," I said.

"Yeah," she said. She sucked her breath in hard and closed her eyes tight until she'd prevented herself from crying.

"Well, he's married..." Leslie said.

"Thanks for reminding me, again!" Heather snapped.

"Sorry," Leslie said sincerely, genuinely surprised by the outburst. "I guess I just don't get why you'd feel so much about someone who's obviously unavailable."

But I understood Heather perfectly.

"Not everyone can control everything about themselves," Heather snapped.

"I'm not sure how you get around it if you feel it," I said.

Leslie seemed baffled by this, but she accepted it without arguing over morals, which I appreciated. Heather was visibly relieved, but she closed up again quickly and seemed unaffected by the vodka or the chocolate or the friendship. Leslie hadn't changed and was confused by how serious everything had become and then unbecome. Heather sat up a little shakily and laughed at something somewhere else. She looked for a moment like she had to concentrate hard on getting the words out clearly.

"So, Rebecca," she said, "do you like Nutella?"

That night I called Brad and told him I'd made two new friends.

"Did you tell them about me?" he asked immediately.

"No," I said, "but what's the difference? They don't know you."

"It's a small school," he said. "You can't tell people about us! Everyone'll think I'm some pervert older guy who took advantage of you."

I twisted the phone cord around my finger and looked at the line of people in the next room, waiting to use the phone.

"What am I supposed to do?" I asked, trying to whisper, my voice cracking. "I don't want to lie to people. You're always telling me to make friends and I finally did. I need to talk about what's going on with me, I can't just pretend it's not happening."

Even as I said this, I knew it wasn't true. I could even lie about being able to lie—to Brad, to myself, to anyone I needed to lie to. It wasn't even about being gay, it was deeper than that; it wasn't even my gender. I knew I'd been keeping secrets for longer than I could remember, since before I knew what a secret was.

He sighed. "Fine, but you can at least change my name. And tell them I go to a different school."

"What?" I asked. "How am I supposed to have dated someone at a different school?"

"We didn't date," he corrected me.

I wished I wasn't in earshot of a whole line of strangers who I knew would judge me if I'd said, "Well, where should I tell them I gave you blow jobs if you were at another school?" But something inside me censored me before I could get it out of my mouth, and before I'd decided what I wanted to say, he was speaking again.

"Tell them you dated me in Maryland," he said. "Tell them you met me there, you saw me when you went home for the weekends. They don't know what's true, you just met them! They're not detectives."

"But how—"

"Tell them I'm another homeschooler guy with a car, who could take you on secret dates in the woods or whatever—I don't care, just make sure they don't figure out who I am, or we're both in huge trouble."

"Isn't lying a sin, too?"

"Not like what *we* did," he said. "Lying is okay if you're just doing it to save your reputation, it says so in the catechism. Anyway, can you imagine what your mom would do if she found out? Or Bob?"

My heart sank: I could imagine telling other people, but not them. I told Heather and Leslie that Brad's name was Joe, and, it turned out, it wasn't that hard to change the other details. I kept the lie up for the next year, until one day when it didn't matter, and I told Heather. But even in Austria, they didn't like him.

"Sometimes he wasn't very nice to you," Leslie said one day. "I know you miss him, but I'm glad he's not your boyfriend anymore."

I made excuses for him and started making him sound better when I talked about him. Lying got easier and easier, in general.

2004. "I liked what you said in history today," I said to Mark Angelo, who had asked to join Heather and Leslie and me for lunch. He was over six feet tall, round, with short, spiky hair. He looked like a bear. Since he was best friends with Heather's older brother, he said it was his job to watch out for her while we were here, which was both endearing and irritating at the same time. "Ragucci is wack!" he said, laughing. "The French monarchy are the descendants of the ancient Israelites? Gimme a break, they were totally into killing Jewish people, they were *not* Jews. And the French Revolution was about overthrowing the Church? Maybe? But, like, it was more about *money*, am I right?"

"Yeah, down with the rich," I said, high-fiving him. "I can get behind that."

Heather rolled her eyes, but now Mark Angelo and I were friends forever.

"Must you make everything about *the rich*?" Heather asked, annoyed.

"Well, what are *you* thinking about?"

"I'm writing a paper about Saint Athanasius," Heather said, sounding important.

Mark's eyes lit up, hearing something he liked. "'God became man so that man might become God'!" he recited. "Saint Athanasius said that, right? I love that guy. Hey, I wanna go to Paris," he said, like he'd seen a squirrel. "You guys wanna go to Paris with me?"

That weekend, Mark, Leslie, and I were off on a series of long trains to Paris. Heather opted to stay behind. Leslie and I sat together, inching closer together in a way that made my body wake up from somewhere. Mark and I sat in window seats, facing each other, both listening to our headphones and looking out the window, occasionally swapping music. "These showtunes are wild as hell," he laughed, and kept listening.

Leslie was indefinitely studying. She made a show of trying to get comfortable and finally said, "Can I just put my head in your lap?"

"Yeah," I said, "sure."

Mark glanced from the window to us and looked up at me, meeting my eyes. I did that thing that's half a smile and half a funny face, a face of admission. He returned my funny smile with his own that said something about everything being cool.

We arrived in Paris early in the evening and immediately found a grocery store. Mark and Leslie discussed the foods they missed from California.

"What *is* an avocado?" I asked, interrupting them, not looking up from browsing the French crackers. I heard no response and finally turned around to find my new friends both shocked into silence, their mouths actually open. They both resumed speech at the same time to declare how *bizarre* it was, in this day and age, that I did not even know what an avocado was, and how this was *wrong*.

We bought red wine, baguettes, mozzarella cheese, tomatoes, and six fat, muscly avocados. Leslie and Mark argued about how to tell when an avocado was ready, and I stood by, surrounded by people speaking languages I didn't know, realizing the world was full of things I didn't know.

There were two large beds in our room, so obviously Leslie and I would share one bed and Mark would sleep in the other. Leslie and I couldn't look each other in the eye for a while.

The wine made everyone relax and talk easily, and we talked for hours. I had never tasted anything so good as the fresh baguette smeared with avocado, with a slice of tomato and a slab of runny mozzarella cheese. The three of us just kept saying how good it was, "so good, so good." Why was it so easy to declare a food *good*, when it was such a complicated matter with a person?

"'God became man,'" Mark said, "'so that man might become *God*.'"

I'd learned this in Dr. Tenerfort's class—a man named Athanasius had written it over a thousand years ago, in his book called *On the Incarnation*, an early Christian text that explained the ins and outs and necessities of the narrative of Christianity: that God became Jesus, a human man, to "bring about the salvation of sinners," to "conquer death," to do all kinds of things, according to the various theologians over the many years. Mark repeated this particular line, though, whenever he felt moved, but usually to justify some intense pleasure, some joy, something a little scandalous.

"The Incarnation *is* scandalous," he would also say. "Plato thought that we were only good for our brains, that our bodies were *trash*. The idea that God would become human was so fucked up to Plato, he'd be completely disgusted by that."

I liked the line about how we were to be God better, though. I didn't know what it meant or how it could be true in any sense, but I liked the idea and completely ignored how gendered the language was.

"Now, libations," Mark said, pulling out a bottle of red wine.

"I know, I know," Leslie said. "We're gods."

"No," he said. "We're *God*."

We didn't have cups or a corkscrew, so Mark opened the bottle of wine with his pocketknife and half the cork fell into the bottle. We passed it around, trading big gulps, picking the cork out of our mouths with purple fingers. Mark told stories about working at the docks in San Francisco with his friend Ernie, whose parents had come undocumented from Mexico. Mark talked about people who weren't white in a way that I hadn't heard before, like the problem was with white people, obviously, and it sounded like new music. Mark missed Ernie and said the two would spend hours smoking pot and walking through the city, just talking about life.

That night, we weren't sad. We ate and drank and fell asleep knowing one another better than we had the day before. Leslie and I had plenty of room in the big bed, but we both reached our hands out a little so that our fingers were close enough to touch, but didn't. What was she thinking? What if Mark saw? We watched each other fall asleep, pretending not to.

Paris was thick and damp with spring. We got cappuccinos and croissants at a café near our hostel. Mark went off by himself, and we agreed to meet him at the Eiffel Tower that evening. Leslie and I set out to explore.

I'd never been to an art museum, and she took me through the Louvre and Musée d'Orsay, explaining everything she'd learned in her high school art class, about why the artists were important and how they'd lived and died. By the afternoon, my whole body ached, like we'd walked the whole history of European art. Staring at a thousand years of human creation, I suddenly felt mortified by my big, puffy bright blue American coat from Burlington Coat Factory. I stood out like a blue mushroom growing through the floor of the museum, as I stared at the plaque explaining that Van Gogh had painted those beautiful irises from the insane asylum, where he'd died in poverty. *That's what happens to artists,* I thought, *and then a hundred years later their work is worth millions.*

Staring up at a painting of Joan of Arc burning at the stake, condemned by the Catholic Church in England as well as the English military. Looking at her, I started realizing the similarity between saints and artists. Joan of Arc wasn't the only one who'd been persecuted by the Church during her lifetime, only to be declared a saint later by the same Church. What a difference a thousand years made. I thought of all the homeschoolers wearing Joan of Arc medals around their necks, praying before her statues, and carrying around her holy cards. Would any of them have followed her in her own day? There was a story about God appearing to people as a stranger, and a similar story about some of the disciples not recognizing Jesus when he came back from the dead because they lacked faith. Staring at the woman on fire, I wasn't sure what she'd had faith in—God? France? Herself? Maybe it was just the stretching out of what was possible that she had faith in, which I knew, and saw depicted across ages of art in the museum, was exactly the thing that people set you on fire for.

On our way from the museum to the Eiffel Tower, on a mannequin inside what looked like a thrift shop, there was a dark gray military-style men's overcoat, just my size. When I put it on, I looked in the mirror and felt like myself.

"What do you think?" I asked Leslie. "It's cheap, too."

"You look good," she said, turning a little red. "Like a writer."

Outside, I stuffed the blue coat into a garbage can on our way into the subway. By the time we got to the Eiffel Tower, it was dark and the tower was lit up.

"Yes!" Mark roared, throwing his arms up in exultation as we approached.

Not many people were still out, and we had the whole monument to ourselves. We lay on benches, stretched out and looking up through the metal bars.

"We're looking up her skirt," Mark said to me, grinning, pointing toward the sky. I laughed. It felt good to be the one looking up the skirt instead of the one whose skirt was getting looked up.

"You two are bad," Leslie said, but she smiled. She was taking endless pictures from every angle, lying on the ground, standing on the bench, crouching, walking far away and then coming closer. Mark and I lay there looking up together.

"Better than TV," Mark said, and I nodded.

I thought about watching TV in the living room at home, with the kids and Mom and Bob. How many times had I seen this weird thing on TV, and now I was right there with it. The whole world started to feel more real than it ever had, like now I was on the other side of the screen. From this side I couldn't see the homeschoolers or the babies with sticky food on their faces, or the moms and dads holding their kids close by the shoulders, in perpetual denial of so much, or the throngs of friars with their hands folded, creeping across the Steubenville campus like ants. It was all blurry now, as unbelievable and as uncomplicated as bright colors and kids' costumes and superheroes on Saturday mornings.

The oldest parts of my brain lit up, from before I started worrying about God so much, when the most holy thing I knew was my brain swelling like an orchestra. The light from the stars and the light from the city were indistinguishable from each other, like the whole city was radiating with heavenly bodies, intertwined planets, lamps and bulbs and eyes and little loves, the secret ones lighting up as bright as the ones everyone told each other about.

Walking back to the hostel, we passed by a church from the Middle Ages. While Leslie took photos, we heard singing. The voices were pristine and practiced, clearer than bells.

"It's Night Prayers," Leslie said, walking toward the door. Mark and I followed. We'd already grown accustomed to the churches of Europe being public places, like indoor parks. If the doors were open, anyone was welcome to come and go as they pleased.

We walked inside, and the slow, operatic chanting sur-rounded us. This church, like the oldest churches, didn't have pews but was just a big, open space. Thirty or forty nuns were scattered across the big stone sanctuary. They wore striking, Jedi-like off-white habits, and they knelt ritualistically toward the altar as they sang their night prayers. Their hoods hid their faces.

Mark, Leslie, and I knelt, too. After a few minutes, I sat back on my feet and looked up. I wanted to soak in this image of these women. How long had this order of nuns been praying night prayers here, every night? They embod-ied something ancient; their postures, their clothes, their rituals, had been here a thousand years, maybe longer, like fingers reaching forward in time.

Who they were, and where they came from, and who they'd loved, and what they'd left to be here—it all sloshed together, collecting like water at a drain. For as long as they wore these clothes and made these movements, they were symbols, icons of something larger than themselves. Their individual traits and characteristics were painted over, covered by sameness. I closed my eyes and tried to imagine the diversity of dreams and desires that must be happening inside their heads, even though they all looked the same on the outside. But their voices sung in such precise unison that they sounded like one voice, deep—not like sounds are deep, because they were women and they sang high notes, but deep like the ocean is, like they were drops of water. It was beautiful and terrifying.

The next morning, we rushed out of the hostel to catch our train back to Austria. We heard chanting before we saw the crowd of protesters marching down one of the main streets we needed to cross to get to the train station. As we got closer, I could tell what their protests were about even though I couldn't read French. A year into Bush's invasion in Iraq, I stood in another country, seeing the real evidence that people on another continent didn't think everything America did was okay.

I wanted to be with them, but I felt light-years away— and not just because they were speaking another language. I knew what they were saying. I knew they were here because they believed what I believed and what every good movie or book or song about it had ever taught me—that there was no good reason for a war. But somehow they were marching against war and I had only ended up in the street to protest abortion access.

I knew Pope John Paul II had been preaching and writing against war almost daily since Bush had invaded Iraq. A few FUS faculty had printed out portions or, in one case, the entirety of his admonitions against war, with big sections highlighted—the pope was clear on the fact that the U.S. invasion was unjust and that it would be a sin to support it. He issued documents and proclamations against the unnecessary use of military force, and I had wondered if this would be enough to get my friends and me into the streets for something besides abortion. It wasn't. While the school sent carloads of students every Saturday to pray outside the abortion clinic in Pittsburgh, I'd yet to see a sign or a handout about attending any anti-war marches. "Well," I heard one student say, "What kind of people do you think would be *there*?"

There was a poster for an antiwar meeting back at the Kartause, but when I got there, it was mostly made up of students who came to argue for the war. Soon enough it was clear that the culture of my school bent toward the Republican Party rather than standing firmly against it in favor of Church teachings against our country's unjust war.

I wrote editorials for the school newspaper, and I prayed and prayed.

17 If I Were A Bell

2004. Friday nights, the Kartause showed movies in one of the big common rooms, an ancient ballroom, with ten or fifteen couches squished together like movie theater seats. Heather was away that weekend, but Leslie and I had decided to stay back, exhausted. Leslie said we should go to the movies. She seemed giddy. She chose a love seat for us, and when I sat down I realized that the furniture was so big and the seats were so deep that everyone was nestled into private trenches, especially when the lights went out and the movie started. Leslie opened a bottle of wine.

As we passed the bottle back and forth, our fingers touched on the glass, and I noticed she reached her finger toward mine instead of pulling it away. I couldn't tell if the wine or Leslie's touch was filling me with a warm, tingling feeling, like I was running in the dark and couldn't see more than a few feet in front of me.

Halfway through *The Bourne Identity*, Leslie was lying across my lap, under a blanket. I looked around nervously, but no one seemed to notice us. She took my hand in hers, under the safe cover of the blanket. I understood now, why movies showed everything around two people going dark, like there was nothing else anywhere. She put my hand beneath the hem of her shirt, on her belly.

My palms were sweating, and I was too nervous to look over at her face. Jason Bourne was running and running, fires exploding around him. My hand felt far away, between Leslie's itchy blue sweater and her belly. She was moving my fingers in hers, stroking her abdomen with my hand. I couldn't move. I felt waves crashing all through my body and let her unfold my fingers. The flames of Hell flashed through my head to the beat of a soundtrack I could hear now, even though I knew I'd never be able to hear it again or find it on any CD. I was terrified of her, and everyone around us, and God, but more terrified that if I moved away, I might never know what I was running toward.

I could tell the movie was almost over because Matt Damon was engaged in a lengthy action sequence and time seemed to be running out on him, and there was a girl he was running toward or after. I was running, too, faster and faster, but not moving. Even when we sat up, we kept our hands together under the blanket. We both looked around, like we were standing there naked in front of God and everyone— but no one looked troubled or interested in us. We'd changed the world under the blanket, but nobody could tell.

"I could set myself on fire," Leslie said, "and I actually think nobody would notice."

I didn't know what to say and was starting to feel terrified of what was next. What would happen when we were alone? All my stuff was in Leslie's room, because I always stayed there, on the floor. But now Heather wasn't there. My mind raced with all the reasons I should go back to my own room, but I couldn't move. It took two of us to carry the blankets and wine back to Leslie's room. She dropped the blankets on her bed and got in.

"Come on," she said. "It's okay. We don't have to do anything, I just want to hold you."

I turned out the light and got into bed, into her arms. She gripped me tight, and I felt her heart drumming through her chest into mine.

All the words I knew started falling away, even "God." Somehow only she and I mattered, and what we wanted, and how it was the same thing. It was particular and vast at the same time.

We kissed and kissed, until I couldn't ignore God pounding in my head anymore, like my dad was yelling at me, pounding my skin's doors, and I just froze up, paralyzed again. Leslie asked me what was wrong, and I couldn't answer, and ran to the bathroom, and threw up.

As soon as we left her room the next morning, I felt like a mannequin in a shop window. Could people tell what I had done? Could they tell who I was? Was I a lesbian now? I tried not to move my hands, not to be too close or too far away from Leslie. I wanted to go back in time. Shame crept through every part of me like syrup spreading across a plate. I couldn't think of a way to get rid of the shame, except to stop existing. I could just disappear, and it wouldn't matter what I'd done—except that, if I died like this, without going to confession, I'd go to Hell for sure. God looked down at me, totally disgusted. Jesus hid his face from me, like my dad used to when he would drive the car for hours without looking over at me. If I so much as straightened my shoulders just a little, I felt a surge of guilt, reminding me to slump back down. "Do you like me?" Leslie asked hopefully, over breakfast. I was annoyed. How could she think about something so unimportant as that right now, when we were practically camped out on Hell's doorstep?

"Of course I like you!" I said, looking around to make sure no one could hear me. I noticed a girl a few tables away was watching us out of the corner of her eye. Could she hear us, all the way over there? The girl looked away when she saw me looking back at her. "But we can't do that again, it's wrong!"

"I'm not talking about us doing anything, I'm talking about how you feel."

"How do you feel? Have you ever liked a girl before?"

Leslie's face got tense. "No," she said defensively. "I just like you, that's all. I've never felt this way before."

I felt my face getting red. Leslie was looking away, biting her lip, and turning red, too. I shook my head in disbelief. So, it was my fault. Leslie hadn't even liked a girl before me. Something about me had changed her. Kissing Brad had felt good, but it was like the drip coffee back in America versus the espresso made in Europe. I remembered all the people who said I could pray it away and change, and I had hoped they were right. I looked in my memory for a movie about what was happening, but there wasn't one. The movies I knew flashed through my head: horrified faces, weeping, closeted femmes married to frustrated, confused men—and dead or lonely butches, hanging in closets.

"What are you thinking about?" Leslie asked, interrupting the spiral. I told her I didn't know. "I know we should just be friends."

"Okay," I said. I couldn't get anything out. My throat was dry; my chest was tense and barely letting me breathe.

"God," Leslie said, staring at me, "you're really freaking out."

She reached across the table and put her hand on mine. I felt her touch ripple through my whole body, and I almost forgot everything else. I pulled my hand away like I had just been burned.

"Don't," I said.

Leslie and I sat a few feet apart on a back pew. We didn't want to look like we were there together. There were two confessionals on either side of the Kartause chapel. Three nights a week, the two university priests who lived at the Kartause offered confession. There was no way of knowing which priest was in which confessional, but Leslie wanted to go to Father Rick, and I wanted to go to Father Kevin. We had decided that if we went to the same person, they'd know we were talking about each other, and that felt more invasive than two different people each knowing half of what was going on.

Leslie was more nervous than I was now. I was used to talking to priests about sex, although I was admittedly more nervous now that it was lesbian sex. But I knew it would be over soon, and I knew how much better it would feel once we'd told on ourselves. Leslie got up, genuflected in front of the crucifix, and entered the confessional. I knelt, now that there was no one to see me, bowing till my body was the shape of how I felt, and I prayed hard: *Just let me do the right thing, whatever it is, just help me do the right thing.*

I took a deep breath and got up. I was relieved to find that the confessionals were still old-fashioned, with screens. I knelt down and saw little glimpses of Father Kevin's white curly hair through the gold filigree of the thin metal screen.

"Bless me, Father, for I have sinned... It's been about a month since my last confession," I said.

"Alrighty," said Father Kevin cheerfully. "Go ahead and tell me what's on your mind."

"Well..." I started. "I... I, uh, I engaged in... in... uh... homosexual acts." Father Kevin was quiet for a minute. I felt like I should keep going. "It was just once—I'm not going to do it again. We talked about it and we're not going to do it again." I was holding back tears now, and I knew my voice sounded sad.

"Hey," Father Kevin said forcefully. "Hey, you listen to me. I want you to read Sister Faustina's diary, about Divine Mercy. Open it to any page and just read some of it! God's mercy is deep, deeper than the ocean, wider than the solar system! He's not going to hold back forgiveness from you! And look, here you are, seeking forgiveness! And it's good that you talked about it with your friend. Friendship is so valuable... but it must lead us closer to Christ, not further away. We must choose our friends carefully. But more than any of that, trust in the mercy of God, who loves you more than you can imagine! He loves you just as you are! You just need to get a hold of your temptations and learn how to say, 'No, thanks!'"

"Thank you," I murmured, trying to take it all in. I sucked in my breath and held it so I wouldn't cry. What he was saying didn't make real sense, considering what the Church taught, but it felt good to hear it. He gave me absolution and forgot to give me any penance.

Leslie was sitting in a back pew when I came out. I genuflected and joined her. Somebody else took my place in Father Kevin's confessional. I knelt down and thanked God for it going so smoothly, then I sat beside Leslie, careful to keep my distance from her.

"How'd it go?" I asked, whispering. A line had formed in the front pews, and we were in the back, so I didn't think anyone could hear us.

Leslie raised her eyebrows angrily and whispered, "Let's go." The cafeteria wasn't open on the weekends, so we went to the Kartause restaurant. Leslie ordered us two beers.

"Well, how was yours? Mine sucked," Leslie spat.

The beers arrived. There were only two Kartause waitresses: an old, grumpy one and a young, pretty one. Tonight, we had the old one. Her face bore the slackening of years and years, but she had two blonde braids pinned across the top of her head, so she looked like one of the little girls in *The Sound of Music*, aged to exaggeration. Leslie got more relaxed after a few sips of beer. She took out her ponytail and started to redo it. She did this whenever she wanted to think for a few minutes without talking.

"What happened?" I asked, keeping my hand clutched around my beer. Confession was like a switch that turned the guilt off most of the time. I knew it would come back, especially if I kissed Leslie again, but I couldn't stop thinking about it. I tried to stay focused on the fact that Leslie seemed pissed and confused, but my eyes kept getting caught up on her neck, her lips, her hands. My mind kept flashing back to being in bed with her, like it was a movie and we were perfect. I blinked and focused on Leslie across from me, running her middle finger around the rim of her beer glass and licking a little foam from her fingertip.

"We just spent the whole time talking about..." She paused and lowered her voice. "He was just, like, fixated on whether or not I'm a lesbian. He asked me if I was, and I said no, and he said, 'Well, then why would you do this? Don't you think you might be a homosexual?' And I told him no, I just like this one girl, and I've never even liked a girl before. And then it was like he didn't believe me."

"Do you think I did something to you?" I asked fearfully.

Leslie looked confused. "You did *something*," she said, laughing. "But not, like, something *bad*."

She paused and shuddered, taking a big swig of beer. I wasn't convinced, but I left it alone. She squeezed my hand, and I felt that rush again through my whole body.

"Whatever," she said. "That's over. And let's not tell Heather."

I'd assumed that somehow Heather would just know, that everything was changed now and there was no way of going back. We talked to Heather about everything—how could we not talk to her about this? But I knew it was easier to believe that it hadn't happened at all if we didn't tell anyone, and that's what Leslie wanted. More time would go by, and eventually days and weeks would go by, and it wouldn't happen again, and eventually it would just be something in my memory.

"Yeah," I agreed. "Let's not tell her."

Leslie smiled at me, a little tipsy. Going to confession had at least made us feel like we were both at square one again, like there was a finish line we'd crossed together, but now we were back at the start, and we just had to manage not to cross the line. Leslie put her hand on my knee under the table and ordered two more beers. Our waitress returned with the next round, her dour expression unmoved by our giggling.

"Do you want anything else?" she said in her thick Austrian English.

"What's good for dessert?" Leslie asked.

"'Heisse Liebe,'" the waitress answered without a beat.

Leslie thought a moment, translating in her head. "'*Hot... Love?*'"

The waitress's mouth opened in a wide grin and she cackled, "Yes, exactly! Hot love!" She raised her eyebrows at us playfully.

"Sure," Leslie said. "We'll have that."

2004. Our spring break was a school-run trip to Assisi and Rome, followed by five free days where we could go wherever we wanted. The school scheduled a caravan of buses to travel all night from Gaming to Assisi, where we immediately attended morning Mass at the Basilica of Saint Francis, before checking into a convent run by nuns who wanted to tell us all about the man after whom our school was named. But they spoke Italian.

The professor touring with us told us about Saint Francis's father, a wealthy guy who ran a fabric company—meaning that he provided the wealthiest, most stylish people their clothing. Francis just wanted to go around in rags and help the poor, and this was embarrassing to his father, who threatened to disinherit him if he kept it up. One day, Francis took off all his clothes in the middle of the street, in the middle of the town, and folded them up, all those fine fabrics that had made his family rich, and handed them back to his father. "My only father is my Father in Heaven," Francis said, and he stood there, naked in front of the whole town. What a badass.

From then on, he lived "like the birds of the air and the lilies of the field," in a complicated, dire, but occasionally blissful poverty. He died naked in the cold winter, on the altar of a church he'd built with his own hands, surrounded by men and women who'd followed him into poverty.

For my confirmation back in eighth grade, we were supposed to pick a patron saint, and I picked Saint Francis because he talked to animals, plants, and planets and called them his brothers and sisters. The lady in charge of confirmation at the church looked uncomfortable, and after class, she pulled me aside and said it was "very strongly suggested" that we pick a saint of our own gender. When I heard that, I instantly picked a female saint so that no one would suspect there was anything amiss about my gender.

Saint Claire and all the women saints cut their hair short as a sign of holiness, but I knew I could never cut my hair short. When I'd tried to get it "short" at the hairdresser as a kid, the lady had given me a Dorothy Hamill bowl cut that I hated. For a while, I thought it might be literally impossible for scissors to cut female hair shorter than a certain length, because people's reactions made it seem so outlandish when I asked for it, until I stopped asking. I chose Saint Catherine of Siena, the patron saint of artists, because I wanted to be an artist and because she had a vagina. All over Europe there were statues of dead saints, broken and decayed into new shapes and colors. I imagined the female thing I was encased in chipping away, like giving my clothes back to God.

In Rome, we were inundated with the preserved bones, fingers, heads, hair, and whole bodies of long-dead saints. Everywhere we walked was significant for a long list of reasons, having survived a series of cultures and the wars that went along with them. Alexander the Great, Julius Caesar, Virgil, the early Christians, Ovid, the martyrs, the gladiators, Audrey Hepburn, and Fellini—they had all been here at one time or another. Time was visible in a new way, the way you could see half an ancient building coming up out of the ground around the subway station.

In the U.S.A., there was a thick layer of concrete poured over everything, and a sign, and a strip mall. The country I was from was a woman with a lot of plastic surgery, wearing new clothes, popping pills in the bathroom to forget what everything looked like before it'd been covered up.

Rome was a bedraggled, elderly queen, wearing one article of clothing from every decade of her life. We walked through her, taking pictures of her scars and her tattoos, trying to decipher her languages.

The school had arranged a special surprise for us: an invitation-only screening of Mel Gibson's *The Passion of the Christ* with the seminarians of the Pontifical North American College, the famously conservative English-speaking seminary in Rome. When I told Brad about it in an email, he wrote back that this was a special gift that Jesus was giving me at this pivotal time in my moral journey. I was going to be able to see what generations of Christians had never been able to really experience: an accurate visual depiction of Jesus's suffering on the cross, which was the suffering that redeemed all of us from sin and gave us the opportunity for redemption—all brought to us by Mel Gibson's star power.

I was trying to redeem my relationship with Brad, too; maybe if we could really be friends, like we'd been telling everyone we were, we could heal a little of the hurt we'd done to Jesus. I thought about all the lies I'd told my mom; she'd asked me a few times if Brad and I were more than friends, and I always lied, like he said I *must*. I was never sure if she believed me. But maybe if we could be friends— just friends—maybe all that lying would turn into something better, something good. Or maybe, if we couldn't be friends—maybe that meant I could be straight, and maybe that would redeem *me*.

But I could feel the pull of Leslie's skin as she sat in the dark theater next to me. Her arm lay on the armrest, and I moved my arm there, too, so that we touched just slightly. She stretched her fingers and squeezed mine quickly, secretly, before gripping the armrest with her hand.

I closed my eyes and prayed not to feel what I was feeling. I moved my arm away, folded my hands in my lap, twiddled my thumbs. The credits were rolling. Heather, Leslie, and I sat inexplicably still and silent, staring at the now blank screen in full light, as FUS students and seminarians filed out of the theater around us, rising from their seats in tears, some of them genuflecting toward the screen, praying dramatically as they exited the theater. My friends and I sat, speechless.

"What was that?" Heather asked finally, voicing the disgust I was feeling, too.

"Too much," Leslie said sternly. "It was just too much."

"Joe said I should think about how my sins cause Jesus to suffer," I said, exhaling deeply as though I had revealed a secret.

"Fuck Joe," Heather said, standing up.

Leslie looked over at me, looked me in the eyes. "Yeah," she said with uncharacteristic conviction. "Fuck Joe."

That night, Leslie and I found ourselves alone in our hotel room, alone and alive. Heather was annoyed with us and wanted to take a walk and find a computer with internet so she could email Frank. When I heard the door close, I asked Leslie what she wanted to do.

"I want to kiss you," she said, and any theoretical resistance I had to it disappeared as soon as she started walking toward me.

When she kissed me, I didn't care who I was, or I didn't have to think about it.

The next morning, Heather, Leslie, and I took turns checking our email at the hotel as we discussed what else we wanted to see in Rome. I felt that nagging feeling, like I had to go to confession, but I still couldn't stop thinking about how to be alone with Leslie again, how to manage getting alone again. I was smiling stupidly at things, feeling like nothing was wrong even though everything was wrong. Then there was an email from my mom, which I knew meant something bad. She never emailed me.

My cousin Jessica had been killed in a car accident. I called Mom from a pay phone in a dark hallway. She asked if I wanted to come home for the funeral. She said she wasn't sure how to pay for it, but she would ask Papa if he could help. We said we loved each other, and she told me to call her back when I'd had a chance to think it over.

"She's not really your cousin," Brad said when I called him. "And that's a lot of money for you to spend—but I guess your family's *rich*."

When I called Mom back that night, I told her it seemed like too much, that I would go to church somewhere that day and just do my own thing. She said she understood and it was up to me. I could hear Brad saying that I just wanted to go because I was dramatic, because I wanted to pretend I fit in with the Tuttles when I didn't. Part of me was relieved. What if I started crying at the funeral and couldn't stop? What if I said something that revealed what had happened between me and Brad, or, worse, me and Leslie? What if Mom rejected me, like Brad and the movies were always saying she would?

Heather went back to the Kartause to finish out spring break alone. Leslie and I decided to go to Spain, but before we left Rome I wanted to go to confession. At the Vatican, they had confession in pretty much every language. There were little signs listing the languages spoken by the priest inside. Otherwise, the process was the same as it was everywhere else, little old ladies and pious students and worn-out housewives all sitting in line for absolution, just like they were in Ohio and Maryland and Pennsylvania, and everywhere else Christianity's fingers reached on Saturday afternoons.

There's an altar in the middle of the Vatican that's the shape of a bed, meant to symbolize the wedding bed of Christ and the Church—the Church which was, supposedly, all of us, our bodies, united in something, even when we felt alone.

When it was my turn, I knelt in the confessional. I could see a youthful middle-aged man on the other side of the screen. He raised a thin hand to bless me as I entered. As I spoke, I could see him nod on the other side of the screen, the expression on his face changing from joviality to concern.

"Is being gay what you've come to confess?" he asked, sounding genuinely surprised. His accent was Irish.

"Yes," I said.

"You don't have to confess that," he said simply. His confidence in his own words was new to me, and he continued kindly. "Do you feel that you are a lesbian?"

"I think so..." I was never sure about that word, "lesbian."

"Well, that's for you to figure out," he said, looking into my eyes shyly through the screen. "And I want you to remember that God loves you. That's all I've got to say, and I'll give you absolution if you've nothing else."

I couldn't remember feeling more relieved, and when I left the confessional, I fell to my knees in the nearest pew and thanked God for loving me. As I stood from the pew, I thought about Father Tim and what he had asked me in that confessional back at home, but I pushed it away as far as I could. I set my Discman to play one sad song over and over. Leslie had lent me a Bob Dylan CD, and I couldn't stop listening to his scratchy voice singing about shelter and storms.

19 Somewhere

2004. Madrid smelled like earthy rain and sweaty bodies. Leslie and I never stopped holding hands, and when people on the street glanced at us, we stood up straight and looked back defiantly. By the time we got to the art museum, our hair was wet, and we were light-headed with exhaustion. In front of a painting by Goya, I kissed her—right there in front of Goya and everyone.

Alone in an elevator, we kissed and kissed and kissed, for what could have been seconds or hours. Lost in each other, we got too accustomed to no one else using the elevator, but the doors opened to reveal us, mid-embrace, to an officious-looking middle-aged woman. We jumped apart, but she'd clearly seen us mid-kiss, and she blushed as she entered the small elevator with us.

For a few seconds, a few floors, someone knew who we were, and she didn't shrink away. It seemed like she was laughing at us a little, like we were in a sitcom rather than a tragedy, just normal people doing something normal. In those thirty seconds something flashed before my eyes: all the queers on TV, their voices singing in musicals even though everyone said it was weird and stupid. I thought of how much our bodies had endured, and Sappho and Oscar Wilde and Adrienne Rich and everyone in between. I thought of *Angels in America* and *Cabaret* and Michelangelo, and all the dancers I didn't know the names of, and the countless dead, the ones who died of AIDS or got beaten up or burned at stakes, and I felt my shoulders spread open a little, like flexing a new muscle in my shoulder blades, like something was growing back there.

I woke up early and we were still on the train. I watched Spain go by through the window, in a light blue morning light. We were almost in Ávila, the home of Saint Teresa, Leslie's patron saint. I thought of all the other Americans who must be on their spring breaks, waking up on trains. Everything in America seemed so new and ugly compared to the layers and layers here. I kept thinking about how so many of us were weaving through all these old countries in our headphones, trying to figure out who we *really* were, just like our stupid young country.

Teresa of Ávila had been brought before the Grand Inquisition, in Spain. She was a Carmelite nun, the kind of nun Leslie was going to be. She told me that when Saint Teresa was called before the Church's judges for being too progressive, the Inquisitors accused her of being in love with her friend, a priest, who was later proclaimed Saint John of the Cross. Saint Teresa hadn't been at all scandalized by the suggestion, and she said, "Yes, I do love Father John. And I love Father So-and-So, and Father So-and-So, and Father So-and-So..." and they got nowhere. And now she was a famous saint, one of the most important writers in church history.

We arrived in the modern Ávila in the morning, and Leslie got us to the medieval part of the city as we feasted on hot dogs from a cart and I sucked down a warm can of Coke.

"The recipe for Coke is different in every country," I said, "so I want to taste it in every country."

Everywhere you went in Europe there were war memorials going back hundreds and even thousands of years, one on top of the next, wars I had read about and wars I had never heard of. I thought about the soldiers, all my age, offered up by their fathers and grandfathers to kill or be killed over religion and property, and, now, oil and freedom and Coca-Cola, which I drank with a harder and harder compulsion, like the writers in the books I loved drank liquor.

At the hotel, we were met by a tall, thin man at the front desk who reminded me of John Waters, though I didn't know who John Waters was at the time.

"Hello," he said in heavily accented English, assuming we were Americans. "You'll be wanting a room with two beds or one?" He raised an eyebrow at us.

"Whatever's cheaper," Leslie said.

He raised his eyes from his computer and looked back and forth between us. "One bed, then."

Leslie and I looked back and forth between each other and him. He smiled coyly, amused by how tense he had made us. "I have here two rooms: one room has one large bed; the other room has two smaller beds. Same price, thirty euros."

"We'll take the big bed," I said, annoyed but resolute. I didn't care what he thought, and Leslie looked up at me with a big smile as we walked away with our keys. We were both a little high from having, in our eyes, come out to the hotel clerk.

For the first time, we had hours, and no one to interrupt us. Soon we were finding out everything our bodies could do together, clean and naked and relaxed with beer and exhaustion and desire. We were so far away from everything we'd ever known and everyone who knew us, like not even God could see us. But I knew that if God was God, God could see us, and Jesus, too. But while we were here together, maybe they had their backs to us, like Bob Fosse dancers, snapping their fingers, imperious and aloof. Years later, I'd learn that we weren't safe just because there wasn't anyone from Franciscan around, but that's what it felt like. What could I fear from men when I was willing to go toe to toe with God?

In the middle of the night, before God or anybody woke up, Leslie lay in my arms with her head against my naked chest, and we whispered to each other things we'd never said out loud to other people.

"I like your eyes," she said. "And I like your arms and your voice. I love when you're at Mass next to me, 'cause I get to hear you sing. Your voice is good! Will you sing me a song?"

The only songs I had memorized were from musicals, and I didn't want her to make fun of me.

"Come on, I like musicals," she said.

I'd never sung in front of anyone else before, except when I sang to the kids when they were babies, and I bounced them around the dining room table in a circle to get them to go to sleep.

She nestled into my chest as I sang, but later that morning, when we were dressed and racing to the train station, she started crying.

"I finally got here, to the town of my favorite saint!" she sobbed, talking loudly since it was raining and too early for anyone to be out in the street, and we were in a little town where most people didn't speak our language. "I get here, and what do I do? I get drunk, and I become a *lesbian*!"

I slogged through the mud, pulling my coat tighter and trying to think of something comforting to say. God was looking right back in my face now, crossing his legs, filing his nails, smirking at me, challenging me to fix the mess I'd created. *This is your mud and your rain and your cold morning,* I thought at God. *Maybe she wouldn't be crying if it was sunnier.*

As we crossed the border into Austria, and the names of the towns started getting familiar, we stopped talking about it, in case anyone from school was on the train. In Linz, before our last leg home, we stopped at a café for an espresso and spotted Mark Angelo with some other Franciscan students.

"How was Spain?" Mark asked Leslie and me.

We looked at each other in the secret way that isn't really secret, and stumbled around in our minds trying to figure out how to answer his question without lying, but also without saying all the first things that popped into our heads.

"Beautiful," I said. "It was really beautiful."

Leslie blushed and looked out the window, smiling and trying not to smile.

As we walked back to the Kartause that night from the train station, alone and out of everyone else's earshot, Leslie talked about how she'd never liked any other girls before, just me. I felt again like there was just something about me that was wrong. Maybe I really was a boy, and that was the joke.

"It's better if we just be friends anyway," I said too abruptly. "I mean, what else are we going to do? 'Come out of the closet'?" I said the words like I was saying "go to the moon" or "grow a third head," like it was clearly, obviously impossible.

"People do it," Leslie snapped.

"Really?" I said, angry at our world for making things so impossible, and angrier at her for suggesting we challenge it. "You think *this* is exhausting and feels bad? How do you think that'll be? Do you know anyone who's out at school?"

It was a rhetorical question, but I also really wanted to know. She shook her head. We were both exhausted. The mountain town was so quiet, I could hear our footsteps crunching the snow and frozen grass beneath our feet. It was a mile and a half back to the Kartause, along a road with no sidewalk. Most people hitchhiked back, but I always thought it was easier to walk farther than to interact with other people. I saw Leslie wipe tears from her face. I wanted to make her laugh.

"Maybe we should just stay friends so we don't go to Hell," I said. She laughed, and I knew it was okay, at least a little.

"Is that what you really want, to be friends?" she asked.

"Yeah," I said, having been taught all those times that if I said a thing out loud enough, I could make it true; that my feelings were just what I said they were.

Later that week, I called home and talked to all my brothers and sisters before Mom got back on the phone to tell me about my cousin's funeral.

"And Brad was there with his new girlfriend! Why didn't you tell me he was dating someone?"

I felt my breath rise into my throat and stop, like a medieval city wall had gone up inside my mouth. I knew she was relieved, like this was confirmation that I hadn't been lying to her.

"Oh, I forgot," I managed to say in a high-pitched choke, trying to make it sound like I already knew. I lied so automatically to Mom now. I stared off into space, trying to settle my mind into the alternate world where I was Brad's cousin, happy for him about the girl he was willing to hold hands with in public, like there was nothing wrong with her. Mom kept talking, updating me about all my relatives.

I tried to think of how to tell her any of it. The news about Brad stung deeper because Leslie and I had been seeing each other less and less, only hanging out together when Heather was there.

Mom was talking about how beautiful the flowers were, how there were so many, like it had something to do with dying young. I was thinking of Leslie, wishing I could find her for one more kiss, but knowing we'd never be able to stop there.

Lily and Beatrice started yelling for Mom's attention, and she had to go before I thought of the right way to tell her anything.

20 Could We Start Again, Please?

2004. After Austria, I went home for two weeks before my summer classes started. The laundry was piling up; the gerbils, fish, and birds all needed their cages and tanks cleaned; both bathrooms looked like four or five children had used toothpaste, toilet paper, towels, and shampoo to create some kind of art installation. Plus, the snake was on the loose, roaming the house.

"But we know he's still alive," Jimmy said. It was his snake, Tom Riddle. "He's around here somewhere... We know because he bit Evangeline's foot one day!"

"What?!" I didn't mind the messes, but a free-roaming snake was alarming.

"It was under the couch," Todd said, unperturbed.

"I was watching *Scooby-Doo! Curse of the Lake Monster*," Evangeline explained.

"And it popped its head out and bit her foot!" Beatrice said, a little delighted. Todd and Evangeline nodded.

"It was scary," Evangeline said, taking the last bite of her waffle. "But then it wasn't."

I took the kids on errands to give Mom a break. I could fit them all in my car if two rode in the back seat, looking out the back window—they fought over these seats. One day at a red light, the man in the car next to mine signaled anxiously for me to roll down the window. I pushed the button to scroll Marianne's passenger window down, removing the barrier between us and the man.

WHAT WOULD JESUS BOMB? That's what my bumper sticker said, and that's what the man shouted indignantly at me, past all the little kids, like he was cursing.

"Yeah!" I shouted back, to put the question back to him.

"How about Sodom and Gomorrah?!" he screamed wildly, as the light turned green.

"That wasn't Jesus!" I shouted, rolling the window back up. The man yelled something else I couldn't decipher, sticking his middle finger up at me as he sped away. A car honked behind me to remind me that I had to go, too.

"What a jerk," Marianne said, folding her little arms.

"Yeah, what a jerk!" Beatrice said firmly.

I looked at the kids in the rearview mirror, and they were fine. Marianne was fine, too. They weren't shaking inside. Jimmy and Lily were laughing in the back seat.

"That was fun!" Lily said.

"Sodom and Gomorrah were *not* bombed, and Jesus wasn't even born then," Marianne said, baffled by the man's ignorance and logic. "Plus, if he cares about what Jesus would do, he definitely wouldn't be yelling at a carful of little kids on their way to *church*."

I looked over at Marianne, really appreciating for the first time that she trusted her instincts about what was right and wrong, and wondering why she was so different from me.

"You're right," I said. "Jesus definitely wouldn't have done that, and he definitely wouldn't bomb anything."

"Jesus was *nice*!" Beatrice chimed in, equally baffled.

"Yeah"—Marianne nodded in agreement—"that's kinda the whole point of Jesus."

The Double T Diner was Nanny's favorite place to take us for breakfast, lunch, or dinner on the way to or from anywhere. I wished she was there as I sat awkwardly with Angie. It was the first time we'd seen each other since high school. Angie was at Christendom College, one of the few schools in the United States that rivaled Franciscan in Catholic zeal.

At Christendom, girls and women had to wear skirts inside the chapels, and tattoos, piercings, and hair dyeing were all prohibited.

Angie and I sat at a small booth in the diner, sipping black coffee, talking about what books we were reading and what we were trying to write. Angie told me that Theresa was graduating from the school of consecrated women and that she was now starting the process of becoming consecrated herself. Theresa was engaged to Jesus, or at least they were dating. I thought about Theresa's face staring blankly into the camera in the picture I kept of her, on the back page of a photo album, realizing I hadn't seen her since we were fourteen. I kept thinking that something about growing up meant I'd feel more normal inside my body, that I'd start to feel right about being "a woman," but the years kept going by, and I still wasn't feeling it. I wondered if she was.

"Have you seen Mrs. Carver at all?" I asked, just before we paid the check.

Angie smiled a funny smile, like she was sharing a secret with me. Did she know about my crush on Mrs. Carver? Could we talk about it? Angie told me that Mrs. Carver now tutored her younger sisters, that they loved her as much as we had.

"I really loved her," I said. Angie said she did, too, but I didn't take the out. I corrected her: "No, I really loved her. Like, I was in love with her."

Angie smiled awkwardly, like her teeth were sinking into quicksand. She sucked in air through her stiffening mouth, eyelids low and fluttering. I knew my fate in an instant.

"Wait, are you kidding right now?" she asked.

I had a second to decide whether to take that half step back into the closet, but the Band-Aid had been ripped off. I had two words to choose from, and I tried to be brave, like people in the movies.

"No," I said, "I'm not kidding."

"You were in *love* with her? Are you serious?" She lowered her voice and looked around the diner as if for the Gestapo. "I mean, I kind of guessed you might like some-one... a girl... because of that letter you wrote me. But I didn't know for sure. Did you just like *her*, or did you think you were, *you know*... ?"

"What's the difference?" I asked.

"I don't know." Angie sat back, appalled. "Do you still like girls?"

I nodded, and she looked like she'd smelled something foul.

"But what about Brad?" she asked. "I thought you loved him!"

"I do love him," I said. "But he's my stepcousin. Or my cousin. I don't know, whatever he is, that part is weird—"

"But you're not biologically related, so the Church says you can still get married. The Church is okay with marrying cousins anyway, sometimes. But anyway, you still feel"— she lowered her voice more—"*same-sex attraction*? Even though you love him?"

Angie seemed to be asking me if I was a pervert. If I didn't still feel it, I'd be lying and backtracking, but if I did still feel it, it seemed to say that my love for Brad was in question, maybe even my ability to love. She was frustrated. We were exiting the diner, and she pointed the key fob to unlock her car like she was casting a spell to save her life. "So, what are you telling me?"

"I don't know," I said. "I just wanted to tell you."

She was silent as she started the car and we pulled out of the parking lot.

"That must be such a hard struggle," she said finally, as if she'd just realized it. This was more generosity than I had expected, and I felt like crying.

"Yeah," I said, looking away and biting my tongue inside my mouth to hold back tears.

"I will pray for you every day," she said sincerely. "I heard there are people who can help you through it, too, places you can go—"

"It's not that bad," I said, like I was talking about a rash. "If I can be attracted to Brad, I think I can be attracted to other guys. It's just, like, that won't keep me from falling in love sometimes."

The radio played the Dido song that played every hour or so, and Angie turned it up, singing along absently.

"I love this song," she sighed. "Sometimes I feel like God plays just the right song at the right moment, you know? Anyway, if you feel attracted to men at all, I think that's the most important thing, because you can find the right man God wants you to marry, if he wants you to marry. Or maybe he wants you not to marry, to be single or be a nun."

"Do you really think, if I'm trying not to fall in love with women, that I should go live in a convent?"

Angie frowned. "I didn't think of it like that. You know, they're saying that a lot of those priests who were in trouble, that they got that way because they were homosexuals, and the Church accepted them and let them be priests anyway. So, I guess they're going to stop letting homosexuals be priests."

"Being gay and being a pedophile aren't the same," I said angrily, but I couldn't shake the feeling that there was, in fact, something deeply shameful about me, something just as bad as Humbert Humbert in *Lolita*.

"The Church says there isn't really such a thing as 'gay,'" Angie corrected me. "But, you know, a lot of those kids were teenagers, and in the medieval times, grown men would marry women who were young teenagers. Once someone has gone through puberty, they're an adult, physically, so that's not pedophilia. And most of the priests were with teenage boys, so I don't think it's that different than when the medieval men would marry teenage girls—one can lead to a true marriage in the Church, and procreation, and eternal salvation, but the other one can't. Of course, no priest should ever be having sex with anyone, but most of this scandal is about them having sex with kids, and it's just not true. Satan wants to bring down the Church, and the liberal media definitely doesn't mind helping him with that. Did you know that the Church has the same rate of priests doing that as any other religious organization?"

"I've heard that," I said. Angie was getting so upset that I was a little concerned for her driving, but we were almost to my house. I was glad I was going to get out of the car soon.

"Anyway, I will pray for you, Rebecca," she assured me. "And I'll pray for Brad to come to his senses and just marry you, for heaven's sake."

She drove the car up our long driveway, smiling brightly at the notion of me marrying Brad. I tried to smile, too. At least she hadn't yelled at me or gotten mad. When she parked at my house, we said good night and promised halfheartedly to see each other again before the summer was out. Would she tell her mom or her sisters? Would she tell Theresa?

When I walked in the house, Mom was sitting in her rocker, smoking and watching TV. Bob lay stretched out on the couch, asleep, and Evangeline lay sleeping on the other end of the couch, her legs and arms sprawled in four directions.

"Hey, you," Mom said. She asked me if I had a good night. I told her it was okay and took a seat on the floor.

Bob woke up and drowsily scooped up Evangeline in his arms to carry her to bed. "There you go, you can have your couch bed," Bob said. "Night night."

Evangeline's feet, still round like a baby's, bounced lightly against the hallway wall as Bob carried her sleepily to the bed they shared with Mom and Meagan, the bulldog, and any other children who wished to sleep there and did, whenever they felt like it. Mom and Bob never got into the kid beds alone like my dad did with me. I tried not to think about it.

Mom lit another cigarette. I wished I could smoke one, too.

"They're all so big now," I said.

"I can't believe I never have to change another diaper," Mom said. "Did you eat dinner?"

"Yeah," I said, but I hadn't.

"You've lost weight," she said. "Don't lose too much, or you might disappear."

She laughed, but I just smiled. I wanted to disappear. I watched her inhaling and exhaling smoke, like a dragon or an angel or a mechanical creature from a carnival ride. Sometimes I wished she could breathe the fire over me and eat me up like we were in a fairy tale.

Maybe if I really prayed, if I really gave myself to God like the other kids at Franciscan did—maybe then I'd be able to get over this thing everyone was always saying I could get over—maybe I could unbecome myself.

That night I sat on my bed staring at my CDs, the meticulously organized collection of showtunes I'd accumulated over my teenage years. So gay.

I opened my laptop and typed out a list of their titles. One hundred, two hundred. I'd never sold anything on eBay, but it seemed simple enough. "LOT OF 200+ MUSICAL THEATER CDs," I typed into the rectangle. Someone sent me thirty dollars. Hiding was easy. I packed up the ones I couldn't let go of: *Les Misérables*, Audra McDonald, *Cabaret*, *Chicago*, and, of course, all the Sondheim. I shoved the box into a closet.

I always went to Dad's when school ended in the summer, but now I drove myself. When I pulled up to the new house on the back road that he shared with Linda and their two little kids, I was still thinking about what the priest had said and how all that time had disappeared. The story was always that nothing ever happened in Dry Creek.

For years I'd been following a script of things I could talk about and things I couldn't. I brought presents for everyone, and I told them about my semester away: the history (avoiding or glossing over anything too Catholic), and the food (not mentioning the alcohol), and how I'd met Heather (but not Leslie).

When the kids went to bed and my stepmom was cleaning up the kitchen, my dad cornered me in the living room as I stood up to call it a night. I knew he expected a hug and a kiss. I glanced at my stepmom, but she was flicking off the kitchen light, going toward the stairs, and suddenly he was grabbing me by the shoulders and pressing his fingertips into my joints. In a swift motion I swiped him away with one hand, and he stumbled backward. The shock on his face betrayed him, as he steadied himself against a shelf.

"Don't touch me," I said, unable to think about it long enough to stop myself.

He looked incredulous, his eyes wide. Years later I realized he was afraid, then: afraid of me and what I might say. I never felt quite as afraid of him again. It was like something had been said out loud. We couldn't look each other in the eye anymore.

21 There's Always a Woman

2004. I stood in the hallway outside of Professor Ritter Blake's office, shuffling my feet on the hard, thin carpet. I'd only been to one other professor's office before, Dr. Davis, who liked my poems, whose office was cluttered, and whose politics and philosophy were fairly Franciscan— still, he said my poems were good and gave me interesting books to read. He was helpful and easy, even if I didn't want to talk to him about feminism.

For that I'd come here, to the lone feminist on campus (it was rumored, anyway). I saw her hair first, because she was so tall. Her thick, curly hair rose up above the crowd of people in the hallway, her curls like the corona of the sun reaching out behind the moon during an eclipse, tingling toward space. Everybody was leaving their classes at the end of the day, moving through the mob, greeting each other, saying "excuse me," facing their evenings with intermingling enthusiasms, their eyes peeled for each other. Professor Ritter Blake's eyes were cast down, however, apparently uninterested in whether she'd run into anything. But she had nothing to worry about. Her hair captured light like a mirror. The crowd parted for her.

As she got closer, she got taller, and I could verify what Leslie had described: that she looked like a supermodel. Her face was square and stern when she wasn't smiling, which was most of the time. But she was so graceful and angular that everything she did looked glamorous. I couldn't stop looking at her, but she either didn't notice me as she passed or was actively ignoring me, heading for her office door like it was the last way to get back to the real world, like the real world was right inside there.

"H-h-hi," I managed as she reached her office, unlocking the door in one swift motion.

She whipped her head back slightly, throwing back her hair. Her eyebrows raised and she looked down at me, sizing me up. I wished I looked different, but I couldn't picture what I wanted to look like. I was glad I'd worn a clean t-shirt. My hair was long now, past my shoulders, like Jesus or Samson, I liked to think, but everyone always just said it was pretty.

"Hi," she replied a little impatiently, entering her office but not inviting me to enter.

As she gathered her belongings to leave for the day, I stood explained that I was the one who had been emailing her about a directed study. She straightened up and faced me.

"Oh," she said. She looked me up and down again, then said, "Okay, well, are you up for it?"

"Yes," I said, with more confidence than I felt.

"Great!" she said, like she was tired. "Then I have to fill out some paperwork, and basically you'll read a bunch of books and we'll talk about them, and then you'll write a paper at the end of, say, twenty or thirty pages. How does that sound?"

There were moments in literature when the protagonist meets the wise teacher, the witch or wizard who knows the old magic or the new magic or the Force or the memory or the future, and everything changes. But I didn't think of any of that; I just worried that I wouldn't be able to do it. I said yes anyway.

"Cool," she said. "Send me an email and start thinking about what you want to do." She walked toward me, exiting the office and readying her key to lock the door. She smiled. "Now, I've gotta get the hell outta here."

"Cool," I said, smiling absently. "Yeah, me, too."

One day as Heather and I sat studying and talking, I told her everything about me and Leslie. She listened and nodded without judgment, asking me questions, laughing with me about all the things she now understood. I felt the world slip off my shoulders for a few minutes as I realized Heather didn't think anything different of me and that nothing had changed.

"So, you're gay?" she asked, smiling.

"Yeah," I said, "maybe I am..."

We smiled at each other for a long time, like we had the best secret.

Heather lived with Natalie, who was taking Professor Ritter Blake's summer class, Medieval Women Mystics, which meant that she spent two hours a day with Matilda, as she welcomed students to call her. Heather wasn't taking any classes, but she was spending hours each week in Frank Blake's office, talking to him "about philosophy." Natalie quickly perceived Heather's crush on Frank and, after a while, even realized, entirely on her own, that Frank had encouraged Heather's affection, and that Frank and Matilda didn't seem to be happily married, and that Frank might actually return Heather's feelings—but Heather was absolute about not telling Natalie about anything that was going on between her and Frank, because she didn't want anyone else to know anything that could get Frank in trouble. I bit my lip to prevent all the things I wasn't supposed to say from coming out.

By the fall semester, the three of us had a reputation on campus as troublesome feminists. News traveled quickly at Franciscan, and it was news if someone admitted to being a feminist. Heather was the most likely of the three of us to get into arguments with people she knew would be scandalized by her liberalism. I started coming up in conversations she had with her household sisters about why women should be priests, or why it was sexist to talk about women's souls being different from men's souls. When one of her household sisters came over to express her concern for Heather's lapsing devotion to "Church norms," the household sister and I got into an argument about whether it would be a sin to smoke marijuana.

I'd still never smoked it, but I was certain that Jesus would've. I kept asking her what the difference was between marijuana and wine, and she kept saying the word "drug" like it made her mouth taste foul, but she had to keep saying it. The Lambs started calling Heather and Natalie's house, where I spent most of my time, the "den of iniquity."

We spent as much time as we could leaving Steubenville for Pittsburgh, blasting music in the car for forty-five minutes each way. Pop songs were just like songs from musicals, I realized, except nobody cared that they didn't already know the story. Natalie had discovered feminism, and we spent endless hours talking about the sexism and sexual repression that we were witnessing day in and day out at Franciscan. None of us had seen much else, but we knew that something else must be possible. I watched other people in their cars, and wondered about their lives and how they'd become who they were.

Just crossing the bridges made the rest of the world feel more real, and the air cleared space to say the things there wasn't any space to say in Steubenville. We rolled down the windows, because there was no A/C in the car, and the wind slammed into us, or we pushed through it. Natalie drove fast, and we sang out loud, and we didn't care how bad we sounded or what we were saying, because nobody knew what we were thinking of, and the country rolling

past us bellowed so loud we couldn't even hear each other,
just ourselves.

There weren't many female professors at Franciscan, and
the cards seemed stacked against all of them. I heard a lot
about what a heretic Professor Ritter Blake was and what
holy individuals the male theology professors were. Most
of them had big families full of children, and hardly a conversation about the Blakes' liberalism went by without a
comment about all the children they didn't have; everyone
was eager to assume that they were having a lot of contra-
ceptive sex, though no one ever proposed that they were
unable to have children, or so virtuous that they had
a Josephite marriage—a marriage without sex, which was
rare, but considered an acceptable path among more
conservative Catholics.

A few of the female professors were nuns, and a few
were married, but there were a couple younger, single
female professors, including Dr. Madison and Dr. Kasey,
a psychology professor who was, notably to me, dating a
graduate student a few years her junior. They participated
in the Charismatic Movement together, and he'd never
taken any of her classes, I was told, but the blurred lines
got a little blurrier. I never heard of Dr. Madison having a
boyfriend, which only made her more interesting to me.
It was a mark of suspicion on her that she wasn't married—why didn't she want a man, or, more importantly,
why didn't any men want her? It implied to most of our
community, as her academic accomplishments suggested,
that she was not an easily likable woman; while getting
a PhD and having a tenure-track job and no husband or
children at thirtyish was not technically "wrong," it wasn't
really *right*, either.

But that didn't deter me. As soon as I could, I took Dr. Madison's Philosophy of Poetry course. I'd never taken a philosophy course, but I liked poetry and I wanted to get to know her. She was so young looking, the first day of class someone thought she was a student. That pissed her off. She shoved a syllabus in the kid's face and sat on the table in the front of the room with her arms folded, over it quickly.

"What is poetry *for*?" she asked us.

I grinned. She grinned back at me. I waited for anyone else to say anything. A few people stumbled.

"Go ahead, Rebecca, what do you think poetry is for?"

"To cut through bullshit," I said. A few people were visibly shocked, and Dr. Madison made an expression of faux astonishment.

"Oh my, Rebecca, *swearing* on the first day of school!"

It went on to be a great conversation, and I started lingering after class, asking extra questions, making up excuses to go to her office hours. Heather had taken a class with her once, too, and one day she casually stopped by after class and magnanimously invited Dr. Madison to a brunch at her house with several other female intellectual-type students of various ages. I never thought Dr. Madison would attend, but she showed up with a big basket of strawberries and cream.

I relished that time with her outside the structures of where we were supposed to be, but it all felt bittersweet. I thought about Heather and Frank, who had something real, I knew, not just a crush in Heather's head and wishful thinking. But Dr. Madison wasn't like Frank—Frank wasn't a believer; he had become cynical a long time ago and just worked here because he had to, because this was the kind of education he'd gotten and the only place that would hire him to teach. But Dr. Madison worked here because she wanted to. She went to daily Mass, too, I'd seen here there.

Was she like me? Was she someone who fell in love with women but was trying to do what she was supposed to? What if we could just be *something*—maybe not a couple, like the Left said two women could be; maybe not just teacher and student, like the rules said we should be; maybe something distinct from the total platonic friendship dictated by the Church—what if we could be something that was what *we* wanted, even if it wasn't exactly what we were supposed to be according to anyone else? And what did *she* want, and how was I supposed to know?

Later that week, I stood talking to Frank Blake in the hallway between classes, and Dr. Madison sidled over to grab my arm and tell me she thought I should sign up for one of her classes the next semester. When she left, Frank glanced over at my arm with raised eyebrows, and I lifted it up as if it were broken.

"I'll never wash this again," I said, and we laughed, like we knew something, even though we had no idea.

During our one-on-one tutorials, Professor Ritter Blake would sit in her swivel chair, and ask me what I thought. Every other week I came to her office, and we discussed whatever book she had assigned me to read. I had to explain and defend the titles to folks in the library or the hallway, or whoever I ran into, who were concerned by words like "feminism" being so broadly displayed on the covers of the books I carried around. They were philosophy texts, mostly, and hard for me to read, so I'd always end up staying up all night trying to think of something smart to say when I got to her office the next day, bleary eyed and clutching a coffee. We'd go back and forth until we ran out of things to say; she rarely did, and most days we ended our sessions because she had to get on the road back to Pittsburgh before rush hour. During the last ten minutes of each meeting, she'd list five to ten books that I could read next, and I'd choose one, write down the name, and order it from the library that night.

One day before I left her office, I got up the courage to ask her if there were any good texts to read about the Church's views on homosexuality.

"Sure," she said, and I could tell she was surprised and trying not to look interested. "I'll send you a list of titles."

"Cool," I said, trying to be cool. She smiled at me generously, and I thought about Heather and Frank, and felt that old, nagging feeling like I didn't know what was real. Frank had a lot of bad things to say about his wife, which I mostly heard through Heather, but so far, I hadn't seen any of it.

"What did you think of the reading?" she later asked, after I'd read a book that covered some musings about the origins of lesbianism.

I got up the nerve to ask her that thing that had been lurking in the back of my mind. I'd read that women could choose to be lesbians as a rejection of men and masculinity, but this seemed to make the whole thing an intellectual decision. I couldn't really imagine someone choosing to be a lesbian, unless she was richer and freer than any woman I'd met. But was it a choice, or a deep-down sort of preference that had formed because something bad had happened to me?

"What were you going to ask?" Professor Ritter Blake was staring at me a little funny, like I'd been staring off into space.

"Do you think people are gay because they're abused as kids? You know, like... sexually?"

She always smiled at me when I asked questions like this, the ones I was afraid to ask.

"I've heard there are statistical links," I said, referring to the time Brad had told me that all the lesbians he knew had been abused and when Father Tim said I must've been abused.

"If being abused by men made women lesbians," Matilda said, "*all* women would be lesbians."

I laughed, but she didn't.

"I'm serious," she said. "And wouldn't that be simpler! Ugh! I wish I was a lesbian!"

I laughed harder now, because I couldn't imagine anyone wanting to be a lesbian. But I knew Matilda was sincere, and for a second I wished I could grant it to her, like the bad movies and angry churchy people always said that I could, as if with magic, I could turn other people gay.

"The thing is," Matilda said, "hardly anybody talks about child sex abuse or about homosexuality. If there's a correlation, maybe it's just that some people talk about things. I don't know if we can know yet, why people are gay or straight, if it's still so forbidden to admit or reflect on, and it's always seen as a negative to be gay or, heaven forbid, *bisexual*! I think if there is a 'cause' of being gay, we won't know for some years. And I think making the claim that it comes from abuse is offensive and just serves this totally baseless notion that there's something *wrong* with gay people, which *there is not*."

I felt relieved, like I had just gone to confession, or gotten all my homework done, or had enough money, or it was Friday.

2004. After I got back from Austria and through part of my junior year, I lived in the city of Steubenville's public housing. There were two sets of city projects, with one close enough to campus that it was basically a part of it. Here a long-running network of students grandfathered housing to each other, to the point that a sizable portion of the people who lived in the projects near campus were students. The non-university-affiliated neighbors were mostly Black people who seemed to live in a different world than the one my friends and I occupied. I heard little of the two worlds interacting beyond saying good morning or good night in the parking lot, though there were a few stories of Franciscan students trying to evangelize their neighbors, to no avail.

Two girls who'd lived in my hallway freshman year had a free room in their unit and offered it to me. They were excited that I would be in Steubenville for the summer, because I could stay at their place when it would otherwise be empty, then live with them in the fall. I didn't know them well, but I knew I didn't want to keep living in the dorm. I wasn't sure what "public housing" meant except that if we could prove we had low income, we could live there for free and just pay utilities. So many good Catholics were doing it, it seemed like everyone had reasoned that, morally speaking, it was totally fine. Still, I kept asking: Weren't these projects meant for poor people? Like, real grown-ups and families, people who weren't in college?

"How much money do you have?" my potential roommate asked me.

I laughed, and I understood her point, but there was something about all of us being white out-of-towners and most of the non-university local folks being Black that felt like we were taking something from Black people. "No, no, no," everyone around me said, and I learned to say, too, "No, it's not about race, it's about how much money is in your bank account, and that's not about race." Our neighbors grandfathered units to each other, too, I was assured. It worked for everybody.

The lady who ran the office didn't like university students much, but that was her problem, I was told, though it stuck with me that she had a problem with us. She was a Black woman, and more than one of my white acquaintances raised their eyebrows at me about her giving them trouble or not helping them, like, *Well, you know how they can be.* I had been taught to recognize any element of the "culture of death," aka liberalism, but I had no idea how to recognize racism unless it was wearing a white sheet and holding a torch.

One of my roommates explained to me that this way, maybe we could evangelize a whole group of people we'd never have close contact with otherwise. But I never saw any of the non-university neighbors looking attracted to or interested in anything about us, and though the university students had been living in these projects for decades, there was no visible Black population on campus, no segment of local folk who had been caught up by the charismatic spirit that now infused the projects—although there was a *small* population of *white* townspeople who had gotten hooked on the Kool-Aid. Of course, anyone who wasn't white could probably tell pretty quickly how racist the Kool-Aid was, but we kept being taught that "racist" meant something else, like the word could refer to only one of two or three particular acts or scenes we'd seen played out over and over again in movies—nothing *we* were doing or could do.

I moved into the unit and spent most of my time at the library, or Heather and Natalie's house. I knew it was wrong to live there—there might be a million ways to argue that it was okay for our cadre of mostly white college students to live in those projects, but they all ignored the reality of what money and skin color mean in America. The ultimate irony, though, was that this university was Franciscan and had espoused an alliance with poor people, a dedication to helping those in need. Instead, the university's students were directly soaking up the resources that would've otherwise benefited poor people in the community they claimed to have set out to serve.

Even before I knew all the facts and all the history, I felt it under my skin: I was taking advantage of something. There was a vulnerability in the system, and I was exploiting it—like a man did, when he saw a place to insert himself, where no one would challenge him or question it or call him on it—that's what I was doing.

George W. Bush was running for his second term, and there was no way he was going to win, I thought. Nearly everyone at Franciscan was 100 percent behind him, fighting a crusade against Satan's army, the Democratic Party. A Franciscan sociology professor was running as a Democrat in a local election, and he was hounded by the college's newspaper, *The Troubadour*, and even other professors. A group of Franciscan students hijacked the candidates' debate, demanding that he justify his registration as a Democrat against his claim to be Catholic, which were inherently opposed, they argued.

Every homily on campus found a way to preach the evils of abortion, homosexuality, and euthanasia, three subjects where the Republican platform perfectly aligned with the Church's rules. Strangely enough, the wars were ignored during these sermons, as were racism, guns, education, economics, and the environment—only a minority of priests ever mentioned any of these issues, publicly or privately. There were a few contrary Kerry supporters, students mostly, who were always getting in debates with people, but they usually ended up saying that they were "just playing devil's advocate." If people on campus were for Kerry, they were mostly silent; openly advocating a pro-choice candidate meant losing all moral credibility. A few people wore buttons, which were an open invitation for harassment.

There were a few brave folks who were openly pro-Kerry. Heather was one. Someone threw a brick through her car window, ripped off her Kerry bumper sticker, and put it in the driver's seat. The closest the rest of us came to supporting Kerry was to say we were thinking about not voting for Bush, if the moment wasn't obviously hostile. Just to say you were thinking about it provoked most Franciscan students into a heated conversation about how the U.S. bishops had declared it to be a sin to vote for any pro-choice candidate and how you were contributing to the culture of death, and the piles of dead baby parts in dumpsters across America, all because you wanted a check on the American war machine or capitalism—a word Frank Blake had explained to me and many others. Till he said it, most of us hadn't known what it was, as if he'd been the first one to tell us what a tree was and had pointed at one and said, "Tree." Then we all went around noticing capitalism everywhere, thinking of him every time.

Both Natalie and I were still on the fence about voting for someone who was pro-choice, so thoroughly had we been convinced against ourselves, torn between what we were learning about the world and our indelibly black-and-white programming. Natalie had made up her mind that she couldn't vote for anyone who was pro-choice, but she hated Bush and had made up her mind that she couldn't vote for him, either. I had endured passionate sermons in church, in classes, and from almost everyone I knew about why voting for Bush was the only moral option. I was sure that wasn't true, but I also wasn't sure I could vote for Kerry. Heather routinely implored us to consider the electoral danger of voting for a third-party candidate in Ohio, and I hid behind the idea that the Republicans and the Democrats were equally evil and that at least a third-party vote would be making an argument for more options.

Dr. Blake and Professor Ritter Blake didn't publicly declare their politics, but I knew from Heather that they were campaigning for Kerry in Pittsburgh. This was damning information in Steubenville, and plenty of people asked me if I knew who Professor Ritter Blake was voting for, in hopes that they'd have some evidence against her moral character. I said I didn't know.

Heather asked Natalie and me if we wanted to go to Pittsburgh to see Kerry speak. We both agreed to go, but Natalie backed out when Heather told us that she happened to know that the Blakes might be there. I was excited by this prospect. Heather had told Frank that I was gay, which made him feel like one of my closest friends. Natalie felt differently.

"They *might* be there, or Dr. Blake *told you* they were going to be there?" Natalie asked sharply. She had been growing more and more suspicious, to the point that Heather was no longer really talking about Dr. Blake around Natalie, insofar as she could help it. Heather admitted that the Blakes would be there, and Natalie huffed something about not wanting to have to interact with teachers on her down time. Heather and I were genuinely confused by this statement, thrilled by the opportunity to spend time with teachers, especially these particular teachers, off campus and outside of Steubenville. Would any of us even exist anywhere else?

On a cold October evening, Heather and I drove to Pittsburgh to see John Kerry and the Blakes. We were both silent with nerves, but Heather blasted the Indigo Girls till we were both deep in thought. I read the directions aloud so that Heather could get us to the place where Frank had suggested we park the car for an easy walk to the Carnegie Mellon campus, where Kerry was appearing.

We waited outside, at the edge of a large mall, where several hundred people had gathered. People were walking around with buttons and signs and hats, some of them supporting Kerry and others protesting, some on the Left and some on the Right. It was amazing to see people who were so liberal that they didn't support Kerry, when it seemed that many people in Steubenville were too conservative even for Bush. It felt like a betrayal of my childhood to even be at a Kerry event without a protest sign. All of a sudden, Heather's face lit up and she started waving. I looked up and saw Dr. Blake waving back, trying to curb his smile. Dr. Matilda Ritter Blake stood behind him, at least three inches taller, confused about who was waving at them. She tried to figure out who we were as we approached, pulling her jacket closer and squinting.

"Hello!" she said, smiling broadly at Heather and me. "More fun than Steubenville, eh?"

"Yeah," I said nervously, taking in that I was standing here, the fourth peg of an actual love triangle. Frank introduced Heather to Matilda, and we made small talk. He was so unimpressive in person that I wasn't sure why both these beautiful women had fallen in love with him—he wasn't short or tall, fat or thin, handsome or ugly, thick haired or bald—he was plain, as bland as a "flesh"-toned crayon. He was funny, though, and soon, he and Heather were laughing, too close together, at some inside joke. Heather nudged Frank playfully, but too playfully. I looked at Matilda. Her whole face had changed, and she was staring blankly at Heather.

"You're the one who actually applied for a membership to Green Peace!" Frank said teasingly, unaware that anything had changed or trying to ignore it.

"I was twelve!" Heather laughed, and Frank laughed, and they both laughed for too long.

"It's really fucking cold," Matilda said finally.

I felt trapped in a movie that I wasn't supposed to see and couldn't get out of.

"I'm going to go," she said. "It's too fucking cold. I'll meet you at the restaurant later, eight o'clock," she said to Frank. "See you later," she said to me.

"Bye," she said to Heather. "Nice to finally meet you."

The three of us watched her walk away, her arms still folded, looking straight ahead, like she was on a runway or a plank.

"Is she okay?" Heather asked.

"Oh, she's fine," Frank said dismissively. "She's trying to get away from you because you're a member of a *terrorist* organization!"

"You don't know what you're talking about," Heather replied, laughing.

They stood close together, their coats almost touching. I dug my hands deeper in my pockets. A half hour later, a voice came over a loudspeaker to tell us that Kerry wouldn't be able to make it.

I had become a citizen of Ohio, and I was supposed to vote at the Days Inn at the bottom of the hill. It was crowded and full of people, mostly Franciscan students, but also a fair number of Steubenvillans, the people we saw at the grocery store and down the street but didn't talk to much.

I'd decided to write in someone I actually agreed with; I'd looked online all morning and finally found Joe Somebody, who wanted to establish a Department of Peace. I walked up to a table lined with little old ladies. One of them found my name on a card, and I asked how to write in a candidate.

"Oh!" one lady exclaimed in excitement. "Your first election, and you're writing someone in! Very good, very good!"

This prompted congratulations from several of the ladies. One gave me a paper ballot, and another took me to a plastic cubicle with a computer inside. I didn't know any of the local Ohio options, aside from the professor who was running on the Democratic ticket and who'd been harassed by students and other professors during his campaign for running as a Democrat. I voted for him and left the rest blank. After I wrote in the name I'd found for president, I turned the page to find a series of questions. Most of them weren't very clear to me, but one was. It asked if I believed marriage should be defined as being between one man and one woman.

I stared at the paper for a few minutes, then I looked up and around the room. I saw a dozen other people with their heads bent inside these temporary cubicles, and none of them was looking around or hesitating. I wasn't sure how I'd failed to know that this question would be asked. I couldn't remember a single student on campus talking about how we'd better vote yes on this question to save marriage, which meant that they never even considered it wouldn't go their way. They assumed that everyone in our fold would know exactly what to do with this question and that no one would deviate. This pissed me off, and I hated that they *knew* the people like me would lose. So I voted no, that marriage shouldn't be defined as being between one man and one woman.

I looked up, and the sky wasn't falling.

A few hours later, I returned to campus with the sense that even if I hadn't voted for Kerry, at least I had been able to tell the truth about what I thought love was. I was early for my next class, sitting on a couch in the hallway. Everyone on campus looked happy, and people were saying that Bush was doing well. I felt something fall in my stomach, and I started to think I'd made the wrong choice. It seemed so impossible for Bush to win again, for anyone outside of our little pocket of extremism to think he was a reasonable choice. It seemed like everyone on TV knew he was incapable of the office. I was counting on them, all those people out there in "the world," to do the thing I couldn't bring myself to do.

I saw Dr. Davis, the creative writing professor, and Dr. Tenerfort, the sweet theology professor, talking in hushed tones as they approached the faculty lounge.

"Looks like Bush'll win," Dr. Davis said, weary in a way that didn't make it clear whether he wanted Bush to win.

Dr. Tenerfort sighed a sigh of relief. "Any news on the marriage question?" he asked.

"Oh, yeah." Dr. Davis smirked. "Yeah, there's no way that's not gonna pass. There's no way this country is ready for *that*. No way."

"Phew," Dr. Tenerfort said, breaking out into a smile. They shook hands. I couldn't recognize what their smiles meant. They looked half guilty but okay with it, like they were being Real Men.

I felt a sick feeling in my stomach. I saw Matilda come out of her office, on the way to her class. She was late, I knew, from the time and her speed. When she saw me, she caught my gaze, shook her head, and said, "Fuck!" under her breath. The intensity in her eyes made me afraid, like she was about to burst into tears. I nodded, and she smiled in solidarity and went on to her classroom. I felt like an impostor. I'd never be able to tell her who I'd voted for, that I hadn't stood up for us when I could have, that I'd acted like Peter when he denied Jesus, like I didn't know myself at all.

I had a key to Heather and Natalie's, and on election night I let myself in knowing I'd find heartbreak. Heather crouched on the floor near the TV, disappointed tears running down her face as she watched the news anchors officially calling more states for Bush. Natalie had already gone to bed. The whole day felt like I'd drunk too much of a sugary drink or eaten too much fried food, the kind I loved, that could turn my stomach, could even, if I let it, kill me.

I remembered being at a fair when I was a kid, my hands sticky with lemonade, carrying around a half-eaten funnel cake, wishing I could eat the whole thing, and puking behind the Ferris wheel after the third or fourth person came up to me and my dad and told me how lucky I was to have a dad like him. Around other people, he'd pinch my shoulders in that way I knew meant I shouldn't say anything. "That's what you get from eating all that sugar," he'd said impatiently, handing me a napkin as I'd emerged from behind the ride, spitting to get the vomit taste out of my mouth.

I felt that taste in my mouth after I voted, too, or wasted my vote. All the arguments flooded my head at once. I fell asleep on Heather's couch, watching her cry in the light of the TV. I couldn't tell her that I was partly responsible for her tears. Something hit me, then, about the desire to keep my hands clean and the ability to pretend that my life hadn't done so much to contribute to the wrongs of the world, when I was starting to see so clearly that it had. Lady Macbeth had imagined the blood on her hands. But I knew, from watching girls wash their hands till they bled, that washing your hands over and over to get the imaginary blood off would just make them crack and bleed—so when had the blood stopped being imaginary, or had it ever been?

Watching Bush stroll victoriously across the screen, I knew I'd been had. I thought about the chicken and the egg, and Lady Macbeth's hands, raw from obsession and delusion, and I wondered if I could ever stop up the bottle of myself from its inevitably problematic spilling out into the world, like I was trying to ride down Niagara Falls in a barrel and keep the barrel from breaking. It seemed like everything I could do in the world was toxic, spilling out onto stolen land, where everything was covered up and made to look like something else. Now I was standing by while this man who went against everything I believed in was taking the keys to the kingdom. I wanted to believe I was different from the long trajectory of oppression from which I sprang. As he took the podium to perform his stupefied triumph, I looked down at my pasty American hands, realizing they'd never been clean to begin with.

23 | I Had Myself a True Love

2004–2005. One evening toward the end of the semester, I unlocked Heather and Natalie's door to find someone I didn't know sitting on the love seat, grinning up at me with curious, pretty eyes. Her skin was olive brown and glowed a little under the lamp. Her blonde hair was pulled back and she wore a large hoodie, but I liked her face right away, and she seemed to already like me, which happened so rarely with new people I felt moved by it.

"This is Jenny Jacobs!" Heather said, emerging from the kitchen with two coffee mugs. "We're out of clean glasses, but we've been drinking rum. Jenny has come over to the den of iniquity because her recent explorations of feminism have been met with rejection and ridicule by the other Lambs," Heather said. "And so, we have been drinking."

Leslie was very active with the Lambs now, and they were especially unfriendly toward me, leading me to believe she'd told them about us.

"You're a Lamb?" I asked Jenny. She was watching me, I noticed, like she was curious about me. She nodded and smiled. "I love the Lambs," I said dryly.

"And the Lambs love you!" Heather said playfully.

"That's what I've heard," Jenny said, but then she looked away from me and started talking to Natalie about people they both knew, and how everyone was worried about Heather and Natalie and their liberalism. I watched her trying to avoid saying that it had anything to do with me, but it was implied and understood. Every few minutes, Jenny would look over to me, and the corner of her mouth would curve up a little, and she'd look shy and not shy at the same time. When Heather and Natalie said they were going to retire for the evening, I said I'd sleep on the couch, which I often did. Jenny asked if she could sleep over, too.

"Well, there's a love seat, so you two figure it out and make yourselves at home," Natalie said, unperturbed. Heather said good night, trying not to giggle. Then Jenny and I were alone suddenly and everything felt electric.

"You slouch a lot," Jenny said after a moment of silence. She put her hands on my shoulders, and I felt a rush through my body. "Holy shit, you're tense," she was saying. "I mean, I can feel the knots back here like rocks. You don't mind if I work on them a little, do you?"

She was already pressing hard on the knots in my back, which I'd always accepted as part of life, part of having a back. I got sleepy as she used her thumbs to wrestle the stones out of my shoulders. I fell asleep for a second and woke up with her pulling me backward to lean on her. Her hands were around my belly now, and when I tilted my head back toward hers, she kissed me, and everything else disappeared. I don't know how much time passed, lost in that feeling of maybe having found someone who understands you, who knows what you know—

Then she broke away from me and said, "Wait." Her face changed, and she looked sad.

"What's wrong?" I asked.

"I've never kissed a girl before..."

My heart sank twenty floors or so, past the concrete basement into the ground, into the roots of wherever we were. She had been so confident—how could she have never done this before?

"Have you liked girls before?" I asked hopefully.

"No," she said, and laughed. "Just you..."

She was older than me, but I was the one who had done this before, I was the one who was corrupting her. But before I could think about it anymore, she was kissing me again.

"Are you okay?" I kept asking between kisses. Instead of answering me, she took my hand and put it underneath her sweatshirt. My body felt like it was melting. We kissed until we heard a door open upstairs and someone go into the bathroom. We froze. It was morning. We heard the shower turn on, which meant that Natalie was getting ready for class. I jumped away from Jenny like a snake had bit me and moved to the couch as fast as I could, where I lay still, pretending to be asleep, pretending that my heart wasn't pounding, pretending I hadn't wanted a pillow or a blanket, or to change my clothes, or to go home and brush my teeth—just pretending.

That spring semester I'd be in Europe again, in Oxford, a place where they actually spoke my language—and a place where I wouldn't be surrounded by Franciscan students. I could be new again, see who I was around other people. But, for the first time, I found myself just wanting to stay in Ohio, to stay with Jenny. I felt like I was being unfaithful to Dr. Madison somehow, but every time I felt that I reminded myself that she was my teacher, that she probably didn't give it a second thought that I wasn't showing up to her office hours as much. I didn't stop going, and that felt dishonest to Jenny. I was accustomed to dividing myself. I learned how to keep my knives ready, how to lie fast.

Before she had met Matilda Ritter Blake and discovered feminism, Jenny had traveled in the most conservative, most charismatic circles on campus. I knew enough to know that in those circles, if you thought or said the wrong thing, you were excluded. When Jenny said that she'd heard of me, I realized how far the circles of exclusion rippled.

Jenny had been a charismatic student leader on campus generally and among the Lambs specifically—until she'd started dabbling in liberalism with Matilda, then Heather, then me. Jenny lived on the Lambs' floor in the dorm, and household activity was supposed to be the focus of her home life. I never went to her hallway because, Jenny said, there were rumors about me and people who didn't like me, and there was no reason to invite bad repercussions.

But the night before she was supposed to fly to Nebraska, she let me sleep over, in the lower bunk, right next to her. We pulled the blankets over our heads like we were kids, and when we heard her roommate get up and leave for early-morning Mass, we kissed and kissed, finally alone behind a locked door.

That was the day I drove Jenny to the airport in Pittsburgh. Nebraska was so far, I couldn't imagine it. I'd be going to Maryland for Christmas, then flying to England, and then it would be summer, and who knows what either of us would be doing then?

"Learn how to text, okay?" she chided. "And I'll text you, like, all the time." She kissed me and handed me a CD she'd made and a letter. "These are so you don't forget me."

She didn't want me to walk her to the terminal, so I just stood outside the car and watched her walk into the airport. I clutched the collar of my gray coat around my neck. When I couldn't see Jenny anymore, I got back in the car and put the CD she'd made me into the Discman I had rigged up to two portable speakers taped to the dashboard of my station wagon. As I pulled out of the snowy parking lot, I tried to sing along, but I couldn't remember past the first line, something about never forgetting someone.

No sound came out of me but a catch in my throat, and I felt in my cells that I wouldn't touch her again, that she was flying away from me faster and further than I'd ever be able to chase, even if I wasn't worried about everyone seeing me running after a plane, or a girl.

When I got to the library to pick up my paycheck, the sweet librarian, Loretta, told me that Dr. Madison had come by and left something for me. I thought it must be a book we'd talked about, but the package was soft. It was a dark, stripy scarf, the European-looking kind that all the cool kids in Austria had. Loretta looked impressed and smiled because I was smiling. As the scarf unraveled, I found a postcard with a beautiful angel painting printed on it, but not a kitschy, corny angel—this one was by a real painter, a majestic angel standing next to a fence in a field that looked American, like two worlds colliding. On the other side of the postcard was the writing I recognized from my homework, telling me she'd been cleaning out her closet and found this scarf I might like, which wasn't her style.

I threw it around my neck dramatically and asked Loretta how I looked.

"Very *you*," she said warmly.

That night Heather and Natalie and I sat drinking wine together. I wore my scarf. Heather was graduating that semester and traveling to France for eight weeks before starting a graduate program in Pittsburgh the next year. Natalie would graduate that May, just after I got back from Oxford, and move back to California. Natalie was sad, but Heather was glad to be leaving Steubenville, maybe forever. When Natalie went to bed, Heather told me that, since she'd graduated now, she and Frank could be together.

"He's looking into flights to France," she said. "He might be able to visit me there, and we could actually spend a few days together... We talked about it, but I don't know if it could really happen. And I think he'd rather wait until he and Matilda are separated."

"What do you want?" I asked.

"I don't know," she said. "I just want him, I don't really care about the rest of it anymore."

Walking to the door of my home in Maryland, I could see the Christmas tree from outside, like in the movies, and hear the kid voices yelling and laughing and playing against music everybody could hear in their heads, even if it wasn't real. I realized that I hadn't changed my clothes in a few days or showered, and I had no clean clothes—but I had fallen in love with someone who might love me back. We spent the whole break texting and talking on the phone late at night, when our parents were in bed and no one could hear us.

Meanwhile, I ran errands with my family, some more pleasant than others. Papa grumpily asked if I could take him to the bookstore, but also said I could pick out a book for myself. Bookstores were my favorite place when I was a kid, but as I got older they started stressing me out. Why were some books always there, and others never were? I'd scan the names in the poetry section and look to each name like it contained the secret of how to become a poet, but none of them did. Not one of them had lived a life just like any of the others, so there was no pattern, no path to follow. I thought about everyone in the world trying to get published. Did I have anything to say?

Poetry was easier to hide inside of, since the story and the pronouns didn't really matter. I'd learned a long time ago that I could lie about gender in poems just by writing "you" instead of "she" or "her." I knew, too, that plenty of writers had spent their careers hiding things in their work that college students would later pick through and decipher by reading their letters in some dark library a hundred or a thousand years later.

I recognized the name "Adrienne Rich" from one of the books I'd read with Matilda about feminism, printed on a thin spine with the title *The Dream of a Common Language*. I took the pale blue book out of its place on the shelf and touched my thumb to the edges of the pages. I went to one page, then another, trying to remember how I knew the name. I read the back of the book. She was a lesbian. I looked up and around me, to see if anyone was noticing me holding a book by a lesbian. Nobody was.

I found the section "Twenty-One Love Poems," and I read them, standing there, poems by one woman about loving another. I don't think I'd ever seen a woman get to be so honest about the thing I'd always been hiding. I realized that in a poem, not like a movie or a TV show, there was only one person talking and making, and it didn't matter how many other people wanted to read it or hear it, like it mattered in the movies. Adrienne Rich wrote whatever she wanted and hadn't had to water it down at all. *These are the forces they had ranged against us, / and these are the forces we had ranged within us, / within us and against us, against us and within us.*

"Becca!" Papa said gruffly, walking by me without waiting to see if I'd heard him.

...*[T]his is how we tried to love,* it said. My heart was beating fast. I ran after my grandfather with the book in my hand. He didn't look at it, just said, "Sure," and put it in his pile. I prayed he wouldn't read it before he wrapped it to put under the tree.

Being home had started to mean holding my breath for a long time, trying not to say the wrong thing and trying to say the right things. Sometimes Mom was so tired she could be harsh with everyone, even the little kids and especially herself. *these are the forces they had ranged against us,* I read, from one woman to another.

I was going to Oxford, and I couldn't stop thinking about Jenny, and I couldn't stop fighting with Mom. She drove me to the airport, and for the whole hour I couldn't think of an easy thing to say to her. I clenched my teeth and sucked my breath in, and she held the wheel tight, like she was trying to hang on to me, and I was trying to hang on to her, and home, and the kids, and shake them away at the same time. We hugged each other like a cup that hadn't been glued back together right. *this is how we tried to love.*

In the D.C. airport, I read the poems again and again, glad that I wasn't traveling this time with a hundred Franciscan students. I finished the book and started it again in Iceland, on a cold tile floor, where I spent my six-hour layover writing a series of emails to Jenny. She hadn't written me back in a few days, but she was just busy, I was sure. I went back to the poems, realizing this was the first time I'd read a lesbian writer who wasn't just rumored to be a lesbian. I didn't understand everything she wrote, but I felt it all, even the one about Marie Curie, a scientist, a woman I knew nothing about. Still, I recognized what Rich wrote, like a torch song from a musical, but on paper:

> *she died a famous woman denying*
> *her wounds*
> *denying*
> *her wounds came from the same source as her power.*

2005. January in England was rainy and gray, but never as cold as it was in Ohio. I was staying in a building near the Oxford city center with thirty other American students from a smattering of schools across the United States. Once I found my room, I called my mom, then my grandparents, then Jenny, but Jenny didn't answer.

There were only three or four students from Franciscan in the Oxford program. This included my new roommate, Helen, my friend from English classes on campus. We hadn't spent much social time together, except for the fateful department party where I'd met Dr. Madison.

During the first few weeks, I found myself thrown together with the conservative kids. They were familiar and nonthreatening. I knew how to talk to them; I knew what to say and not to say. The overall crowd was a little more diverse than Franciscan, but mostly white and middle class. Two kids were rumored to be queer, but whenever they came back from the "Gay, Lesbian & Ally" meetings on campus, they were plastered and made sad jokes. It felt lonely to think of going with them.

We all lived in a sort of dormitory with classrooms and a big living room, kitchen, and dining room. Unlike Austria, the classes here were intense, and reading took up most of everyone's time. I could make calls easily from my room and spent the first few days talking to Heather. She was fighting with Frank because he and Matilda had just bought a house, which of course was not the same as getting a separation.

Helen had done the Oxford program the previous semester, so she told me things like how to do laundry, where to buy cheap "chips and cheese" at 3:00 A.M., and how to check out books from the library. Helen wasn't Jesus freaky; her religiosity was private, more medieval than charismatic, but I sensed that she was ultimately an obedient Catholic. Helen introduced me to Grace, her friend from the previous semester who was in the program from a school in California. I told her she reminded me of Bernadette Peters, and she laughed a big laugh.

"A Vietnamese Bernadette Peters, huh? Well, I'll take it. I love that one she did, what's it called? *Sunday in the Park with George*. About the painter. You can call me Bernadette if you want. Grace isn't my real name, either, it's my American name. So it's all relative."

"What's your real name?" I asked, stunned that I met someone who liked my favorite musical, the one about the artist who couldn't decide between being a perfect artist and being present to live his life.

"I'll tell you when I know you can pronounce it," she said with a big, beautiful laugh.

One day, Jenny wrote me back—one line, telling me to call her at a certain time on a certain day.

"Hello?" said a voice, but it didn't sound like the girl I knew. She was tired and raspy and irritated.

"Hey, it's me," I said. There was silence. I waited, and she breathed a heavy sigh. Suddenly all the "checking in" emails I'd sent to her seemed ridiculous and excessive, and I felt ashamed. If she had wanted to talk to me, she would have, of course.

"Hi," she said finally, and when I waited for her to say more, she didn't.

"Well, I guess I just wanted to talk to you. Why haven't you written me or anything?"

After a long silence, she seemed to gather the energy to tell me. Her voice was flat and depressed sounding. "Look," she said, as if she'd rehearsed this, "I think you got the wrong idea about our relationship, and I'd like you to not contact me anymore."

My face flooded red. My heart boiled under my skin, and I didn't know where to start. "The wrong idea?" I repeated, not caring how loud I got. "What do you mean?"

"I mean, it was weird, but we were just friends."

My stomach collapsed inside me, and I fought back tears. I hung up convinced that I was crazy and foolish. Everything I'd said and written to her inundated my mind all at once, conversations on top of poems on top of emails and text messages and her eyes under a blanket, in the middle of the night.

That semester my mind got quiet, like the second a vacuum turns off, or the moments after gunfire or fireworks. Little muted bombs kept exploding inside me and ravaging landscapes that I had only just begun to know were there, bombs with Jenny's face, Jenny's hands, Jenny's funny voice. I wore Dr. Madison's scarf all around England. Grace introduced me to Fiona Apple and we listened to "Paper Bag" over and over.

One night I came back to my room to find Helen sitting in her bed holding Grace. A dozen other people from the program, including the resident director, and all the kids from Grace's school were gathered around the bed with red eyes, some holding hands. Grace's face was buried in Helen's chest, but I could hear her sobbing. The RD, Amber, came over to me and ushered me into the hallway.

"Grace's mom killed herself," Amber said, her voice just below a whisper. I barely heard her, but the words echoed like repeating thunder between my ears. I stammered, asking questions. Hadn't Grace's dad just died?

I took a deep breath and went back inside my room. I knelt by the bed and took her hand.

"Hey, Chicken Butt," she said, smiling and squeezing my hand.

It was rude to talk about money, of course, and Grace didn't actually ask for help; she told the RD and Helen, and they dispersed the information that Grace needed several thousand dollars, quickly, to get back to Vietnam for the funeral, and that once there she'd be able to get money from her family to pay us all back.

I kept thinking about Grace's mom, whose name I hadn't known before and couldn't pronounce. I heard it now only through Grace's half sobs. Helen told me, when Grace was asleep in her bed, that she'd gotten a phone call when they were together, dropped her cell phone, and started screaming, sobbing on the floor. Helen didn't know what had happened exactly.

"She couldn't live without *him*," Grace said when she woke up, eerily calm, staring into space.

Grace returned from Vietnam quieter than she'd been before. She mostly wanted to sleep and go out for dinner.

"Look, Chicken Butt," she said. "This place is expensive, so I'll pay, okay? I don't want you to worry about it. The truth is my family is kind of wealthy. So, you know, it's not a big deal. And I still owe you anyway, for helping me get enough cash together for that stupid ticket. So, this is my treat, partly it's a thank-you, okay? And if you don't know what to order, you let me know, food is sorta my thing."

After we'd been seated by a waiter who knew her, Grace ordered a bottle of red wine in French. She sat back in her high-backed chair and folded her arms.

"So, my parents are dead," she said. "That's why I look like shit all the time. What's your problem?"

I laughed and acted like I didn't have to answer, but she pressed.

"Seriously, girl, what is up? You look like you're in a morgue all the time. Heartbreak? Some guy I need to beat up for you? What's the trouble?"

I figured I must be doing my act pretty well, if she thought it was a boy right off the bat. The rawness of the preceding days swelled inside my skin and burst out like ants from a silky brown sand hill.

"Do you care if people are gay?" I asked, focusing my gaze across the cobblestone street, glazed in rain. It looked British enough to be a movie set.

Grace threw her head back and laughed, her long earrings jingling against her neck, her smile wide. "What? Oh, Chicken Butt, what's that school you go to? Saint Francis? You've gotta get out of there. Of course I don't care if people are gay. Except I do, because I prefer it! I love gay people! So, I guess I do care. Who's gay, Chicken Butt?"

"Me," I said. "I'm gay."

Grace's mouth opened wide, in an exact O shape that somehow still turned up like a smile. "No way," she said. "You are? Chicken Butt! What does Saint Francis think about that? Are you gonna get in trouble? Does Helen know? Shit, I have so many questions, sorry. This is amazing."

I laughed, because this was certainly the happiest response I could imagine. I felt a lightness take over my body. Grace was the kind of person I'd seen on TV. It hadn't occurred to her to reject me; it was like I'd just told her that I was a superhero. She looked at me differently, like there was something more behind my eyes that hadn't been there a few seconds ago, like they were roads to somewhere inside me where she wanted to go to find out what had happened and what would happen. Still, I knew she might change her mind, like Jenny and like Leslie.

"You know God doesn't hate you, right?" Grace said, looking right into my eyes. She could see that I wasn't so sure. She took my hand and pressed it. "Those assholes are gonna molest little kids and tell you that *you've* got a problem because you wanna kiss a girl? Gimme a break. You're fine, okay, Chicken Butt? You're just as good and just as bad as everybody else."

I laughed again, sat up straighter, shook my head in disbelief. Grace asked me if I'd ever had a girlfriend, and I told her about Leslie, then Jenny.

"That's shitty," Grace said firmly. "She wants to break up with you, she should have the balls. She's gonna tell you you misinterpreted things? Ugh. Fucked up, Chicken Butt. Fucked up. She couldn't handle it! She couldn't handle being a lez. Ugh, I'm so sorry."

It felt good to hear someone else say it out loud. We sat for hours at a little table in the window, drinking wine and eating French food that I couldn't describe or pronounce.

"I'm never going to be able to remember this to order it again," I said. Grace tried to teach me how to pronounce it, but I couldn't wrap my tongue around the words.

"It makes a big difference," she said, as we left the restaurant, "not having words for a thing. It makes whole parts of the world totally invisible."

"And yourself," I said, knowing it was true without being able to explain it. She looked at me with that shock of recognition. Stepping into the street, I realized I was drunk and laughed. Grace laughed, too, and asked if she could sleep in my bed.

"I'm having nightmares," she said, and I saw that ghost pass over her face again, through her pupils, flaring her nostrils and putting that fragile little squeak in her voice, that ghost we'd been running from all night.

Grace slept in my bed almost every night for the next month. Most nights she stayed up later than I did, but she would creep into our room and wrap herself in my arms, holding my hands in hers, and fall asleep. She'd wake up early, too, but for a few hours every night her black hair would lie in my face, just under my mouth, and she'd tell me to "be a good spoon!" which meant to hold her tight around her waist. Helen thought it was odd that Grace kept sleeping in my bed, but said something about grief and comfort and the power of friendship.

I realized Grace was a habitual liar when she told me she was related to General Mao. The details of her life became more outlandish as time went on. The only part of her lying that bothered me was that she thought I was someone who couldn't tell the difference, and I wasn't.

I asked her one question that ended everything. She often stopped by our room in the mornings, and one morning she sat on my desk eating a honeydew melon she'd sliced in half and ate out of like a bowl with a spoon. She told me about a boy she'd met at church and how she was trying to figure out how to ask him out. It stung a little that she slept with me and didn't want me like that. Would she have wanted me if I was a boy?

She spooned some of the melon into my mouth and kissed me on the cheek, but a few minutes after she left, I realized that I had only twenty pounds on my desk instead of forty.

I looked everywhere and thought only the best. When I caught up with Grace later, I asked, "Hey, could you have accidentally taken twenty pounds off my desk this morning?"

I saw that thing flash in her face, a secret recognition, a game her eyes were playing, challenging me to keep challenging her.

"How could I *accidentally* take twenty pounds?" she asked, then told me she was in a hurry and disappeared down a hallway.

That night, Helen told me that Grace had been caught stealing from almost everyone in the program during the previous semester. She'd been given "another chance," and everyone had chalked it up to bad behavior in the face of grief and death. I asked why Helen hadn't warned me at all.

"It's wrong to tell people's sins, isn't it? That's, like, *gossip*, isn't it? And aren't we supposed to just forgive her? How else can people get redemption and change unless we forgive them?"

I could see the strain on Helen's face; she was doing her best, too, now wondering if she had done the wrong thing in the name of some Bible verse that turned out not to apply. I thought about this for a long time. How often had someone's forgiveness compromised someone else's safety? I never minded too much what Grace had done; I figured she had her reasons to lie and to need money that she might've assumed came easily to anyone else spending a semester in Europe. But what else was happening here, hidden behind the guise of forgiveness and the possibility of redemption? And which stories weren't even true?

A chilly night a few weeks later, toward the end of our program, I heard a ruckus in the hallway in the middle of the night. I was up late writing one of my last papers, drinking a room-temperature British Coca-Cola. I popped my head out my door to see three girls from Grace's school in California, running down the hallway, coats flying up in a gust as the door to the stairwell closed behind them. I grabbed my old gray coat and followed them.

In the stairwell I heard a joyful chorus of giggling and exclamations about snow. When we got downstairs, half the students from the program were funneling into the main lobby and outside into the street in various states of amazement and exhilaration, smiling faces tilted toward the heavens like they were at the altar, taking Communion straight from God, more natural than Communion in any church. My friends Jay and Ethan were there, standing in their dress coats and ties, grinning. Jay opened his mouth and stuck his tongue out, opening his arms wide when he saw me.

"I've never seen snow before!" Jay's voice bellowed musically. "Grace!" he called when he saw Grace coming out through the school's front door. "Grace, look, it's real!" He quoted something in Greek and rushed over to her.

As soon as she stepped out from under the overhang, she caught a snowflake on her cheek and wrinkled her nose in surprise. The streetlamps cast their faint yellows on the bright white snowflakes against the dark night and the gray cobblestones, shining in their eyes the way newness does.

Grace started singing "I Could Have Danced All Night" and dancing theatrically with Jay, like they'd already rehearsed and everything. Eventually Jay tripped and they collapsed in giddy laughter. Grace came over to me, shivering, with no coat.

"This is so beautiful, Chicken Butt! It's, like, the most beautiful thing I've ever seen! Fuck the ocean! What is this? You can get this in Ohio? I'm moving to Ohio!" I smiled at her. "So, you've seen it before? Then why are you here?"

She stepped the last step toward me, and she was leaning against me, under my chin like I was her umbrella. She laid her head on my chest and put her arms around me, under my coat. I felt like people might be looking at us, but I didn't care. No one from Steubenville was out here looking at the snow, no one to carry the story back home where it mattered.

"I'm seeing you see it," I said.

She stood on her tiptoes and kissed me lightly on the lips.

"You're going to make some girl very happy someday, Chicken Butt," she said, and she unlocked her hands and walked away from me as suddenly as she'd come. I accepted somebody else's cigarette and was glad I had something else to put in my mouth.

That semester my gray coat disappeared, and so did Grace, just before finals, and nobody I knew ever heard from her again.

PART 4
I'M ON FIRE

The angel of the Lord appeared to him in flames of
fire from within a bush. Moses stared in amazement.
Though the bush was on fire, it did not burn up.

—Exodus 3:2

2014. One night I got home from teaching to find an email from my dad. I hadn't seen his name since I'd asked him a few years before not to write to me anymore. I looked at the name for a while, the familiar shape of it in bold at the top of my inbox, where I wanted to see the name of a poetry magazine, or a university where I'd applied for a job, or nearly any other human being. The letters of his name blended together into one shape, a ghost ship.

He told me he was dying. He had cancer now, all through his body, he said, because of all the treatment he'd gotten for diabetes. He'd neglected himself for most of his life, sometimes even going into diabetic comas after binging soda and candy, and he'd needed two kidney transplants. The second kidney came from his friend, because he was such a good man, everyone said.

He'd be in Pittsburgh that weekend, if I wanted to see him. I put my laptop down. My wife, Alexis, came into the room.

"What's wrong?" she asked.

"My dad's dying," I said. "He just emailed me. He'll be in Pittsburgh this weekend."

"Fuck him," Alexis said. "He molested you. Now he wants you to come hold his hand or whatever?"

I don't remember what I said after that or what she said, but I told her I was okay enough for her to go pick up something for dinner. I sat alone on the couch waiting for her to come back. Everything tasted like sand in my mouth.

I'd spent the years since college trying to make something of myself, and what had I made? When I looked at myself, I couldn't see anything, like a vampire looking into a mirror: a butch looking into culture and seeing nothing looking back—like looking into the nothingness of a father who leaves or only comes back to hurt you.

My dad would die, I realized. There was cancer all through his body—he didn't have any physical power anymore. I imagined him in a hospital bed, skinny and slumped over. But I was still afraid of him, at that moment, in every cell. Alexis's words rang in my ears. I'd tried to pretend it hadn't happened, that he was just an asshole.

I wanted Alexis, but she was at the store, and even farther away from me, like a movie I was trying to watch again like it was the first time, and it would never be the same, and I didn't know why.

The living room was a collage of Alexis and me. I wasn't sure how long we could stay together; everything had been straining us lately, money and work and family—she was twenty years older than me, and lately, it had started to seem like it mattered. I couldn't say how, but when we woke up every day, it seemed like we had such different paths in front of us, and they weaved less and less together.

I thought of my dad again, stretched out like Eliot's "patient etherized upon a table." My mind rushed with the truth of it. I couldn't wrestle with the question anymore: Had he or hadn't he? He was dying and I had nothing for him, no compassion, no sentiment, just a cold, shivering ex-vigilance. I felt like I'd feel it forever, no matter how long I was out or married or teaching or writing poems. I thought about all the times I'd told my students to have hope, that it could get better. Could it?

I was an adjunct, and it felt foolish to think I could have any real impact on my students. I taught them first-year writing, then they went on to have professors who could teach them in their majors, who could teach them more than one class, and about things they were passionate about. I hardly ever came across English majors or students very interested in writing, since those students often skipped the classes I taught. I was, by definition, a supplement, a fun part of their first year who they'd likely forget by the time they were seniors. Maybe it was better that way, I thought, seeing myself reflected in my father's email, like I was only the words he could generate out of his little imagination.

I went up to the bathroom and looked in the mirror. I couldn't think of anyone I wanted to talk to. Everyone seemed like an enemy who couldn't understand. I wanted to talk to Sara, was but she was too far away to talk to anymore. I thought about that dark church in France, cool and beautiful and old enough not to worry about its meaning anymore. I closed my eyes over the sink; I couldn't look at myself anymore. *Ugly butch,* I thought. *No real friends, just like Sara knew would happen.* I sat on the edge of the bathtub.

Alexis had been raised Catholic, too, but not like me. She let me put up a few icons, but not all over the house, she said, just in the bathroom. I looked up at Saint Rita, with the bloody stigmata on her forehead, like Athena had just sprung out of her forehead, and Saint Francis, talking to animals like a dyke dog lover, and Our Lady of Perpetual Help—they were like celebrities who'd been in the magazines my whole life, always wearing different clothes, changing their minds and reinventing themselves.

Everything good left my mind, and I thought of my dad again, in the passenger seat of some car, getting driven out to Pittsburgh by the brother who didn't want to talk to me anymore—was it because I didn't want to talk to my dad? Or because I was a big queer? I didn't know, and I'd tried to keep the lines of communication open, but he hadn't responded to my messages.

I wasn't sure that swallowing all my antidepressants would kill me, but I learned later that it would have. I held the bottle in my hands for a few minutes, thinking about running a bath and swallowing the pills in there. Why did people in the movies always do it in the bathtub? Maybe because it was a little comfortable. A hard womb. I was so tired, I just needed it to be over.

I couldn't think about Alexis. I shoved my brothers and sisters away from my mind. They'd all be fine, I thought. They were grown up enough now. I stood in front of the sink and poured a handful of pills into my palm, swallowing them with handfuls of water grabbed greedily from the faucet. I sat on the floor of the bathroom, under the saints. I rubbed my eyes like I was finally done with something. I closed my eyes and wondered if I'd fall asleep. What a relief it would be for everyone, I thought.

Then it was like a song turned on in the background, like I was a character in a movie. All of a sudden I wanted to stay alive, the same way you want a drink when you're really thirsty.

I had poison inside me, I realized, and I had to get it out. It was instinctive. I stuck my fingers down my throat the way I'd refused to do as a ballerina, to get smaller. I was saving my own life now, a micro-superhero.

I reached my fingertips as far back into my throat as I could and felt them tickle against my tonsils, and the stirring at the base of my heart meant I would vomit. Usually just when I had the flu, or was nervous, or had seen my dad, or had gone to Steubenville. Finally, I erupted the pills up my throat, out of my body. I could still see them floating slimy and pink in the toilet, and I kept throwing up until nothing came.

I didn't kill myself that day, but I ended my life as I knew it. I broke something between Alexis and me—and from there I went on to break everything else I could since I couldn't break myself.

When Alexis got home and I told her what I'd done, she made me call my therapist, and I left a message. She called me back half an hour later, her voice shaking.

"Are you safe now?" she asked me, and I could tell she was angry, because I'd never heard her voice sound like this before, like she was shaking me, like moms in the movies, crazy with love.

I promised to see her that Monday, and I promised that Alexis wouldn't leave me alone till then. They were both so mad at me I could feel it in the sound of their voices, like it was matter, like it stuck against the oxygen and hydrogen in the air like a virus. Still, I held my breath, wrapped up in a blanket on the couch, and Alexis squeezed my hand. I rested my head on her lap, and we watched *The Sound of Music*.

26 I've Got Your Number

2005. The population of Steubenville whittled down in summer to those of us who couldn't go home. During finals, the priests would preach homilies about not "slipping back" when people left town. We all made up reasons to be there that obscured what was really happening, that we didn't want to face our own realities, whatever they were.

I was lucky enough to keep my library job through the summer, but most people had jobs through the summer conferences. The university made a lot of money from these gatherings of youth, middle schoolers and high schoolers who traveled in from all over the country, who came to Steubenville to revel in the Holy Spirit. Most of the students who came to the school learned about it through these conferences, and many of the people who brought high schoolers to the conferences were alumni. Every few weeks in the summer, the campus would be flooded by youth groups and homeschoolers and the adults who led them, and high school students would crowd the campus like ants swarming a half-eaten hot dog.

In the summer, I'd drive home to Maryland from Steubenville for long weekends, leaving at night to avoid the humidity of the daylight hours. I listened to music as loud as I could and took solace in picturing myself driving off the side of the road and how easy it would be for everyone else if my suicide looked like an accident.

Then I'd get to Maryland and see the faces of the kids who loved me, the ones who didn't think I was weird. They'd known me before I knew how to pretend, even before I knew what I was. In the midst of their love, I'd feel ashamed of wanting to get rid of myself, and that would give me enough energy and evidence to resist. I resisted and resisted.

During my last visit home that summer, I got a call from an unknown number on my cell phone.

"Hello, is this Rebecca Mertz?" asked a familiar voice. Everything stopped for a second. I wasn't sure if it was really happening or if it was wishful thinking that made me think it was her.

"Dr. Madison?" I asked in disbelief, as Todd and Evangeline burst into the room. Todd was chasing Evangeline, and they were both yelling, growling, and screaming at each other.

"Quiet, you guys!" I said, holding my hand over the phone. "Go play somewhere else, please!"

"Bye bye!" Todd yelled loudly toward the phone, and Evangeline jumped up around me like popcorn, squealing loudly, "I love you, bye bye! I love you, bye bye!"

"Are you babysitting, Rebecca?" Dr. Madison asked skeptically.

"No, it's my brother and sister. I'm at home in Maryland right now."

"Oh, I apologize! I thought you were in Steubenville all summer! I hope you don't mind, I got your cell phone number from Johanna Gael."

I knew Johanna from English classes and the library, but didn't know how she'd gotten my number either. I'd taken a class with her the fall before going to Oxford, but we weren't close friends.

Dr. Madison continued: "I'm calling to see if you're available this Sunday to go on a hike with me and another student I think you might enjoy talking with, Rebecca McFadden. Johanna will also be joining us. Rebecca McFadden is an avid hiker, and Johanna Gael is interested in learning. And I thought you might like to come along for the fun! We'll pack a light lunch, hike a few miles, and perhaps go swimming in the lake there, at Raccoon Creek State Park. Have you been hiking before, Rebecca?"

I heard Todd crying from the next room, which made my heart sink. "Yes," I said. "I'm sorry, I have to go, my brother hurt himself."

"Oh." Dr. Madison sounded irritated. "Alright, well, we'll meet after noon Mass at the chapel at school. See you there!"

Todd appeared in the doorway, uttering a high-pitched, heart-wrenching little wail, his face distorted from crying, his mouth wide open with pain, though I couldn't tell if the pain was physical or emotional. Evangeline appeared right behind him, a look of wide-eyed concern on her still chubby five-year-old face.

"Todd hit the wall!" Evangeline reported breathlessly. "He hurt his toes! On the bench!"

"Owwww!" Todd wailed in anger and hurt, as if to verify her story. Remembering his toes, he fell to the ground and clutched one foot. "Becca!" he yelled loudly. "I fell!"

I scooped him up and kissed him and kissed his toes, and he stopped crying. I tickled him, and he was laughing again. He leapt from my lap and started chasing Evangeline around the room, and soon they were out the door. I looked at my phone, not knowing how I'd gotten so lucky. I thought about swimming with Dr. Madison, Dr. Madison in a bathing suit, Dr. Madison surrounded by green leaves, and what we might talk about in the woods. I wasn't sure this was really possible, and I knew it wasn't normal—but if it was happening, it must not be too abnormal. Maybe it was just unusual. Other students were going, too.

But I had to tell Mom.

"That was one of my professors," I said. "She's taking some students hiking on Sunday and asked if I could go..."

"So, you're going?" Mom sighed heavily and shook her head.

"I thought I could just leave Sunday morning instead of Sunday night, and I'll get there in time for it."

"Whatever, Rebecca, just do what you want."

"Well, it's not like I make you happy when I'm here anyway," I said. "You hate everything I do!"

I stormed past her into the dining room and saw Todd and Evangeline sitting at the table, looking from Mom to me and back, nervous. They'd been eating cereal, which was strewn across the table, and the floor. The half poodle and the bulldog were sitting patiently beneath the table, waiting for more food to descend, but Todd and Evangeline had stopped eating, Evangeline with her spoon held in midair, watching Mom and me.

"Well, you don't like anything I do, either!" Mom countered, lighting a long menthol cigarette and storming away.

Todd and Evangeline looked up at me with wide eyes. I nodded with my eyes wide, too.

"I don't like fights," Evangeline said. She patted my big hand with her little one.

"I do," Todd said thoughtfully, taking a bite and leaving the spoon in his mouth. He grinned and held the spoon between his teeth, growling.

I sat in the chair at the head of the table, and Evangeline climbed into my lap.

"Me, too!" Todd said, and he climbed up, too.

"Becca, I love you," Evangeline said, snuggling into me.

"Me, too!" Todd said, making a clinking sound with the spoon still in his mouth.

"I love you two, too!" I said. "But no climbing with spoons in your mouth, okay?" I tried to retrieve the spoon, but Todd's teeth held it firmly in place. "Toddy," I said, "please let me have the spoon." He opened his mouth wide, giggling, and I removed the spoon. He curled into me like he was apologizing for his resistance.

"Thank you very much!" I said.

"Can I fly when I grow up?" Todd asked.

"Yes," I said firmly.

"Me, too?" Evangeline asked.

"Yes!" Todd said, squirming off my lap.

"Yes!" Evangeline squealed, delighted by the answer, and the two of them started running in circles around me, flapping their arms like wings.

I drove to Steubenville early the next morning, arriving on campus in just enough time to meet Dr. Madison and Johanna Gael. Dr. Madison was bright-eyed and bushy-tailed in high-end hiking boots, but I felt like a zombie during the hike. Johanna was nervous and easily frustrated, but she never actually complained. The other Rebecca, a grad student in her first year, talked to Dr. Madison incessantly about hiking until she left, just before the swimming. I wasn't sure why Dr. Madison thought we'd like each other, but when she seemed as irritated with the other Rebecca as I did, I realized she must not actually know her very well.

When we finally made it to the lake, we laid out our towels in the grass and put down our bags. Johanna sat in the grass with a book, and Dr. Madison and I walked out into the water. It was cold, and I dove right in, but she took a few minutes. When she had adjusted to the temperature, she looked over at me and smiled.

"I'll race you to the buoy," she said.

"Go!" I said, and we both dove under.

I surfaced, touching the rope attached to the buoy, looking around for her. Dr. Madison's head popped up just a foot or so away from me.

"Oh, I let you win!" she said breathlessly.

"Thank you," I said, reaching out my arms to keep afloat. I leaned back to relax into the water and feel the sun on my skin. We both swam alongside each other for a few feet. I felt my leg brush up against hers, quick and smooth and soft. I pulled it away fast and blushed.

"Rebecca!" she exclaimed. "Are you making a pass at me?"

My mouth dropped open a little, and I smiled, speechless. She laughed her loud, high-pitched laugh, which sounded like a flute or a bird.

"How did you learn to swim?" she asked, when we got a little farther in and it was easier to tread water.

"My grandparents," I said. "They have a pool... and when we were babies my grandmother would just drop us in the pool... and, you know, make sure we didn't die. And the ocean. They have a house in the Cayman Islands, too," I said. I was used to pausing while people reacted to this news in various ways. She smiled inquisitively. "It's really beautiful there," I said, trying to keep it simple.

Now we were standing where the water reached to just under our arms. I picked up dirt from the bottom and held it up to see it without my glasses, looking for some signs of life in the nearly square, man-made pond that Racoon Creek wanted us to think was a lake. There were a few tiny pieces of colorful plastic.

"Oh, gross!" Dr. Madison said, coming closer to observe the dark gray sludge I was letting drip back into the water between my fingers. "What are the Cayman Islands like?"

"The water is turquoise," I said.

"And it smells salty everywhere."

"Well, if you go back, you should invite your favorite professor!" She laughed. This stunned me a little, and suddenly there was the possibility of going away with

Dr. Madison, staying in my grandparents' house, making coffee, swimming, sitting on the beach, sitting in the airport—my mind sped up with all the implications of what she'd just said, until she interrupted me with "Let's go back and see if we can get Johanna in the water."

I tried not to look at Dr. Madison's body, but I did. Her bathing suit was black and modest. She put her towel around her shoulders, and I put mine around my waist. Johanna was reading but looked up from her book to smile hello at us.

"Come into the water, Johanna!" Dr. Madison prodded. "It feels wonderful!"

"Oh, I don't know," she said. Johanna's voice sounded like the song of a little bird who was just about to go extinct.

"We're here and you've got your bathing suit on, right?" I asked.

Johanna smiled warmly at me, but then looked down at herself, and her face changed to a frown. "I feel ugly in my swimsuit," she said quietly.

Dr. Madison looked at me fearfully. She had no idea what to say to this.

"You look great, Johanna Gael!" I said firmly, and added, "As usual!"

"Yes, and who cares, anyway? Who's here to see you?" Dr. Madison spoke with determined cheer, as if her tone of voice could boost Johanna's spirits all by itself. And maybe it did. Johanna stood up a little nervously, clenched her fists, and said with determination, "Okay." Then, smiling big with relief: "Okay, I'll do it!"

Johanna stood up and made it into the water slowly, one step at a time, though she wouldn't go where she couldn't stand up easily. Dr. Madison and I swam around her, and the three of us splashed each other, and I told them good things I could remember about Oxford. When we got back to the grass, the three of us lay a while in the sun, on our bath towels.

"Doesn't that sun feel good on your skin, after all that walking and swimming?" Dr. Madison asked.

Johanna had scooted herself a few feet away, into the shade. Without sitting up, I reached over to my backpack and rooted around until I found a bright yellow plastic bag with two little books in it. They were a volume of Dorothy Wordsworth's letters and a beautiful edition of William Wordsworth's and Coleridge's poems, which I had bought for Dr. Madison in Oxford.

"Oh, Rebecca!" she exclaimed when I handed them to her. "You carried poetry all through the hike!" She drew the books out of the bag and admired them, with her mouth still half open in surprise. "Will you please read one? Read us a good nature poem for the end of our day!"

I protested, but finally agreed and thumbed through the Wordsworth and Coleridge book until I found one that wasn't too long. Johanna sat in the shade, grinning with newfound pride and affection for the two of us who had helped her into the water. Dr. Madison lay on her belly, on her towel, in the grass, her hair drying softly around her face and her head propped up on her hand, looking up at me as I read the Wordsworth poem about the rainbow.

27 Pick-A-Little-Talk-A-Little/Goodnight Ladies

2005. That summer, Natalie graduated and went back to California. One night on the phone, she asked me if Heather and Dr. Blake were "more than just friends." I hemmed and hawed, but laughed at just the wrong moment, and Natalie heard everything I hadn't said out loud.

The next week, I ran into Dr. Blake on campus, and he asked me if I'd come see him in his office for a moment. He seemed unsettled, and once the door was closed, he frowned angrily at me. He seemed taller and more powerful than he had only moments earlier.

"Heather told me that you mentioned something to Natalie about us," he said as quietly as he could. I could tell he was trying to keep his voice down. I felt his anger in the air as thick as the morning fog.

"Well, she asked me if you were more than friends," I managed to say.

"And you said *what*? What *exactly*?" He was shaking, talking through clenched teeth.

"I just kind of laughed—"

"You laughed!" he interrupted me. "You laughed? Do you know what would happen if anyone found out about us? Do you think me getting fired is laughable? Do you know what that would mean for me, for Matilda, for Heather?"

"No," I said, trying not to cry. Suddenly my ally, the only adult who knew my secret, who didn't judge me, was now backing me into a corner, the corner of his little office, which had been like a refuge all those times I hadn't had anywhere else to be myself. I stepped back from him, into the cramped, off-white-painted concrete corner, trying not to fall into the ugly green leather chair that always just sat there. I wanted to stand up, not to cry, not to be disappointed or feel betrayed, and not to sit just because it was easier and there was hardly another way to stay in the room.

"She's not going to tell anyone," I said as firmly as I could.

"I don't think you understand what kind of risk you put me in by telling her *my* business. It's my business and it's Heather's business, not your business! You should've told her to ask one of us if she wanted to know something about us!"

"I didn't mean to put you at risk," I said, "but it's not just your business. Heather's my best friend! Natalie's my best friend, too, and I don't want to lie to her."

"You lie to her all the time, don't you?" he snapped.

I felt hot tears break through my eyes, and for a second, I couldn't see anything. I sniffed and wiped my eyes and said, "Natalie doesn't even talk to anyone from here besides me and Heather, and she's all the way in California!"

Frank grabbed me, hugged me tight, and kept saying, "It's okay, it's okay, it's okay, I know you didn't do it on purpose."

I broke away from him, thanked him for forgiving me, so that the conversation would be over, and from then on, I avoided being alone with him. Soon Frank and Matilda were openly separated and divorcing, and Frank and Heather were officially together, in Pittsburgh.

I didn't know how to talk to Natalie anymore without lying or without threatening the wrath of Frank or Heather, so I mostly stopped talking to her. She left messages, and I'd feel my lungs get cold and dry, and I'd avoid calling her back.

The pollution was more perceptible in the August heat. The air was hot and thick most days, and you could see thick white clouds rising in the morning, like the grass and trees were sweating. Everything would wear a thick fog, tinged with the scent of whatever chemicals the plant had released. The air smelled rotten, like the things that nobody could say out loud, like they'd materialized from thin air, all the evaporated, aborted thoughts and feelings and insights, reeking of decay and poison. I wasn't sure anymore whether the things we weren't allowed to say were poisonous, like "they" said, or if they got sour from always being held in and contained.

Whenever the Coke plant performed a certain function (the name of which I never learned), the air would be heavy with a bitter scent that you couldn't escape, even if you held your breath. It was the natural response to hold your breath, because it smelled and even tasted foul; then you'd gasp and gag a little, and take a big swallow of air like a drink you needed, just because it was air and there was no other version of it available. Thinking about places where it cost more to live, I wondered if the air was really cleaner there, or if the poison was just more covered up. Maybe the most dangerous part of the poison had no smell, I thought. I could barely remember the air in Maryland or in Austria. It didn't seem possible that it could be that much better anywhere else.

I was about to be a senior, and I knew where everything was and how to learn what I didn't know. I lived off campus, in a two-bedroom apartment that I'd found and rented by myself. When my friend Helen mentioned that she needed a place to live, I offered my extra room—but then I wondered, *What if I come out? What will she think?* I decided to tell her.

"Helen," I said, "I have to tell you something before you get too excited."

"Oh no, is it, like, all painted obnoxiously chartreuse or something?"

I laughed. "No," I said, more nervous than I'd thought I'd be. Suddenly I thought Helen might also be mad that I hadn't told her before. "I have to tell you, just, like, before we live together... I wanted to say—because I don't want you to be uncomfortable, is the thing... and, I mean, if you don't want to live with me now, or whatever... that's cool..."

"Oh, Mertz!" Helen exclaimed. "I've already lived with you! What could be so terrible?"

I laughed. "I know, uh—I just, uh—I'm gay."

Helen's eyes got wide and compassionate at the same time, and she stretched her hand out to mine. "Oh, Rebecca!" she exclaimed, squeezing my hand. "Oh, are you kidding?" She laughed, hard. "Oh, I don't care at all, you're wonderful! You're my dear friend, of course! I definitely want to live with you! At least you're not going to be praying for me to stop reading about feminism!"

"Definitely not," I said, and we started talking about keeping olive oil and tea and good coffee in our apartment, and how we'd play music all the time.

I told Helen about Jenny, and she listened with a satisfying mixture of shock and kindness, saying things like, "No, no!" at all the right moments. But I got more and more depressed as the semester went on, and I wasn't great at hiding it. Helen said she'd taken a class with the psychology professor Dr. Kasey and that she had talked very compassionately and nonjudgmentally about gay people. I knew Leslie had talked to Dr. Kasey, too, and that Dr. Kasey probably knew all about me from her, so maybe I wouldn't have to say much out loud if I didn't want to.

When I finally got up the nerve, I went to Dr. Kasey's open office hours and knocked. She opened the door quickly and smiled so big that I thought she must be thinking I was someone else, but she already knew who I was.

"Hi, Rebecca," Dr. Kasey said, without me having to introduce myself. She welcomed me in and gestured to a chair. She asked why I was there, and I said that Helen had suggested I talk to her. Before I knew it, she was explaining that she was a therapist, but that we could just talk, it didn't have to be therapy, or it could be spiritual direction, she said, she did that, too. Or it could be both, or whatever we wanted. She emphasized that whatever I said in her office was just between me and her.

"Well, you pretty much know all about me already," I said, looking away. I hadn't realized how hard it would be to sit across from someone I didn't know yet who knew all my secrets.

"Well, I'd like to hear it in your own words," she said. "I like to hear everyone's story in their own words."

"My roommate Helen says I could be depressed," I said. "And I, uh... I made a joke about wanting to kill myself"— I laughed—"but I was just kidding."

"Wow," she said, nodding her head. "Why did you say that?"

I laughed again, but she didn't laugh with me.

"Do you think about killing yourself a lot?" she asked.

I fumbled. "What's a lot?"

"More than once a week?"

I looked away again, thought about it, and nodded. She asked me question after question, and before long I was talking about Leslie and Jenny, and Brad, and Mom and home, and how confused I felt about everything. I told her about my brothers and sisters, and homeschooling, and just being sad all the time, and the priest back in Maryland, and what he had asked me, and what I had said.

"Do you think someone molested you?" she asked.

I nodded. She asked me if I knew who it was. I said I didn't.

"A man?" she asked. I nodded. "So, your same-sex attraction would make sense, then," she said. "If you learned that men are sexually predatory or violent, of course you'd want to seek out love and sexual attention from women."

I stared off into space, and her voice got fuzzier and fuzzier as my mind drifted from the chair, the room, the building, the campus, like driving on a highway between my parents. I didn't like the idea that I fell in love with someone because someone else had hurt me. Dr. Kasey talked about God a lot, and she asked me if I thought that God loved me and what God would say about me killing myself.

"I want to be good," I said. "I don't want to want to kill myself. But I don't want to be someone who *hurts* God. And I don't *think* being gay is wrong, but I don't want to live my whole life wrong, you know?" She nodded. "I just don't know how I'm supposed to live, how I'm supposed to be in the Church or be out of it. Neither one of those seems right, you know?"

She asked if I could come again that week, and we made an appointment for the next day. As I left her office, I thought about what Frank and Heather and Matilda would think. I knew they would be skeptical of Dr. Kasey. She was charismatic; she held her hands up in Mass and prayed over people. But she seemed happy, and Frank and Heather and Matilda never seemed happy, even now that Frank and Matilda were separated, and Frank and Heather were officially together. I wanted to be happy, somehow, or at least not want to die.

If the Church was right, then being gay was harmful to the universe, which I didn't want to be if I could help it. In nine months, I'd be graduating, and I'd have to choose what to do next with my life. Every time I thought about leaving school, I had to fight to catch my breath, and I drew a blank on what to do next or what kind of person I wanted to be when it came time to decide. I expected there to be some moment of clarity when I realized that either the Church was right or the Church was wrong, but the moment kept not happening. I started seeing Dr. Kasey twice a week.

2005. That fall, Dr. Madison took over teaching Women Writers because the regular English professor took a leave of absence. On the first day of class, Dr. Madison took her seat at the head of the table and asked us what value could come from studying women's writing. We didn't know.

One day after class, Dr. Madison asked if I'd help her move a dresser from an antique store downtown to her house. After we finished moving it inside, she offered to cook me dinner. Her home was neat and simple, no family pictures or much art on the walls. The kitchen was small, but big enough for the two of us to move around comfortably. I sliced onions, tomatoes, and eggplant, and Dr. Madison prepared two pork chops for the frying pan. She wore an apron and offered one to me, but I declined.

"Too girlie?" she asked, laughing.

"Absolutely," I said.

She laughed again. She taught me how to press the garlic, slice the eggplant, and lay everything out on the pan to bake in olive oil. When the vegetables were in the oven, she put the pork chops in a pan and turned on the heat. She asked if I was twenty-one and if I could drive safely home after some wine.

"Oh, yes," I said. "I come from a long line of drinkers."

She asked me if I still thought about Willa Cather, and I blushed, remembering our first exchange about whether Cather was a lesbian.

"Yes," I said, smirking. "Maybe."

"So why is it so important that she was a lesbian?" Dr. Madison asked, taking her wine to the stove and turning her attention to the pork chops. "Does it change her books for you?"

"All her characters' love is thwarted, you know? It seems like she's writing out what it's like to be gay, but she's making them heterosexual so it's not too shocking."

"I don't think that makes *her* a lesbian."

"Me, either. I think she loved women, that's what makes her a lesbian. But all her love stories are tragedies. That's pretty gay."

She studied me for a few seconds, like she wanted to say something she didn't know how to say. Then her face changed, and she laughed and said, "I think you just like to be shocking."

When we sat down to eat, she asked me again about the Cayman Islands and what it was like there.

"Do you wanna go?" I asked, eyes down, like I was fifteen and asking her to a dance. I looked up furtively for her reaction, watching her face closely.

She smiled at me quizzically. "Are you serious?" she asked.

"Yeah," I said, unsure if Nanny and Papa would agree, or how I could afford it, or if all the things could ever fall into place, to get me and Dr. Madison to one of those beaches together, in a long, open quiet.

"Well," she said with a giggle, "I am free over spring break if you'd like to arrange permission to issue a formal invitation."

"Noted." I smiled, catching her eyes before I brought mine back to my plate, trying to focus on eating when so much else filled my mind, like little windblown seeds scattering, taking root; like new words forming inside a language.

We did the dishes together and had a cup of tea. Then I knew I should go, and I thanked her for the food, and she asked if I was okay to drive.

"Please be very careful," she said, leaning against her front door, raising her eyes toward me. Sometimes our bodies were so close I thought we'd touch, and it seemed more unnatural not to. What would she do if I reached for her? Did she want me to?

"She was totally flirting with you," Helen would say whenever I got home and told her what Dr. Madison had said to me that day. Soon it was impossible to tell the difference between Dr. Madison's way of acting toward me and the way Leslie and Jenny had acted before the silent revelations that they wanted to be more than friends. So, I waited for the revelation, which I assumed couldn't come until I had graduated, if it ever came. I knew, beyond anything else, that Dr. Madison was intensely aware of rules—the letter of them usually concerned her more than the spirit.

Sometimes I felt everything that couldn't be said like a headache, as though my computer and the CD player and the TV and the radio were all playing at the same time, turned up as loud as they could go, through headphones that were glued to my ears. I was shaking and rattling, and nobody could turn down the volume.

I wrote a few poems that alluded to how I felt, and Dr. Davis frowned. We were sharing his bag of chips and drinking warm Diet Cokes from the box he kept in his office.

"A little dark," he said. "Pretty dark, I mean. Do I need to worry about you or anything? Or is this just you being a poet?"

I laughed and told him not to worry. He made a joke about Sylvia Plath and handed me her book.

Some nights I sat almost naked on the floor of my bedroom, my back against my bed, knowing again, for sure, that it was all impossible. I could see curling clumps of my long hair bound up in the carpet along the molding, where the vacuum had pressed them against the wall rather than taking them. Dead skin of mine, I knew, maybe skin that Jenny had touched, before she changed her mind. I knew Dr. Madison would change her mind, too, and maybe Helen, and maybe everyone I'd ever get close to, the way my dad had, too. I thought about how his hands grabbed at me when I was a kid, like he was trying to keep me still and close. What if the homeschoolers and Dr. Kasey were right, and he had ruined me, or broken me? What was the point of trying if I was already broken?

I kept a pocketknife in the top drawer, for these moments when I found myself on the floor, unable to imagine getting up. I liked to stare at it and wished I had enough courage to use it on myself. There was only one way for me to stop being confused. I looked at the knife for a long time, like I could see everybody's faces in there, asking me to stay. I started cutting my wrist one or two times, where the veins were. The knife wasn't as sharp as it needed to be, and it was hard to even break the skin. When I finally did break the skin a little, I thought about Todd and Evangeline and Beatrice and Lily and Jimmy and Marianne. I didn't want them to have to think about me like this. It would be better if I could keep this from them, and I couldn't do that if I were dead.

I grew a slow, green resentment in my veins toward everyone I loved, for being in my way, for impeding my nonexistence. Maybe when the kids got older, when they would be able to understand, when they were already grown up and had their own lives—maybe then I'd be able to leave without hurting them so much. This thought was consoling, and I went to bed imagining what it would be like to disappear without hurting so many people. *Maybe someday,* I thought. *Maybe years from now, maybe when they're older.*

I left a little scrape on my wrist, barely noticeable. When I told Dr. Kasey about cutting myself with the knife, she looked alarmed and sad, and made me promise to call her if I was ever thinking about doing something like that again. I promised that I would.

Soon enough, Nanny and Papa asked what I wanted for graduation. I asked them if I could go to Cayman with a friend and stay in their house. I expected them to say no.

"Of course!" Nanny said. "What a perfect idea! We'll probably be back from there by then from our spring trip, but you'll have a wonderful time."

When we hung up the phone, I was still stunned. Surely Dr. Madison would back out, now that it was a real possibility—but what if she didn't? I called her.

"Oh, Rebecca!" she celebrated. "How wonderful! Thank you! We're going to see the ocean! The *real* ocean! But"—she hesitated—"I'm afraid to fly... You might have to hold my hand."

The next day, I sat in Dr. Kasey's office, freaking out. I'd told Dr. Kasey how I felt about Dr. Madison. She knew how much we hung out, but Dr. Kasey hung out with students all the time, and she didn't see anything unusual about Dr. Madison hanging out with me. Being at Franciscan was like living on an island where we'd all been stranded—we were a people set apart, like all the old books talked about, meaning that outside of our community, everyone was suspect. That meant a lot of students became administrators and even faculty, eventually, and the lines all blurred. And ultimately, everyone's goal was salvation and holiness— even at Franciscan, it was understood that a student could be just as holy or spiritually insightful as a teacher, even more so. Holiness was the great leveler of everything and everyone. The only boundaries that really mattered were the lines between us and them.

But Dr. Madison didn't hang out with students all the time, just me. Dr. Kasey said I should just channel those feelings the way God would want, into friendship. She said God definitely wouldn't want me to be in a homosexual relationship with anyone, especially my teacher.

"Yeah," I said out of habit. But this was therapy, I remembered. I could say *anything*. "Well," I said, "but maybe he does. Isn't that possible?"

Dr. Kasey inhaled deeply and spoke carefully. "Does God want you to love women? Yes. Does God want women to love you? Yes. But does God want you to express that love sexually? No, I don't think so."

I sighed with irritation.

"But guess what's a lot more important than that?" Dr. Kasey said. "God wants you to stay alive."

"Is that really more important? Isn't it more important to be good than to be alive? The saints are always dying, getting killed instead of sinning. Like Maria Goretti, when the guy tries to rape her: she resists and gets killed instead of letting him 'take her virtue.'"

Dr. Kasey looked reprovingly at me. "In some cases, being good is more important, but if you're asking me if God wants you to kill yourself, no, in no way would that be a moral choice for you. So, get that off the table."

I clenched my teeth and my fists. I thought about how some saint had said all our sins bore into Jesus's body like nails, like plastic bottles of Coke boring into the planet, and all the documentaries I'd seen about America and science and "the environment" we still weren't sure we were a part of—why couldn't I die if I wanted to? What was the point of staying alive when you knew you were just going to mess everything up?

"It's getting a lot harder," I said, "to hold all this... to keep everything inside."

"Of course it is," Dr. Kasey said sympathetically.

"Well," I started slowly, then the words spilled out fast. "I think I should tell Dr. Madison I'm gay at least."

Dr. Kasey looked wary. "I don't think so," she said. "You've said yourself in here that you've been attracted to men in the past. So is 'gay' even the right label for you? The Church teaches that it's not a good idea to label yourself as gay when in fact you're a lot more than any one word."

I nodded, ignoring the logical gymnastics involved in that point, just trying to wade through this feeling, trying to find something to hold on to, something that I could say was worth pulling myself though the muck for.

"So, you don't think I should say anything to Dr. Madison?"

"I don't know that that would help you right now, Rebecca," Dr. Kasey said. "Although you might want to stop spending quite so much time with her. And when you get back from spring break, I think you should consider letting me pray over you with my prayer team. God is the only force real and powerful enough to help you. God loves you more than any woman ever could, and God will be there for you when all the desires of this world fall away and you're alone. God will still be there. And God loves you, just as you are."

"How can you say that?" I asked, not angry, just imploring. How did this make sense to her and not to me? If I could make it make sense, I could stay right where I was, I'd never have to move on or lose anyone else.

"God loves you just as you are. That doesn't mean he wants you to give in to every impulse you have. Our culture has taught you that these impulses you have toward women are your whole sexuality. That's just part of your sexuality.

And all of your sexuality can and should be channeled, if God wills it, toward your husband in a marriage, toward producing children. That's the way that sexuality can be so meaningful and beautiful. Everything else is so much less than that. Don't you think?"

"So, do you think I'm a pervert?" I asked.

"No," she said. "Or, more specifically, I think everyone is a pervert in some way or another... I think we all have to struggle to make sure that our sexuality is, you know, channeled, in the right direction. Everyone struggles with that!"

"Yeah," I said. "But it's not like I'm saying I don't want to wait until marriage or something. Like, I understand that's a struggle, too, and I get that. I get why it's a good idea to wait to have sex until marriage, because if you don't, it can really hurt you. But I don't get why it's wrong for me and Dr. Madison to fall in love, or me and Leslie, or me and Jenny. Why is it wrong?"

"Because it's not the way things are supposed to be," Dr. Kasey said, sighing.

I couldn't hold back my tears anymore, and I let my eyes get red and salty with them before I collected myself and blew my nose.

"I just wish I could die," I said, forgetting who I was talking to for a second. I covered quickly with "You know, sometimes, not all the time..."

"Rebecca," she said with tears in her eyes, "you are such an amazing person. If anything ever happened to you, I would feel that loss for myself and for the whole world. I know that God has a plan for you to do great things! You're so smart! But you're also so strong and so good. You're so good, Rebecca. I can see, in the future, years from now, how much you've done for God and his Church, and how, once you get over this... this... gay thing... you could be *a saint*."

I bit my lip, sucked in as much air as I could fit in my lungs, and nodded a slow, steady nod in a direction my head didn't want to go.

"Please think about letting us pray over you," she said. "It has really helped a lot of people."

"I'll think about it," I said.

"Good," she said. "Good. We'll have to keep talking about this next time, okay? But in the meantime, will you promise me you won't hurt yourself?"

"Yeah," I said, "I promise."

2005. One night Johanna Gael walked into the library and marched straight over to the circulation desk, where I was sitting. She seemed bursting with good news.

"Have you ever read *Turn of the Screw*?" she asked, her voice exploding out of her mouth. She was excited and didn't wait for me to answer. "Never mind, it doesn't matter... The thing is, I realized all of this shit from my childhood, and I just want to... well, I want to print out this letter I wrote about it and burn it! Do you think we could do that at your house? We can't do it at my house; I live with my parents."

I wasn't sure why Johanna was coming to me for this celebration. We'd had a few classes together now and gone on that hike months ago. We always talked in the hall, but I was never sure if she liked me or not. Still, my curiosity demanded I say yes, and I was happy to be included.

"Of course! You got me to go *swimming*!" she exclaimed.

A few nights later, Johanna, Helen, Dr. Madison, and I gathered in my living room. Johanna had invited Dr. Madison, in whose class she had read the pivotal tale that had changed everything. I thought about *The Turn of the Screw* and wondered what kind of childhood Johanna could have suffered that had made this particular novel about ghosts and manipulative children such a cathartic experience. Dr. Madison gave each of us a bowl of ice cream and explained that "catharsis" literally meant "to get the shit out."

"Well, that's what I'm doing!" Johanna said. "For twenty-five years"—she raised her spoon of ice cream—"I've hated myself."

Her voice trembled, and everyone got serious. This was more naked honesty than any of us were used to encountering, and I felt the shock of recognition, the quick breathlessness of hearing someone say out loud something I had no words for, that beat like blood through my body, physiologically familiar.

"The details don't matter... but I hated everything about myself," Johanna continued, tears in her eyes, "and I lost myself in books, and school, and everything everybody else wanted... so I didn't have to look at myself in real life, and I... I hurt myself. Over and over again. I tortured myself, for years, since... well, it doesn't matter. And then the other day I read that book, and for some reason the book, it made me look at myself... And I realized that what I hated wasn't me, it was the things that had happened... things about other people and how they made me feel..."

I looked around, and everyone had tears in their eyes. Dr. Madison and I locked eyes for a second, and I smiled, to make her smile, and she did.

"And now I feel free, like I could fly!" Johanna was saying. "So I'm glad you could all be with me to eat this ceremonial ice cream, which is the first ice cream I've had in six years! And now," Johanna said as we finished eating ceremonial bites of ice cream, "who has a lighter?"

Johanna held several pages of typed text in her hand, which she held over a frying pan, which Helen swore would contain the fire produced by burning a few pages. Johanna took a few deep breaths and lit a corner of one page with the lighter I had provided her. The pages went up in a big red flame, bigger than any of us expected, and she dropped the papers into the pan.

"Oh, no!" Dr. Madison exclaimed. "Out, out, out! Everybody outside!"

As the little flame got bigger, soaking up all of Johanna's secrets, I raced down the stairs with the frying pan, followed by the three women squealing and giggling. When we got out into the dark yard, I flung the fiery pages onto the grass.

"Johanna! Stomp on them!" I said. "Stomp out all your shit!"

Johanna laughed wildly and squealed in fear as she extended one foot to stomp on the flames, which were already going out. Everyone joined her, laughing and yelling, tearing up the burning pages of Johanna's self-hatred with our shoes. When the fire was out, and the pages were all torn up and scattered through the yard, the four of us stood around breathlessly, looking at one another. Johanna laughed. I had never seen her smile so big. She was beaming from ear to ear, looking back and forth between all of us like we had just climbed a mountain together, and we were all still dizzy from being at the top.

"That's what literature can do," Dr. Madison said.

One night, Helen and I found ourselves at a house party with Dr. Madison's friends, the Reids. Dr. Reid was a new theology professor from New York City, young and enthusiastic and well dressed, who was hosting a visiting priest; that night, the priest gave a talk and held court in the Reids' living room. Dr. Madison said there would be good food and music and plenty of other students there.

When I arrived at Dr. Reid's house for the party, Ella Fitzgerald was playing from somewhere, just loud enough, and innumerable children were running around the house. It was as big on the inside as it was on the outside, and it was filled with art, books, dolls, origami objects, glitter, headbands, paper and glue sticks, and stacked-up copies of *The New Yorker* and *National Geographic*. Helen and I looked at each other with happy understanding—this house wasn't like most FUS houses, at least none that we'd ever been to. The walls were painted bright colors, yellows and greens and oranges and blues, and there was art everywhere. The fact that music was playing—jazz, no less (music by *Black people*), not Christian music, not classical music or monks chanting—was already a departure from most school-related events.

"But didn't you live with a terrorist cell?" Dr. Reid was asking Father Raphael, the visiting priest. Dr. Reid asked every question like he was really curious to know the answer; he was easier to talk to than any of my other professors had been, even Dr. Davis. Dr. Reid, a smiley, classically handsome man in his late thirties or early forties grinned expectantly at Father Raphael and greeted me with a smile as I joined the circle.

"Yes, but I didn't know they were a terrorist cell! That's how peaceful they were!"

Soon the conversation about Islam turned into an analysis of the many similarities between Islam and Christianity.

"Don't men in Muslim countries kiss each other and hold hands?" a student asked. A few people snickered at this question, and Father Raphael smiled.

"Yes!" he said. "That is a custom among heterosexual men! And, indeed, this relates to what we were just talking about! Christian men in medieval times, just like many Middle Eastern men today, would exchange affection in the way of holding hands or kissing on the cheek, and it wasn't sexual at all!"

Dr. Madison looked right at me from across the room and chirped, "I guess that means we can kiss each other now!"

I laughed out loud and felt my face turning red, as everyone in the room laughed a little nervously and looked between me and Dr. Madison. Helen's eyes were wide as saucers.

The dean's wife saved us, chiming in, "Yes, we should all be more affectionate! What a beautiful thing that would be. Now, I have a question, Father Raphael. What about the question of women in Islam? Is it true that they're more sexist than Christians?"

"Superb question!" Father Raphael exclaimed, and he launched into a brief history of women in Christianity and Islam. I needed another beer.

In the kitchen, I found Mrs. Reid beginning to assemble dessert. She was a short, delicately featured woman with blonde hair cut short, but not like a nun, more like a movie star. I'd watched her zip around her party like a bee in a garden, laughing through the maze of people she'd assembled, laying out plates of food, and gathering up napkins, and herding children like it was all choreographed. But in the kitchen, she was more still, standing at a counter, cutting up peaches for a fruit salad.

"Hi!" she exclaimed when she saw me, licking the juice of a peach from her finger. "Sorry, I'd shake your hand, but I'm a mess. I'm Sara, by the way—not 'Mrs. Reid.'"

We talked for a few minutes about nothing in particular, in the way that you do, with a light glare over your eyes, when you meet someone you know you'll talk to again. A little kid came up and interrupted our discussion of Bob Dylan, but Mrs. Reid said she'd be getting my number to invite me for dinner sometime. I looked around at all the bright colors and people she'd assembled around her, in this gigantic house full of books and art and music and instruments, and thought I'd certainly like to come back.

When I went back to the living room, Dr. Madison looked over and smiled at me, like she had been looking for me. I raised my bottle to her, and she raised her red cup at me, and we smiled at each other, but I still couldn't tell if we were both smiling at the same thing or not.

2006. Jesse was the only boy in Women Writers. Lean and muscular and graceful, he was a punk, but I didn't know what that word meant yet. He wore dirty black clothes, black boots, and a leather jacket, but he still always looked like a ballet dancer. His voice was soft, and he talked about literature the way most English majors used to talk about it but didn't anymore. He talked about books emotionally, like the point of them was just to fascinate and move him—Jesse, in particular—and that his job was to report to us whether this had happened, to describe the happening or the not happening inside himself. This irritated Dr. Madison no end.

"This girl is isolated," Jesse said, about Virginia Woolf's *To the Lighthouse*. He stretched his booted foot out into the center of the circle Dr. Madison made us sit in. He flexed his ankle before us, like punctuation. "She writes like a bird hanging out of a tree? With her beak sort of trying to reach the ground." He spoke, then turned back to his notebook drawings, as if his comment had been perfectly clear. Dr. Madison grimaced and shook her head. Jesse continued: "Wasn't she gay? Virginia, I mean?" His question was innocent. He wasn't a homeschooler or a Jesus freak; he was a local Steubenvillan who had gone to public school and never knew what conservative Catholicism was until he stepped on campus.

I grinned, and Dr. Madison frowned. Jesse always referred to authors by their first names—another of Dr. Madison's pet peeves. She pursed her lips and exhaled deeply through her nose.

"*Woolf*'s private life isn't relevant here," she said severely. "And these kinds of speculations are anachronistic."

"Don't we usually talk about the lives of the writers?" Jesse asked, even-keeled though he was challenging her. "Wouldn't it be relevant if she was gay?"

Hope flooded me for a second, till I saw Dr. Madison's face. Her lips curled, as if she was really considering what to say. She looked at me with an expression that explicitly, wordlessly warned me not to get involved. A flash in her eyes reminded me that she was the teacher and I was the student, and that I'd better not forget myself today. I felt my face sink.

"Well, unless you have some evidence to support your claim—your *accusation*, rather—that Woolf had homo-sexual proclivities, I don't think it's something we need to discuss here. She was married until her death, which is some evidence against you. And I don't think it's fair to slander someone without any evidence, is it?"

"I think she had an affair with her friend, a woman friend," Jesse replied calmly, thinking. "I saw something on TV about it."

"That's nothing but liberal propaganda," Dr. Madison said harshly. "There's no evidence to support that the re-lationship was sexual."

I felt a few punches in the stomach, a blow to the mouth, my teeth shaking, a spectral spurt of blood flying across the circle, all invisible. My mouth opened halfway to say some-thing, but nothing worked. Dr. Madison was flushed and flustered, and Jesse looked confused. I waited for myself to say something, too, but I didn't. When I finally looked around at the other students in the class, they seemed a little disgusted and a little relieved that Dr. Madison had axed the subject.

Jesse nodded as if to yield the floor, and he bowed his head toward the papers on his desk. I recognized the shame in his body. We were sitting next to each other, and I could see his notes and doodles without even turning my head very much. Dr. Madison had started talking officiously about Modernism. I clicked my pen and wrote in the top left corner of my paper, where Jesse would be able to see: *VW was G-A-Y!*

He smiled when he saw what I wrote, and when he was sure that Dr. Madison was looking away, he scribbled, *Yeah! That's dirty talk, I guess.*

I thought for a minute before I responded. I looked up at Dr. Madison. Was she watching us from the corner of her eye, or was I imagining it? I didn't care. She was talking to someone about Beckett wrestling with God and saying that God would never come.

I guess I'm dirty, too, then.

I felt my heart start beating faster as I wrote it. I remembered stories of teachers reading notes aloud in class, and I thought this might be the moment, right here and right now, when that would happen to me and Dr. Madison would know everything. But she was still pretending like she didn't notice us.

Me, too, Jesse wrote.

When class was over, he asked me to walk him to his car. Usually I hung around and talked to Dr. Madison after class, but today I was rebelling. "See you later," I said.

"She's weird," Jesse said, once we were out of Dr. Madison's earshot.

"Is she?" I laughed. "She's great when you get to know her."

Jesse cocked his head to one side, raising his eyebrows. He'd taken out a cigarette and put on sunglasses once we'd left the building. He smiled, and lit his cigarette. "I mean, she's great *looking*."

"Yeah," I said, then laughed again. "I mean, I don't know what you're talking about, I only think about Jesus."

Jesse laughed. "Well, Jesus is great looking, too." He inhaled the smoke like he was taking his first breath after swimming the length of a pool. "Do you want a cigarette?"

"Sure," I said, and I took the Marlboro Red he offered. He lit it for me and smiled.

"I didn't think you were queer," he said, tilting his head to inspect me. "And I wouldn't've pegged you as a smoker."

"Affirmative," I said, as we walked down the main hill on campus to the library parking lot. When we got to a beat-up red clunker, Jesse threw himself onto the hood and inhaled again from his cigarette.

"So, you like the weird chicks? That's cool," he said.

We laughed. It felt good to tell the truth to someone. I smiled but didn't say anything. He nodded understandingly.

"It's hard here. I mean, it was harder in high school, I have to say. No kindness. No Jesusy sunbeams, you know? And I was a big whore, too. I still am, but I'm getting better. I'm becoming Catholic at Easter this year. It's helping me. I don't want to just fuck around for my whole life. And I like girls sometimes. I dunno. I don't want to be like this, you know?"

"Yeah," I said, but I wanted to ask him why—why was he jumping off the cliff I was trying to figure out how to climb up to the ledge of? But my mouth felt like it was at the bottom of the cliff and he was at the top.

"I mean, I don't judge other people," he said, sensing my nervousness. "I hate that shit, but what has being gay brought me? A bunch of blow jobs and feeling shitty about myself, and a *lot* of lying."

"I know what you mean. It doesn't seem like something that can make you feel so fucked up should be something you accept about yourself."

He looked away.

"I don't know how much God cares about it, though," I said. "You know? Like, maybe war is more of a problem..."

He laughed and agreed, but we were quiet for a few minutes. He said he had to go, but he didn't get up from the car.

"Ugh, I have to go take a shower," he said, "and I hate them," he added, more passionately than I had heard him say anything. "I like to feel the dirt on my skin. It's like the days all add up and become part of you... And when you shower, you just wash it away. You wash yourself away. That's not my thing."

When I got home that evening, Helen wasn't there. I kept hearing Dr. Madison's voice in my head, saying "homosexual proclivities" and "slander" over and over again. In three weeks, we were set to spend a week together on a tropical island, alone.

My mind raced with visions of Dr. Madison's disgust, if she ever found out or when she found out... Would I be able to keep it secret forever? As far as I knew, that's what most queers did, though I wasn't sure how a lifetime of lying was morally superior to being in love with a woman. But didn't she already know? Surely, she must. I thought of the ocean again. Jesus kept shaking his head at me. What a mess I'd made this time.

When Evangeline was two, she looked just like the little girl from the movie *Signs*, who always rejected glasses of water, saying, "It's contaminated." I figured the kids would be okay without me. They'd figure it out.

Without thinking too much about it, I'd assembled all the pills in the house in my bedroom. I didn't know what could kill me, but I had Tylenol and ibuprofen and some prescription that Helen had for migraines. I figured that swallowing all of it would be enough, although the fact that I wasn't sure was enough to make the whole thing seem a little pointless. I didn't want to wake up with my stomach bleeding or my brain damaged—although at least then I wouldn't have to make this decision. At least things would be interrupted, and maybe someone would have to tell me what to do.

I opened the bottle of Tylenol and poured a mouthful into my palm. At some point I had gotten myself a big glass of water. I siphoned as many pills into my mouth as I could fit and took a big gulp. As I swallowed hard, I happened to see that there were several glasses on my desk and book-shelves, holding liquid in various states of biological decline, and for some reason at that moment I saw in my mind the toddler version of Evangeline proudly pronouncing, "It's contaminated," over and over.

I spat out the water. I ran into the bathroom and reached my fingers into my throat to make myself throw up. I shook and sweated from vomiting, or rage, and the desire to hurt myself, to punish myself for getting myself in this position in the first place. I choked, and my throat stung. I couldn't get Evangeline out of my head.

I thought about Dr. Kasey and my promise not to hurt myself and my promise to call her if I got this close again. I forced myself to find her number and dial it into my cell phone. I didn't know what to say exactly. "I almost... I almost swallowed some pills..." I said. "I put them in my mouth..."

"What? What pills?"

"Tylenol. You can die from that, right? That would be embarrassing if I mixed that up..."

"Did you swallow the pills?"

"I put them in my mouth and spit them out," I said, softening it a little for her.

I thought of sitting in that circle of chairs in Women Writers, and walking across the bottom of the ocean in flippers and a mask and a snorkel tube full of water, and the view from my grandparents' house on the beach and what the house might look like from underneath the water, and the kids running around in the sand, chasing lizards, and Dr. Madison laughing in the sunlight and telling me I was disgusting.

"Rebecca," Dr. Kasey said, waking me from my daydream, "Rebecca, why don't you come to my house? You have a car, right?"

She told me how to get there, and I drove over, robotic. Dr. Kasey's house looked like a cross between a priest's house and a nerdy boy's dorm room. The furniture was used but clean. The decoration was minimal but included posters of John Paul II and the Sacred Heart, the kinds of things students put on their walls. There weren't many books, and they were all psychology textbooks, theology books, or prayer books. There was a pile of board games in the corner.

"Wanna make cookies?" she asked.

I agreed but didn't say much, feeling more grateful than I knew how to express that she'd dropped everything to have me over. We cracked eggs, sifted flour, measured out sugar and vanilla and extra chocolate chips. Everything—the color of the egg yolks, the shimmer of the sugar—seemed more real, brighter, than it had before I'd bent over the toilet with death.

She poured me a glass of Tang and I sipped it gratefully, realizing my mouth tasted sour and mean. She asked me questions about my day. As the cookies baked, we started a game of Scrabble. I usually played with my dad, and beating him was the only justice I'd ever known.

"How'd you get so good at this game?" Dr. Kasey asked when I used all my letters in one turn.

"My dad's mean," I said.

"Do you promise me you won't try to hurt yourself again?" she asked, offering me a hot cookie.

I promised again, shifting the letters around on the tray.

"Rebecca," she said, "there is a battle going on right now, for your life, for your soul. God is fighting for you, Rebecca, because God loves you! More than you can imagine! God is fighting for you; God is fighting against Satan for your life. Satan would like nothing more than for you to yield to these impulses you have to hurt yourself, either by following your same-sex attractions or by literally hurting yourself and taking your own life. What would that mean for Satan? Another soul that belongs to him! And not just any soul! A special, loving, good person who could do so many things for the Kingdom of God! Think, Rebecca, think how you could serve Christ and his Church if you conquer these temptations. All your gifts, all the gifts that God has given you, you should use in service to him! You will have *great* love in your life, even if it's not the exact kind of love you want."

I felt my brain racing backward toward the stillness of the egg yolk planets, waiting to be broken up and transformed into something totally beyond themselves.

"Satan is strong and has a lot of allies in this world," Dr. Kasey said.

I nodded and asked, "You mean, you really think the devil is trying to get me to kill myself?"

"Do you ever feel... unsafe? Like you're not alone?"

Well, I did. When I was alone, that was when I couldn't avoid thinking about my dad, and the things I couldn't put into words, and the constant vigilance in my body that I could never explain, and about trying to perform that I was fine for everyone all the time. I nodded.

"Like you need to catch your breath sometimes, in the middle of the night?"

I nodded again. "I'm scared of the dark," I said. "I feel like something bad will happen. Sometimes I wake up and I can't move, and I have to catch my breath."

Dr. Kasey nodded significantly. "Satan's demons haunt us in all kinds of ways, Rebecca," she said. She bowed her head and raised her hands over my head. "Lord, please protect Rebecca from your enemies and keep her heart pure, a pure receptacle of your love..."

I felt my hands start to shake a little, and I stuffed them quickly into my pockets. Leaving her house that night, I could taste the air, like it was coffee. I felt the scent seeping into my cells and sinking into me. Who knows what it was doing to my body? I was glad I wasn't going to have any babies, and whatever I was breathing in would just be poisoning me.

2006. When I was a teenager, my grandfather took me to the Cayman Islands National Museum because I wanted to know who lived there originally. I'd learned that there was no archaeological evidence of Indigenous people on the islands. Instead, Columbus happened upon them in the sixteenth century, calling them Las Tortugas because they were mostly populated by turtles. The islands were then settled by pirates and deserters from Cromwell's army—British guys who got to the Caribbean and never wanted to leave.

In 1670, England took formal control of the island, introducing slavery. Before slavery was abolished in 1833, it's estimated that just over a hundred white families enslaved nearly a thousand African people. The turtles went extinct. The islands had become more or less independent in 1962. Yet like everywhere I went, the rich people were almost entirely white and the poor people were hardly white at all.

My grandparents had bought their house there in the seventies, and everyone they employed to take care of it was Black. I had tried to ask about this as a child, but by the time I was in college it was something I was trained to shove to the back of my brain and down the back of my throat, to not try to understand. Every question about it I tried to formulate resisted simple language, like I had to think of new words every time.

The week before Dr. Madison and I were supposed to leave for Grand Cayman, my grandparents told me that they'd decided to extend their stay, so they could be there with us. There'd been a pregnant emptiness stretched out before me—what would it've been like to be alone with Dr.

Madison, with no one there to perform for? And now I knew I'd never know. My blood got hot when I thought of telling Dr. Madison that instead of having the house to ourselves and not having to meet anyone new, now she'd actually have to meet my grandparents, and they'd probably expect to share every evening meal with us. I was happy to be seeing them, in spite of how much I feared the separate parts of my world colliding. Dr. Madison was too excited to be seeing the Caribbean to care who we'd be sharing the house with.

"Oh, don't be silly, I'm happy to meet your grandparents," she laughed. "We can still sit by the ocean, right? With margaritas?"

Like race, money, too, was a subject without a language. I knew my grandparents weren't rich, or poor, either, but I knew they often spent their money on the wrong things— or, at least, that's what other people in our family said, in and out of words. It wasn't polite to talk about.

I wondered if Dr. Madison would be able to keep up with all the things we weren't supposed to say.

When we landed on Grand Cayman, I saw Nanny and Papa waving from the little balcony, where they had waited for me to get off of planes for my whole life. I felt that same flash of fear I used to feel right before my parents would be in the same room: people I loved were about to talk to each other, and it might end disastrously. But within moments, I realized that Nanny and Papa and Dr. Madison, and I in their company, were all far too polite for anything too explosive to happen.

As Papa drove the car to the house I'd gone to so many times as a little kid, I realized how alike the four of us were, accustomed to spending our energies trying to blend in despite all obstacles, each in our own way trying to pass for something we weren't every day. Now we were four white people in the Caribbean, white enough to pretend we were rich enough to belong there, to pretend we weren't there on credit.

The Caymanian air was hot and salty and smelled so familiar. I'd stopped coming here with them in high school, partly because Mom was always worried about their drinking. I was nervous that Dr. Madison would judge them, and that they wouldn't let me drive, but they'd rented us our own car, a purple convertible.

"This is for you two to run around in," Papa said, kissing my cheek and handing me the keys. I could smell the chardonnay on his breath, and it felt warm and familiar and homey.

Dr. Madison grinned at me, her eyes wide, like she couldn't believe it.

Every day we got up earlier and earlier, because there was nothing to not look forward to. Dr. Madison and I would sit with our coffee from five or six until ten or eleven. She graded every morning, and I read or wrote in my notebook about how I wanted her to be in love with me, but she probably wasn't. I wrote tiny, so she'd never be able to read it at a glance.

Every day we left the house for a few hours and snorkeled at local spots. Dr. Madison marveled at the underwater colors, but they weren't at all like I remembered. Most of the Reef was gray or brown instead of orange and yellow and green and blue, and there were far fewer fish than when I was younger. I wasn't sure if I'd imagined it being brighter and more interesting than it was until my grandfather told me it was "the damn pollution." We went to the Turtle Farm, where professionals were bringing back the turtle population, supported by a turtle zoo and a gift shop and the kind-nesses of rich donors.

Every night we went out to dinner, swapping stories and sipping cocktails.

"Is he dead now?" Nanny would ask of some friend Papa would bring up. Dr. Madison and I would laugh.

"Of course, he's dead!" Papa would bark impatiently. "They're all dead!"

The islands were so close to the equator, to the Sun, that we had to wear sunscreen constantly. Dr. Madison asked me to put sunscreen on her shoulders and her back, like we were in a John Hughes movie or *Some Like It Hot*. I fumbled with the straps of her bathing suit, trying to persuade my hands not to shake. *She knows, surely.* Other people had said they knew I was gay before I told them, so why shouldn't she? When I stripped down to my bathing suit, she told me I had a nice body.

"Don't be self-conscious," she said. "You've got nothing to worry about."

The sun made her skin shimmery, and she wore her hair down all the time instead of tightly pulled back, like she did at school. The salt water made it curly. I let myself look different, too. I bought a green blazer in a thrift store and wore it with a t-shirt and jeans one night, with my hair down. For a second, I looked like a boy in the mirror, like a flicker of another life. That night Dr. Madison got cold and asked if she could wear it, and Papa took our picture, smiling big.

"You two look like you're in high school!" Nanny ex-claimed. Dr. Madison looked like a college girl I might be dating in some parallel universe that came right up to ours but never touched it.

Dr. Madison let my grandparents call her Alexandra, but reminded me, even in our bare feet, when we were sliding into each other on the hammock, after my grandparents were asleep, and drinking our third margarita, "*You* have to call me *Dr. Madison*."

"You're not a real doctor," I said, laughing.

"I am, though," she insisted. "You should come to me for all your medical inspections!"

"Dr. Madison," I said, sitting up. "Did you just make a joke? Did you make a little joke just then?"

"Don't flirt with me." She laughed, slapping my chest. "I make jokes all the time. I made that joke yesterday about the turtle. You are making a joke out of me right now, aren't you? Stop laughing! Rebecca Mertz, stop laughing right now!"

For thirty dollars, we boarded a boat out to the sandbar, where for decades fishermen had been gutting their fish and feeding the guts to the rays. Now they flapped around the sandbar every day, waiting for the fishing boats like dogs lurking around a kitchen. I had to coax Dr. Madison and tell her that the stingrays wouldn't hurt her. She finally took my hand, stepped down into the surprisingly shallow water, and planted her feet in the soft sand.

"Okay," she said, "I'm in the water. Now you go enjoy yourself."

"No," I said, "you have to touch them, they feel amazing."

I stood with my feet secure in the sand and stretched my arms out before an oncoming ray, like I'd learned to do when I was a kid. The big old man ray locked his yellow and black eyes on my palms and swam over to me. He let me hold him while he flapped his big slippery wings on top of my arms and made eye contact with me as sure as any dog or cat or person. Dr. Madison looked on, laughing in delight and a little fear.

"Touch his belly," I said, trying to keep my balance in the waves without moving too much, which would scare him. She reached out her hand and touched his soft, silky belly.

She gasped audibly. "He's so soft!"

In the early evening after a hot day, we'd linger in the surf outside my grandparents' house or walk up and down the beach. Along the shoreline were huge mansions that had been gutted by Hurricane Ivan a few years earlier. I had marveled at how big and grand they were as a kid, but now they were broken down and abandoned, too expensive to bring back to life. We came to a big white one that had a balcony looking out onto the beach. Its doors and windows were blown in, and I took a step closer to it without thinking.

"Do you want to go in?" she asked. I was a little shocked by her willingness to break the rules. She smiled, like she was offering me a shot of whiskey.

The glass hadn't been cleaned up, and there were still a few shattered pictures on the wall. I imagined the dinner parties, the thousands of dollars spent to decorate and entertain in these gargantuan beachfront rooms, now abandoned, filled with sand and broken glass. I thought about how glass was made from sand, how it all washed up together like decimated generations after an invasion.

We climbed the stairs, and there were still beds in the bedrooms covered in shards.

"Look, a balcony!" she exclaimed, and we stood out there, without a camera or any witnesses. As the sun set, she pointed out a funny-looking house in the distance. It looked like two houses with a bridge in between.

"We could live there," she said. "You in that one, and me in that one."

She grabbed my hand for a few seconds again and dashed back inside the house and down the stairs. Those few seconds felt like a few hours; it felt like I was dancing down the stairs with her, and she was singing about feeling some way she'd never felt before, and we both knew the choreography. But once we left the house and she let go of my hand, everything went back to normal.

"C'mon!" she said. "Let's see what weird fish your grandpa tries to get me to order tonight!"

When we landed back in Pittsburgh, I had ten voice mails from my dad, each more intensely angry that I hadn't answered the last one. My cell phone hadn't worked in Cayman, and I hadn't told him where I was going because I knew he'd make me feel bad about it.

"Rebecca, this is your father," he fired off in the tenth message. "I don't know why you're ignoring me, but I don't appreciate it. I had to call your *mother* to find out where you are. I refuse to do that again. I'm your *father*. I deserve to know if you're alive and well or not. You've got no right to do this to me. Call me back *immediately, immediately, immediately* when you get this."

My heart burned, and I remembered the men who'd left Cromwell's army because they'd been to the Caribbean and never wanted to leave. They'd seen how beautiful the world could be, how warm the air could be compared with where they came from, the seduction of the blank slate. I got it.

But nothing was blank. The blankness of anything was the lie, the thing everyone always pretended was real that wasn't.

As we waited in the security line at the airport, I thought about the sea urchin shells, thin and more fragile than

Communion wafers, that we'd packed up so carefully in toilet paper and tissue and cardboard. Dr. Madison had kept a small glass jar of sand, some for her and some for me. Would any of it survive?

Waiting for our bags in Pittsburgh, we saw some Franciscan students, and she frowned secretly at me.

"It was fun while it lasted," she said.

32 People Will Say We're In Love

2006. A few days after we got back, I was on Dr. Madison's doorstep with the things of hers that wouldn't fit in her suitcase. She had the sand.

"What's the matter, Rebecca?" she laughed. "Are you nervous? Come in and dry the dishes while I rinse. Don't be nervous, spit it out!"

I laughed at the way she enunciated "spit it out" so carefully, so properly. I followed her to the kitchen.

Placing a dish on the rack, I closed my eyes like I was on a roller coaster. I took a breath and spat it out: "I think I'm gay."

I heard a little clatter under the water, like she had dropped something and scrambled to grab on to it again before I noticed that she'd reacted. She smiled the smile I knew was fake, and she nodded, like a sigh. She thought for a minute about how to respond, and I knew at that moment which path we were about to travel. I felt all the smiles sputter out of me. There are people who you always want to say the right thing to, and I knew at that moment that I had just done the opposite of that.

"Well," Dr. Madison said, nodding every few words. "Wow. Well, that is your cross, then. If that's what you are, then that's what you are."

"Yeah," I said, frowning, "I guess so."

"And it's your own business, to tell or not tell whoever you want. It's nobody's business but yours." She took a few minutes to decide on her next question: "Is Heather gay?"

"No." I laughed. "But that's funny, that's what everyone says..."

"What do you mean, 'everyone'?"

"When I tell people I'm gay, the first question is always 'Is Heather gay?'"

"What do you mean, when you tell people? Who else have you told? Does your family know?"

"No," I said. "Just some people at school... Helen, and uh..."

"It's alright," Dr. Madison said abruptly. "You don't have to tell me, of course, it's your own business. I assume Dr. Kasey knows?"

"Yeah, I mean, I just started telling other people recently. I've been talking to her about it, Dr. Kasey. I wanted to tell you before our trip, but I just wasn't able to get it out... and I didn't want to weird you out... I didn't want to ruin our trip." Now all that seemed like excuses, like I'd deceived her. "I don't know, I just didn't know how to tell you until now."

"You don't have anything to be sorry for, Rebecca," she said calmly. "But it is late, and we should talk more about this another day if you need to talk about it again, alright?"

"Okay," I said, relieved that at least if the conversation was ending, it wasn't ending in rage or tears.

"Thank you for trusting me with this, Rebecca, I am very honored. And I will pray for you, that your struggle will bring you to a place where you can live your life authentically for the glory of God."

I didn't mind anything that she was saying because she wasn't screaming in anger at me, and at least I could be grateful for that. When I got home and told Helen, she was thrilled and kept exclaiming about how brave I was, how Dr. Madison and I were going to end up together, and how we'd be so happy.

The next day on campus, I stopped by Dr. Madison's office, as I usually did between my morning and afternoon classes, but the door was closed and locked.

When I saw her later, she said, "I have to tell you, I'm a little hurt that I'm the last one to know."

"You're not... you're certainly not the last one to know—"

"Can we take a walk later?" she asked, cutting me off. "After your next class? Meet me at my house, and we'll walk around my neighborhood?"

I could feel my whole body shaking as I parked my car in front of her house. I wished I had a cigarette or a drink. I took some deep breaths and went to the door. I had barely knocked when Dr. Madison appeared, her coat on and her keys in hand.

"Let's walk," she said.

We walked in silence for a few minutes before she finally started talking.

"I was thinking," she began, folding her arms sharply. "And I'm wondering if you have feelings for me."

I laughed out loud at her directness and because I was nervous. I felt short of breath, too, and I realized I couldn't concentrate on walking if we were going to have this conversation.

"Let's sit down," I said. "I need to sit."

We sat on a curb, down a hillside, out of the way of any likely passersby.

"Okay," I said, "so..." and I tried to couch it a little: "So, yeah, I guess I have feelings... but I mean, it's confusing. I know you're my teacher, and I know you're... older, and you're probably not gay, of course, and I know you don't have any feelings for me."

"Then why would you pursue a relationship with me?" She was angry, and her face was turning red.

"Well, I like you!" I said. "And I mean, I wanted to be friends with you, and I thought you wanted to be friends with me."

"If you're attracted to someone, and you can't be with them, then it's your duty to keep your distance from them. That's the only moral thing to do in that situation."

"According to the Church, I'm not supposed to tell anyone I'm gay anyway! Didn't you ever suspect that I was?"

"How could I suspect you were gay when I see you at daily Mass all the time!"

This burnt. I could smell the ashes of what I used to feel for her rising up. I shook my head, and turned away, and started transitioning into autopilot.

"Well, what does that even mean, anyway, being gay?" Dr. Madison had angry tears in her eyes. "Are you sure you're gay, I mean? How do you know?"

"How do you know you're straight?" I asked.

"I'm not 'straight.' I'm a human woman and certain things are biological. I mean, is it just sexual?"

I could feel the tears welling up somewhere inside me. She had no idea what she was talking about, and that stung more than anything. I'd been full of secret knowledge and hoped she was, too.

"No, it's just like if you're attracted to men. You don't just want to have sex with them, there's a lot that leads up to that, and for me, what leads up to that... well, it happens with women, not with men."

She nodded, then stood up and folded her arms again, like she was warding me off. "I need to think about this," she said. "At the very least, our relationship needs to be more professional in the future."

"Okay," I said angrily. I waited for her to say something encouraging, but she didn't.

I sat in my bedroom, feeling like something was over. Now I could call my dad back.

The phone rang on the other end twice before he picked up the cell phone he'd just purchased. His voice shook with anger. He told me how disappointed he was, and his voice felt like his hard red stubble used to feel against my face, leaving marks, making little wounds of my skin. I thought about standing at his tall bathroom sink, brushing my teeth, with his groin behind my head, and how he always leaned in or pulled me closer.

He was talking about how my little brother and sister wanted me to come for Christmas, that they'd said it was all they wanted for Christmas. It was only spring, and already he wanted me to be thinking about the next winter and who I'd be hurting on Jesus's birthday.

"I'll have to think about it," I said, trying to breathe normally. Jesus was putzing around my room, acting like he couldn't hear what I was thinking, even though I knew he could. I felt sick to my stomach, thinking of the choice and how it was just part of my blood: Who would I make happy this year, and who would I make sad? There was no movement without collateral damage.

Dr. Madison had emailed asking that I come by her office on campus, so I sat in the chair I'd sat in so many times before. This time she didn't close the door but opened it a bit when I arrived, as if to signal that this was a professional, not a personal, conversation.

"How are you doing, Rebecca?" Dr. Madison asked cheerfully, after a moment of weird silence. She leaned back in her office chair, oddly positive, considering our last talk. "I was wondering if you're going home this weekend for the break," she said casually.

I said I was, trying to search out from her face what was going on.

"Well," Dr. Madison said, picking up a gift bag from behind her desk, "I was hoping you could deliver this to your grandparents for me. It's just a small gift. I'm so grateful to them for our vacation, and there's a thank-you card in the bag." She smiled. "I was also wondering... I was wondering if you were planning on telling your family when you go home this weekend."

"Telling them what?" I asked, genuinely not sure.

"You know," she said, glancing up at the door, "what you told me."

"No," I said, surprised, "I wasn't planning on telling them *this weekend*..."

"Oh, good!" Dr. Madison exclaimed. "Because I have some thoughts about that."

I shuffled my feet and looked over uncomfortably at the open door.

"I've been thinking, before you tell your parents, or anyone else, you should really be sure yourself. You should be sure about what all of this means to you, and how you're going to live your life, how you're going to be in the world."

"Whaddyou mean?"

"I think you should have a handle on it for yourself before you discuss it with your family."

"Why?"

"Because I think it will be easier for them to accept in that case."

"Easier for them to accept?"

"Yes. If you're confident in your commitment to live according to the Church's teachings, it will be easier for them to accept this part of you."

"Well, I don't know if I'm going to live according to the Church's teachings," I said, "so I don't know about that plan."

"I know you feel that way now"—Dr. Madison looked at me urgently—"which is why I think you should wait to talk to people about this."

"You don't really know what it's like not talking about it," I said.

Her eyes were angry now. "Look," she said, "you can't tell me that deep down you don't know it's wrong."

I met her eyes and spoke as evenly as I could. "Deep down," I said, "I do *not* know that it's wrong."

Dr. Madison threw up her hands in frustration. "So *the Church* is wrong, then?"

"Well, maybe—" I began, but stopped.

She was shaking her head dramatically and half laughing at me. "Either they're wrong on this, which means they're wrong on everything, or they're right on this because they're right about everything else. What do you believe, Rebecca? Do you believe that you're smarter and that your feelings are more important than thousands of years of Church teaching?"

"Of course not," I said. "But I also don't think you actually *know* what you're talking about... what it's like to be told that who you love, that loving someone, makes you immoral."

Dr. Madison scoffed. "Oh, we're not talking about love, Rebecca. This is about sex, isn't it? You said so yourself!"

"Sex is about love," I asserted. "Or it should be, right?"

She leaned back in her chair again, looked away, and shook her head. Now she looked at the open door, too. "Please go," she said, so I did.

I'd see her around campus after that, and we'd greet each other awkwardly, not pausing to catch up. At one point she emailed me to tell me where I could pick up a box of my things. Not long after we stopped talking, I heard that she'd started dating a man. Within a year, they were married.

When I became a teacher, I became more and more amazed that she'd gotten so close to me, been alone with me so much, gone on vacation with me. What did she get from me? Why had she kept me around? The only thing I was sure of was that we weren't allowed to say what we really thought or felt—how could any of us know what we really wanted, or who we really were?

Above my desk I'd pinned that Wordsworth poem we both loved, torn out of the Norton anthology, like a rainbow pin I'd been trying to wear:

My heart leaps up when I behold
A rainbow in the sky:
So was it when my life began;
So is it now I am a man;
So be it when I shall grow old,
Or let me die!
The Child is father of the Man;
And I could wish my days to be
Bound each to each by natural piety.

Dr. Madison's anger made me feel like I'd done something wrong, that not saying anything had been lying. Was I just a liar, like my dad? There was no one I could tell the story to, besides Dr. Kasey, who always said it was part of therapy that she could never repeat what I said to anyone. But there was so much to tell her, I felt, if I wanted to get better; so much I had to say that I didn't know how to.

At my dad's house, I'd bite my tongue. I thought if I had really grown up there, I wouldn't have a tongue left at all. I felt further and further away from my mom's house, too. There was hardly any of me that could be anywhere. I wrote more poems.

33 Nothing

2006. Dr. Kasey wanted to save me, and I wanted to be saved. So, after four years of resistance, I found myself at a Festival of Praise, the thing people came to Steubenville for from miles around.

Everyone assembled in the gym in ecstatic prayer. The best musicians on campus competed to play those nights. People sang and raised their arms and got "slain in the spirit" (the Holy Spirit took over their bodies, and they gyrated, fell to the floor, passed out); people "got a word" and received some message from God, spoke in tongues. The gym's doors were propped open, music and light pouring out of them. I wasn't sure that I could just walk in, but I did, and no one stopped me. I felt like, at any moment, someone would come up to me and tell me I wasn't good enough to be there.

The building was surrounded by FOP staff, who wore headsets and looked like low-budget Secret Service agents. People were milling around the lobby of the gym and sitting on the floor in groups of two or three, deep in prayer or conversation. The gym was so dark and full, I could lose myself in singing without getting self-conscious. For a brief moment, it was like I was living in a musical, and I understood why people loved this so much. They were praying with their whole bodies—it wasn't dancing, not exactly. Once, maybe, it had started out as dancing and been repressed, bent into this.

I was supposed to meet Dr. Kasey and her prayer team partner, Brother Chris, in the chapel when the prayer teams started. I knew it was time when I saw that more and more people were breaking away from the orgiastic musical worship scene and started flocking toward the chapel. Only the most impressive charismatic students, the ones who were clear leaders in so many other contexts, now assembled in groups of three or four across the chapel, ready to receive other students one by one and pray over them. A few groups had started, their hands raised like medieval statues, rendered in stone, permanent, channeling a silent, ancient power. I started biting my tongue and the inside of my cheek, just like I was back at my dad's.

Among the students, Dr. Kasey and Brother Chris were like prayer celebrities, and there were many legendary stories of their prayer team and the miracles they had achieved. It was no surprise that they got the best spot in the house, the Adoration Chapel. This was Jesus's room, where the tabernacle contained the Communion wafers that had been changed into Jesus's real body by the priests. I was acutely aware of the power that stood before me: Dr. Kasey, my counselor and professor; Brother Chris, her platonic spiritual partner; and, of course, Jesus, the King of Kings. I trembled appropriately.

The lights were dim in the chapel. Brother Chris was a tall, thin, stern-looking person who looked like a lot of the gay men I'd seen on TV. He slumped, too, which by now I read almost immediately as the sign of a sexual hang-up.

Not knowing what else to say, I said, "Hi, I'm Becca."

Brother Chris looked immediately annoyed. "Peace be with you," he said shortly, more like a character in a Bob Fosse movie than a priest giving a blessing.

Dr. Kasey bounced over to us, her usual overfriendliness somewhat tempered by her obvious efforts to comport herself with a level of dignity that matched the situation.

"Hi, Rebecca," she began, and explained to me that we would just talk for a few minutes about what I wanted, what I needed prayer for. I wasn't sure, though, what I was supposed to say. She assured me that whatever I said, it would be okay. I bowed my head to let them know I was ready. *Okay, God,* I thought. *Let's do this.*

Dr. Kasey and Brother Chris stood in front of me, each raising their hands, their hands wavering near the other's, never touching.

"Lord," Brother Chris began, like he was pulling up at a fast-food window to speak to the Lord. "Lord, open our hearts to your will tonight and help us see your wisdom in all things. We come here on behalf of Rebecca, she is here asking for your help tonight, Lord."

A few minutes passed as Dr. Kasey and Brother Chris each mumbled imperceptible words under their breaths, bobbing their heads from side to side as if to music. I looked back and forth between them hopefully, thinking they could and would help me, but not sure what I'd have to give in return, or give up. The hero in a story always had to trade something for something, and I was ready to get it over with.

"Rebecca. Rebecca," Brother Chris said again, which annoyed me, "what are you bringing to the Lord tonight? What burden do you wish was lifted from your shoulders?"

I knew enough to know that this was a pointed question, like the arrow points all over the body of Saint Sebastian, who Leslie had told me was the patron saint of "the gays." I looked up at Dr. Kasey, pleading for guidance, but she just nodded encouragingly in that "you know what to do" way. But I didn't know what to do. It seemed like this should be the moment for total honesty, like therapy, like it would just be a waste of my time to posture now. So, I thought about it, tried to get down to the crux of it.

"I just don't think God can love me," I said, finally nailing it.

Dr. Kasey looked surprised, maybe even moved, but Brother Chris looked like I had just thrown up on Jesus.

"What?!"

"I mean, I know he can love me, I know it in my mind," I said. My throat was dry, but I was determined to tell the truth, to get the help, to change. "But I just... I don't believe it. In my body. You know?"

Brother Chris's eyes were wide, indignant. "Why?" he snapped. "Why would you think God doesn't love you?"

"I don't know," I said honestly. When it came down to it, I could imagine God loving gay people. Other gay people, just not me. But I didn't want to bullshit anymore. "I think I've always felt this way."

"Well, what do you want us to do about it?"

Clearly, Brother Chris was scandalized, and miffed by the scandal. Dr. Kasey looked shocked as well, but not by me. "Brother Chris!" She regarded her prayer partner dubiously.

"I'm serious!" he said defensively. "What are you hoping to get out of this, Rebecca?"

"I don't want to be sad all the time," I began. "I want to feel... good, like other people do." I thought about all the other people like me who were, at this moment, crouching down in the dark with strangers, to feel better about something. Did any of them know what it was?

"Following God isn't about feeling good," Brother Chris said sternly.

"I know," I said, "but I don't want to be depressed. I want to do whatever I'm supposed to do, whatever God wants me to do..."

"Then start by admitting why you're really here," he said a little too loudly.

"Chris..." Dr. Kasey interjected, surprised.

"What exactly about you is so unlovable?" he asked.

It was obvious now: he was asking me to tell him I was queer, like secret parts of each of us were waving to each other from behind our masks—but something deep down in me resisted the easy explanation that God only loved straight people. Even I didn't believe that, especially when I wasn't thinking about myself.

"Well?" he asked again.

"I don't know," I said, "a lot of things..."

"I don't think we can help you," he snapped.

"Brother Chris, I think Becca's just being honest about her doubt, and certainly—"

"No," he said. "We can't do anything for her if she doubts the Creator's love for her."

I knew a whole host of saints had gone on record about their doubt, their hard times when they felt like God didn't love them. Yet Brother Chris was standing here right next to Jesus, claiming to have nothing to say to me.

"Really?" I asked, and that was all I needed to say. He was indicted. The more I stood up for myself, the more I felt the floor I was standing on start to crumble beneath me. I felt exhilarated, too, though, like I was reaching the top of something, and I was about to find out what was there. And what was there was the string you pull to open the curtain, or rip it in two, to show what was always back there, which wasn't what's supposed to be.

It was just this man, and men like him, and he had no answers, and he knew he wasn't as smart as I was.

Dr. Kasey asked me to wait outside while she talked to Brother Chris without me. I tried to stand up straight as I left the Adoration Chapel and slid into a back pew. All around me, other people were still looking for ways to get up the mountain. I started biting the inside of my cheek again, looking up at the big Franciscan crucifix, looking Jesus right in the eyes. I had been following him, and he had brought me here. I tasted a little blood inside my cheek and realized I was crying. Wiping tears away, I saw Leslie in the pew in front of me, turned back to look at me. Her hair was longer now, but she still had the same kind, pretty face.

"What's going on?" she asked. She looked scared. The whole world seemed quiet, but I couldn't find any words.

"I broke up my prayer team," I said, laughing even though it was the opposite of how I felt.

Dr. Kasey rushed up to my side, asking if I was alright, putting her arm around my shoulders, squeezing me. As soon as she touched me, I felt something crack open inside me. Defeat and shame filled me, and I hunched over even more, trying to bend myself away from where I was and disappear. I pictured myself swallowing pills, leaping from a cliff—anything to get away from these feelings. I tried to swallow them, but I felt like I was going to throw up.

Dr. Kasey started talking about how I didn't do anything wrong. There was a familiar knot in my heart muscle, and I could dissipate it with force. I raised my eyes to Leslie and saw that she was looking at me even more anxiously, glancing back and forth between me and Dr. Kasey. She asked what happened.

"Brother Chris was mad at me," I said.

"No," Dr. Kasey contradicted me in that saccharine way that always crept under my skin, "He was frustrated by the situation, but he wasn't upset with you."

"Why would he be mad at me?" I asked her, and looked her in the eyes and confronted her, without words, about betraying my confidence. Leslie looked at me in that way she used to, like we were surrounded by idiots and we had to take a train somewhere, fast. I straightened up.

"I've got this, Leslie," Dr. Kasey said patronizingly. Turning to me, she asked, "Do you want to sit and talk for a while, or go pray together at the Port?" Her face assumed that I would go with her, clearly the wiser choice. I looked back and forth between them.

"Can you just take me home?" I asked Leslie. She stood and held her hand out.

Dr. Kasey looked like we had just sworn off Jesus right then and there. She looked crestfallen. This night was not going as she had planned at all. I'm sure she thought that Leslie and I were going off to sleep together, but I knew all of that was over between us. When we got out of the chapel, I felt something surge in my stomach, and I had to bend over behind a bush, lean against the chapel, and throw up.

"It's okay," Leslie said, when we were in her car. "Sometimes Dr. Kasey makes me want to throw up, too." She handed me a bottle of water. People from California always had water.

Leslie didn't ask me any questions. When we pulled up in front of my house, she put her car in park. We sat silently for a few minutes before we both agreed that we didn't have to talk. We forgave each other in as few words as we could.

"Are you going back to California after graduation?" I asked.

"Fuck yeah," Leslie said, and we both laughed, because she'd been talking for four years about how much better it was there, so of course she was going back. I knew we were friends again—not the kind you hang out with, just the kind you know are out there, still rooting for you, even if they're far away.

Up in my room by myself, I got out the pack of cigarettes I kept in my nightstand and opened the window. I sat at my desk, deciding whether or not to smoke one.

I noticed a pile of mail on my desk, including a fat envelope I recognized as my latest batch of poems, returned from Dr. Davis. *At least that will make me feel better,* I thought. I opened the envelope hurriedly, remembering that the last batch I'd sent to him had contained a poem about Dr. Madison. I didn't use any pronouns, but I'd alluded to the object of my affection in the poem wearing a pink shirt. Even boys at Franciscan wore pink shirts (one household even had "pink shirt day"), so I didn't think it was anything particularly revealing. Anyway, it was a great poem. It was also the only poem that had a comment of any kind.

Seems lesbian, Dr. Davis had scrawled out on the paper. Nothing else, no notes, no compliments. I bit the edge of my tongue so I wouldn't cry and wrinkled my nose up angrily. *Fuck him,* I thought.

I got up and climbed out onto the roof. Sitting up there in the middle of the night was like watching an aquarium when the lights were turned off, every tiny movement a mystery. But then I realized I was inside the aquarium, too, just as trapped as everyone else.

Finally, I lit a cigarette and was glad I had something to depend on besides people. I wasn't scared of dying anymore, wasn't scared of Hell anymore. How could Hell be any worse than trying to live with all these secrets? At least in Hell, if you were on fire, you didn't have to pretend you weren't.

34 There's Gotta Be Something Better Than This

2006. The spring I was going to graduate, Brad married the girl he'd been holding hands with at our cousin's funeral. Bernadette—she even had a saint's name. They were both off working for churches in different states, but they decided to get married in Steubenville, since it was such an import-ant place to them, he said, and such an important place to the whole world. Suddenly, Brad was back in Steubenville and kept coming up with reasons for me to join them on their wedding errands. One afternoon in the car, on the way to pick up the bridesmaids' dresses, he said, "Becca should be a bridesmaid, don't you think, Bernadette?"

I started saying no, that was Bernadette's department, and Brad said it was only right, since I was his best buddy and I couldn't be a best man. Bernadette looked like she was being tested and had no intention of failing.

"Oh, sure," she said. "Yeah, we can get you a dress today, no problem!"

I glared at Brad, catching his eyes in the rearview mirror, and he smiled guiltily at me. He knew I hated wearing dresses and always said how much he liked to see me in them.

I stood in the fitted, strapless lavender gown in the middle of the shop where God and Brad and Bernadette could all see me, in addition to an overeager shop lady and several well-meaning, middle-aged women passersby who wanted to tell me how good I looked—I felt like I was wear-ing someone else's nakedness up on a bright stage, having had no warning that I'd be giving this performance. While Bernadette did something with her dress in another part of the store, Brad leaned against the wall and gazed at me in the dress.

"Your tits look great," he said under his breath, with his hands in his pockets.

On the big day, the church was full of Tuttles, even Bob, but Mom had stayed home. She'd been suspicious of Brad for a long time, though I hadn't told her anything. She made excuses about it being too much to get all the kids back and forth from Maryland to Ohio for just a weekend. Scott Hahn, the one whose voice I'd heard coming through mom's car speakers all those years before, was there, too. He had been Brad's teacher, and Brad asked him to do a reading. They asked me to read something, too, so I stood up in front of everyone, in high heels and a dress, and read a psalm about what love was.

At the reception, I drank enough whiskey to forget what I was wearing. Brad and Bernadette had their first dance, and then everyone joined in. I sat at a table with Brad's friend Clark arguing about women's ordination; Clark was losing, but had admitted that he no longer thought it was "cool" to pray outside abortion clinics. As I shot back the last sip of my whiskey sour, legs crossed like a real woman, I heard some old, familiar words.

"This one goes out to Brad's cousin Rebecca," the DJ was saying as the opening bars of the last song in *Rushmore* played, the one Brad knew I loved, because of the the kid with a crush gets to dance with her, even though she's too grown up to be attracted to him, like Brad wanted people to think he was. He motioned me over, smiling. I decided not to look at Bernadette.

Part of me knew I was just dancing for the story of the dance, and a bigger part of me knew that the rest of me just didn't know how to say no. Across the room Bob sat with his brothers and sisters, laughing and drinking and talking in funny voices. He went back to the hotel room early so he could leave for Maryland the next morning, but not before patting me on the shoulder and telling me he was proud of me.

Then Clark asked me to dance.

When Brad and Bernadette had driven off to the hotel near the airport, and everyone else had left the reception except the wedding party, Clark asked if I could give him a ride home. Brad's mom raised her eyebrows at me, impressed. When we got into my car, he bent his face toward mine and kissed me, right there in the church parking lot.

Clark was a beautiful man, and he asked my permission to keep kissing me. Hours had gone by when my cell phone started ringing. It was Brad. Clark laughed and took his hand from under my dress. We were covered in sweat and laughing.

"Wait, have we gone further than they have tonight?" Clark was giggling, and I shushed him to answer the call. I wondered for a second if Brad had realized his mistake, if he was calling for a getaway car.

"Bernadette left her driver's license in your car," he said. "Can you bring it out to the airport hotel?"

Clark and I crafted a story to explain why the two of us were still together at two in the morning. We wondered if Brad and Bernadette had "done it" yet. When we got to the hotel, Brad and Bernadette were sitting in the lobby, not changed out of their wedding clothes. Clark and I exchanged looks. Clearly, they had not done it.

Brad locked eyes with me when he saw that I was still with Clark.

"Why are you here?" Brad asked Clark.

"We were hanging out," I said, and Brad looked crestfallen. I handed Bernadette her wallet, and she apologized for leaving it, hugged me and thanked me, and told me how silly she felt. I told her I didn't mind, and Brad and Clark talked for a second in the corner like they had a secret. Bernadette smiled awkwardly at me, and I made for the door.

"Yeah, let's go up," Bernadette laughed, and grabbed Brad's hand. As she led him toward the hotel elevator, he looked back, forlorn.

"Becca, will you come, too?" Brad asked, holding hands with his wife. I wasn't sure if I heard him right.

Bernadette pushed him in the chest. "What is *wrong* with you?" she asked.

I thought of a hundred things to say, but I just wanted to get out of there and let them figure it out themselves. Back in the car, Clark didn't seem to be in on what was happening.

"I'd say they have *not* done it yet," he said simply, giggling. I laughed with him, but I just wanted to go home and sleep. I dropped him off at his friends' house, a few streets away from mine, and got into bed by myself. The next morning, I made coffee and called Heather.

"Hey," I said, "I'm *definitely* a lesbian."

35 It's Hot Up Here

2006. The closer we got to graduation, the more events there were to celebrate what a wonderful time we'd all had over the past four years. Most of my friends had graduated already. The week before graduation, the university hosted a dinner for seniors. Students, some faculty, and various staff and administrative folks, along with the most active friars, gathered at a banquet hall to eat mediocre food, listen to speeches, and watch awards get passed out.

I sat at a table with Helen and a few other English majors I'd gotten to know in classes over the years. I'd never hung out with them per se and was grateful for this; they knew nothing about me except what I'd said in classes, what I wrote in articles, what I was in public—just a liberal, not a lesbian. Meanwhile, the president of the university, Father Eugene, grinned with enthusiasm as he gave the introductory remarks. He spoke of all of us going into the world to spread the messages of love and obedience to Christ's Church. I looked over at Dr. Madison, but she was avoiding my eyes, clenching her mouth into that fake smile I hated.

"As you go out into the world, know that we are so proud of you," Father Eugene was saying, "and that we'll always be a home away from home here, any time you need us; we will always be proud to welcome you home; we will always be proud of our 2006 graduates of Franciscan University of Steubenville!" He'd always been oddly long-winded.

I saw Leslie at her table across the room, and she raised her eyebrows and smiled at me. I wasn't sure Father Eugene knew what he was saying, if he or any of the other faculty or staff here could ever actually be proud of me.

As dinner concluded, faculty members milled around with students. Dr. Reid came to my table.

"Congratulations, Rebecca!" he said. "I wanted you to know you were in the running for our award!"

Dr. Reid was on the writing society's interdepartmental committee, along with Dr. Madison and ten or so others, which gave out an award each year to a senior of any major for being an accomplished writer. I tried to imagine Dr. Madison at a table discussing whether I should get an award. Did she argue for me or against me, or say nothing at all?

I told my parents that I'd decided not to walk in the graduation ceremony, that I'd prefer to celebrate with my two families separately. Dad was mad and tried to persuade me out of it. I knew he wanted a picture of me and him, me in a cap and gown, that he could frame and point to when his friends came over, to prove how smart he was to have a kid graduate college—a girl, no less—with his hands all over me like a support system I'd never asked for.

But on graduation day, everyone I knew in town was attending it, working at it, or participating in it. So I put on a red dress and went to the ceremony. I would see Leslie and Heather later, but for the moment I was alone, thinking of the people I wouldn't see again. Jenny was there, too, for some reason, off in the crowd somewhere, not present for me, but present. Just as I was changing my mind about coming, I ran into Mark Angelo, who was in town to celebrate some younger friends. He asked if I'd like to sit with him at commencement in the big gym. We found a seat in the back row, and he passed me a flask.

"Tequila," he said. I was relieved and took a long swig.

Father Eugene was talking about the virtues of our graduating class and what virtuous men and women we all were. I didn't feel like a virtuous woman, or a woman at all, even though I was wearing a dress and my long hair was down.

"Wanna go to Wendy's?" Mark Angelo asked in a loud whisper, after his friend had walked. I'd never wanted to go to Wendy's more in my life. We made it back in time to see everyone mulling around in their caps and gowns, posing for pictures with parents and teachers and siblings and friends. I saw Dr. Madison in her doctoral robes, laughing and talking to other people's parents. She passed me and offered a compulsory congratulation without stopping.

I saw Dr. Davis at a table, getting a piece of cake, so I joined him. He smiled, shook his head, and turned fully away from me. Waving to someone else, he walked forward to join his wife and children at the other end of the long plastic folding table dressed up in white tissue paper. He didn't look back. I stood still for a few minutes with my cake, searching the fields for a familiar face.

Leslie was taking pictures with her family and the other Lambs. I knew I was really welcome there. Heather and I would go out to dinner in Pittsburgh later that week, but she'd said she couldn't bear to come back to Steubenville, maybe ever again.

I started to walk over to say hi to Frank Blake, but he was standing with a philosophy student and her family, posing for pictures and chatting with her parents. I noticed the way he smiled at her, the way he put his arm around her waist and let it sit there while her parents snapped a photo, the way he was fully charming them.

If I zoomed out from Frank's hand and just beheld the scene in its totality, it could've been a beautiful spectacle— after all, we had read an awful lot of books together. Happy mothers and fathers laughed and toasted and ate cake off paper plates. I missed my family. I missed being able to talk without first making sure I wasn't spilling any of the innumerable lies I was holding.

That night, when I got back to my house, there was a folded blue index card stuck in my door with my name on it. When I opened it, it just said, *I'm sorry I hurt you*. There was no signature, but I recognized Jenny's handwriting. I leaned against the porch railing, holding the little card. I could still feel that hollow feeling of Jenny saying that I'd gotten the wrong idea about us, like I'd imagined it all. I knew, now, that I'd burst her life into flames, that what she felt for me and done with me had thrown everything into flux, even Jesus. She wanted to be a religious education teacher, to work in churches—who'd let her do that if they knew about me? I looked at her small, neat letters, the turquoise ink on blue paper, and I couldn't be angry at her anymore. She was as mixed up as me, I knew. She hadn't even been able to sign her name.

PART 5
YOU'LL HAVE TO KILL ME FIRST (THE RESURRECTION)

You duped me, O Lord, and I let myself
be duped...

—Jeremiah 20:7

2016. Six months after the last time I ever tried to kill myself, I found myself, for the first time in my life, sitting in a room that *just happened to be* mostly lesbians. I'd been in groups of women my whole life, and I'd been in spaces welcome to queers—but I'd always been part of a minority, until I started the Intensive Outpatient Program at Western Psych. There were ten or eleven women who consistently came to the group, and seven or eight or nine of them at any given time were queer people assigned female at birth. We joked that we were a variety pack, representing every stage of the closet and every point of the gender spectrum, all ages and sorts, from punk, to librarian, to corporate vice president, to the two college-age girls who laughed sweet-awkwardly when the rest of us didn't know what they were talking about.

To get into this room, I'd had to say my trauma out loud over and over again. I sat across from a series of health and then mental health professionals who needed to hear my history of abuse. I gave them the greatest hits. Every time I said it, it got easier and easier to say out loud. No one ever reacted with surprise or disbelief.

"My dad molested me," I had to say over and over. "And then I was sort of in a cult..."

I'd been in individual therapy for years at an LGBT center in Pittsburgh—long enough for a string of diagnoses and the opportunity to learn how to say the things I'd been trying not to say my whole life. I had to learn the new language of surviving "whatever we must survive," as James Baldwin said.

I'd spent my whole life struggling against the grain, and now everything was supposed to be okay. I'd been so angry for so long. I was angry at God and my mom for making me, for not being able to protect me. I didn't have anything left to feel toward my dad. I was mad at myself for going to Franciscan instead of Bennington. I was mad that the world had been so hostile my whole life—and now it was all over, supposedly, like a war.

I'd seen movies about people in psych wards, but I wasn't in the psych ward exactly. It was a plain room with a purple floor. I went there for three hours on Tuesday and Thursday nights and Saturday mornings for about four months, and sat in a circle, and learned about how to get control of my emotions so they wouldn't kill me.

All I wanted to do was finish my book. I was angry that it had been interrupted. I'd known for a while now that it was my only real prospect for improving my life, getting better jobs. To write it all down, to get it out. The longer I was an adjunct, the less and less attractive I'd be as a full-time hire. I'd have a better shot of getting a full-time job with a book published, any kind of book. I spent so much energy trying to survive that I didn't do academic research anymore. I applied to fewer and fewer jobs as time went by. Every year, it felt more impossible. So I kept writing—but the more I wrote, the longer I needed to sit with my pipe and watch television to recover, to remind myself that the parts of my life I was writing about were over. Then Alexis had to leave. Then it had gotten really bad.

The group therapist was passing out workbooks, plain packets like I used to get of poems in graduate school, except this one just said "Skills Training Manual" on the front. Some part of me wanted to laugh, but my laugh was broken. I'd been trying to hold in everything too long. I didn't want to learn things anymore. That part of my brain had blood all over it.

This was the part of the movie when the shit had hit the fan, and there was nowhere to go but up. My marriage had ended, but now I had an on-again, off-again girlfriend who let me live in her spare apartment. Teaching two classes and not having to pay rent was enough to keep me fed. Three times a week I caught the bus to go to the University of Pittsburgh, where I'd first run away to.

I had a killer inside me, and it was me. The killer smirked every time the therapist who led the group challenged me to feel my feelings instead of shoving them away, to accept my reality instead of imagining how much better it would be if it were different. I was afraid to feel everything, afraid that if I felt the anger I'd bottled up, if I let a little through, it might never stop. My anger was the ocean, and my thumb was stuck in a wall, and I was convinced that if I moved, the ocean would flood me, my whole town, my whole world. I'd kept my finger stuck in there so long, my body had grown up around being stuck there, like a plant that's funny shaped from reaching itself toward the sun.

Even through my degrees in English, I didn't learn what "dialectical" meant until I spent nine hours a week in a Dialectical Behavioral Therapy treatment program. It was concerned with the integration of opposites, the dialogue between extremes. It was both psychoanalysis and clear, practical application of research psychology to help people deal with their emotions in real time. It was abstract *and* concrete. I learned there how to start tolerating contradictions without feeling like I was compromising myself. For years I'd blamed myself for going to Steubenville instead of Bennington, until my therapist finally challenged the notion that this had somehow doomed me.

"Maybe it would've been better at Bennington," she had said. "Or maybe something terrible would've happened there, too. You can't know. It might've been better, but it could've been worse, too. You *can't* know."

I'd thought of all the bad things that could've happened and realized that the Catholic Church didn't have a monopoly on homophobia, confusion, or abuse.

For years I'd been going to her, wondering if it was possible for me to get better, and she had sent me to the DBT program, knowing she couldn't do it by herself. She was in touch with my treatment team at Western Psych, where I had a group therapist, a boisterous, hilarious woman from Long Island, and an individual therapist, a funny lesbian.

Like surgeons or mythological characters, my therapists let me count to ten and fall asleep, and one held me still while another tenderly withdrew my thumb from the wall, and we filled the empty hole with concrete and diamonds. Like the witches in a kids' book, they spirited me away to safety, to some far-off place where I could heal and figure out what to do with myself—not some other person who'd had a different life, but me, *my*self. When I let myself feel my feelings, I realized the anger had already come out, mostly toward myself, over the years, and the things I was really afraid of were over now.

One day when I was feeling discouraged, I remembered my therapist recommending that I watch musicals and that I should see *Hedwig and the Angry Inch*. I had heard about *Hedwig* in the nineties, watching Rosie O'Donnell's show every day at four o'clock. Back then I'd blocked it out, like something I knew would break the glass walls of my world—I'd've gotten cut back then, and I might not've even realized it.

I sat on the secondhand red leather couch I'd bought at Habitat for Humanity for fifty dollars, looking into the mirror of John Cameron Mitchell's character—the boy forced to become a girl, who became a woman, who could take off their clothes and stand bare-chested singing "Midnight Radio" to the audience as both.

I'd never seen my own gender looking back at me so neatly, and I realized all at once that I existed in the dialectic, in the space between the opposites, in the both-place.

I sat in the office with the individual therapist and decided not to hold back.

"Do people get over this?" I asked. "Wanting to kill themselves? I mean, does it ever go away?"

She looked me directly in the eyes. "Yes," she said firmly. I asked how. "You have to take it off the table," she said. "It's like a door, and you have to board it up, or delete it, or move outta that house altogether, to a house with no door!" She laughed. "Maybe that metaphor is limited."

I knew they all were. I felt like I'd been building my life on top of the door, even when I pretended it wasn't there. At the same time, I kept dusting the seals and making sure it wasn't even locked. Sometimes I held on to the doorknob, just to feel like there was somewhere I could go where everything about me wasn't true. What would my life have been like if my dad hadn't sliced me in two so completely? What would it be like to grow up now, after *Glee*, when there were people from every letter of the rainbow on TV, singing their teenage hearts out?

"You will always be you. But you have to feel it, too. You can't get through this without feeling whatever it is you're avoiding. You want to kill yourself because you want to escape, and that made sense, for a while. That's what Acceptance is about," my therapist said, referring to the skill in our workbook.

I hated "Acceptance." I'd only been able to carve out my identity, to stay alive, by not accepting things, and here was a workbook on how to stay alive telling me that I had to learn how to accept the things I couldn't change. Like the past.

"But *you* are not set in stone," my therapist was saying. "If anybody's life proves that, yours does. You can change the way you think and the things you do, and it can make all the difference. But only you can do that... Unless you're dead." She paused for effect, and it worked. "If you die, you can't change anymore, you'll die just like you are now, and you'll never get better."

I squished my lips like I did when someone told me I should drink more water. I knew she was right, but I hated it. How was I supposed to take the door away?

"I can't just pretend it's not an option," I said. "I have a big imagination..."

"Well, why don't you use it for something else?" she challenged me.

From then on, every time I thought of it, I covered the door with another layer of concrete. Then dirt. Then a garden. Then a city.

I graduated from the Intensive Outpatient Program around the same time as two other lesbians, one in college and one a few years older than me, married with a kid. I took a bus to meet them at a vegetarian restaurant on the South Side of Pittsburgh, known for having tattoo shops on nearly every block. We sat in the sunshine, a fancy business mom in a sun hat, a college-aged sports-dyke, and me, in my cutoffs and tank top, hairy and red as Esau.

It felt like the last scene in the movie about our time together, learning how to live after coming up against the death inside ourselves. We drank beer and laughed, and Susan, the mom, teared up talking about how she never thought she'd feel this well again, and that's how all three of us felt.

"We should get tattoos," I said. "Like, something little that we could all three get."

Susan brought up the semicolon tattoo trend that was happening all over social media, for suicide awareness. We all had tattoos already, and soon enough we were in the lobby of a place playing loud, unrecognizable music, and a small blonde woman covered in blue and green ink was asking where we wanted our semicolons.

I chose my neck because I wanted it to always be visible, in case someone else needed to see it. I knew enough about tattooing at that point to ask if I could get a deal on a second small, simple tattoo; the most expensive part of little tattoos was opening the gun, not the amount of time they took, so a lot of artists would give a second tattoo for just twenty or thirty more dollars versus fifty or sixty if it was gotten on its own. I got a *Hedwig* drawing out front on my arm, like a badge, like a bloody purple heart on my sleeve.

That night I watched it again and texted with my new friends. I rubbed Aquaphor into my new tattoos and felt like Jesus with his resurrected body. My therapists were like the women who went for Jesus in the cave after he was dead, found out he was alive, and helped him back into the world. They had assured me I was alive; they told me to stick my finger into my own side and see what I'd survived, and tell my friends not to be afraid. The cave was like the closet, and neither one was a metaphor—both were the very real place you went after you were crucified, after your friends betrayed you and you were humiliated, stripped naked, destroyed in front of everyone.

And what happened in the closet-cave? I'd been curled up, waiting for someone to come along like an angel of God, to bring me back from the dead. But that wasn't how it worked. In reality, it was just people talking to each other, through centuries—carvings on walls, poems, radio waves, TV signals, and the internet—telling stories to show each other what we can survive, the chorus of survivors, of bad women and queers, of teachers and artists, repeating that same thing over and over in all the different languages: *Get up, come out: resurrect yourself.*

37 Skid Row (Downtown)

2006. I had no idea what to do after graduation, but my rent was cheap, so I stayed in my apartment alone that summer, working at the library and researching MFA programs. One day I got a voice mail from Mrs. Reid, or Sara, as I had to remember to call her, inviting me to dinner at their house. This seemed totally different from going to a single, childless professor's house for dinner. Sara said something about college students living away from home and needing a home-cooked meal. I was thrilled to go back to the house full of music and books and art. When I got there at the appointed hour, I was met by the Reids' oldest child, Zoe, who explained that her mother would be late for dinner because of a meeting that she'd forgotten about.

"She forgets things sometimes," Zoe said, laughing, "by which I mean often."

Zoe led me through to an expansive porch covered in potted plants: flowers, ferns, and little trees. The tile floor was strewn with gardening gloves, tools, and bags of fertilizer, intermingled with the signs of child life—a doll, tiny plastic food, a few trains, nail polish, books. The Reids had two little girls and a boy. The trees were ageing magnolias. I imagined the scent of the magnolias competing with the power plant fumes that left a thin layer of black on everybody's windowsills. That was the price of raising your children here in Catholic paradise—dangerous air and water. I didn't know what brought the Reids here or how conservative they were. I wondered, again, like a song stuck in my head, what I was supposed to do with myself.

The inside of the house, crowded with plant life, art, and color, reminded me of being in Europe; there was a sense of beauty and design about the complex layers of living—

it wasn't decaying and giving up, like most things in Steubenville were. In this house, people cared about things like beauty and books. The art was framed. *Maybe they're different,* I thought again.

Dr. Reid met me in the kitchen, wearing an apron and unloading a dishwasher. He introduced me to Zoe and Faith, his two daughters, who immediately started asking me questions about which movies and music I liked. They seemed somewhere over eight and under twelve. The little boy, Charlie, appeared holding a truck and told me he was four. Throughout dinner, we heard about Zoe's and Faith's respective problems, which were mostly related to the fact that the family had moved from New York to Steubenville. The girls were each appalled by particular things about Steubenville, which they found to be generally appalling. Faith was appalled by people's grammar, and Zoe was appalled by the level of importance that football seemed to hold in the community. Charlie kicked his legs under the table and nodded along with his older sisters.

"It's like on TV—the football players are the coolest people. I thought that was all sort of an exaggerated stereotype of history, I didn't think it was *real*!" Zoe was saying.

I had never met such assertive little girls. After dinner, they interviewed me about my life and interests while their little brother fell asleep on the couch listening. No sooner did I answer one question than they asked another. It was a relief to sit with a family and not feel uncomfortable, or like I had to hide things. Instead of being shocked that I liked musicals, or Italian movies, or "scandalous" works of literature, the Reids were impressed. When I made sarcastic jokes, they thought it was funny and smart, not rude or inappropriate, like Dr. Madison always did. I felt like I was in a movie, with the kinds of people I had only seen in movies.

When Sara finally appeared, we had covered my favorite musicals (Faith and Zoe loved them, too), political movements, books, cities, movies, directors, professors, classes, sections of the bookstore, and restaurants in Steubenville. The girls jumped up to greet their mother, who had brought cake. The whole family and I spent the next few hours telling each other stories and getting to know each other, stories overlapping and interweaving.

"I don't want to stop talking to you!" Sara said, as we stood in the kitchen after the girls and Dr. Reid went to bed. "Do you have to get up early in the morning or anything?"

She made more tea and started asking me about my parents and family. Before long, I was telling Sara about how hard it was to leave home, how hard it was to go back, and how hard it seemed to figure out where to be at all.

"Well, you know," she whispered, smiling. "This place is a little weird."

"Yeah." I laughed. "What's a nice girl like you *doing* in a place like this?"

She laughed a deep laugh and clapped her hands together gleefully, explaining that finding a full-time teaching job in theology wasn't easy, and that this is where they had landed for Kirk, as she called Dr. Reid. I said that she must love him very, very much, and she laughed again.

"Oh, Rebecca, I hope you come back soon! Are you a babysitter, by chance? I really like to leave my kids with people who I *actually* like, and some of these girls who sign up to babysit or advertise at the college are *really* weird. They've said some things that I really didn't appreciate to my kids, about the girls wearing tank tops or listening to 'secular music'! For God's sake! Crazy!"

"Yeah," I said, "but if I'm going to babysit, I have to tell you something..."

I had already decided to come out to her sooner rather than later. I couldn't bear losing these people, too.

"I'm gay," I said, looking quickly at her face for my fate. She smiled and squeezed my hand. I kept talking fast, to get as much out as I could before she freaked out. "I used to say bisexual, but I don't think that's really true. I don't know. Maybe it's something that I can change, or maybe it changes, I'm not sure, but I just didn't want you to have me babysit your kids and be your friend without telling you, if it would be a problem for you. I don't know if I agree with the Church or not, or how I'm going to live my life, but I want to be honest."

I was looking away, focusing hard on the red blinking of the metronome on top of the piano. Every part of my body was poised to flee, to run fast, if necessary.

"Rebecca," Sara said with conviction, still fiercely squeezing my hand, "I have *always* disagreed with the Church about this. I want you to know that first. And thank you for telling me. I really appreciate how afraid you must have been to tell me. But please, don't be afraid, my friend, please. I am your ally in this, okay?"

I shook with relief, like I'd exhaled a lungful of some new medicine. My back straightened up, and I relaxed. I could tell I looked confused as well as happy. I had expected this revelation to, at the very best, awkwardly end the evening. I was prepared for her to cast me out.

"Oh, please don't worry!" Sara exclaimed, reading me like an open book. "This doesn't change anything I already said! I hope you'll babysit every week! Seriously!"

I laughed in a way that felt like crying.

"And look," she continued, "you might as well know that I'm a really weird lady! I've never fit in anywhere, so this isn't new, and I just figure the Church will catch up with us eventually!" She paused and looked a little sad. "And, just so you know, Kirk has many great qualities, but he is much more concerned than I am about theological correctness... he yields to the Church's authority over his conscience, which is sometimes a good thing and sometimes not. But he's... he's not hateful, please know that. I wouldn't tolerate that. But if it's all the same to you, we could just keep this between us?"

"Sure," I said, like a cough. I felt a little bubble burst inside of me, in the back of my mind somewhere, but by that time I was good at ignoring anything that wasn't an explosion or a torch about to set me on fire.

"And my kids know that intolerance is unacceptable in our family, but I don't want them to be in a position where they have to keep something from their father... Does that make sense?"

"Oh, sure," I said, absently pushing my hair behind my ear. Of course, they were kids.

"I don't want you to outright lie, of course, but maybe 'don't ask, don't tell'? Would that be okay?" I nodded and tried to smile. She continued: "I really think the Church's teachings on sexuality are like the teachings on science in the Middle Ages. The Church is so far behind the rest of the world, and it's causing a lot of suffering. The Church is focusing on these issues right now in this way that makes dialogue impossible, and the victims of that are people like you, whose lives are sort of on hold..."

I couldn't believe how it felt to hear someone else say these things. I nodded, and Sara talked of her gay and lesbian friends in New York and how different it was there.

"You have to get out of here," Sara said solemnly, squeezing my hand again. "But even after you leave, I'll still be your friend, okay? So, you won't be, like, leaping out there into the world with nobody on your side."

I marveled at how sure she was that we could be friends, especially since she was so clearly a grown-up and I was so clearly someone in between. Before I left that night, we decided that I'd babysit Charlie within the next few days, as a test run.

A few weeks later, we started making plans for me to give up my apartment and move into the empty third-floor bedroom at the end of the summer, to be the live-in nanny.

In Steubenville, everything in the ground grows up drinking poisoned water, and most of the people do, too. But even in a place where you know the air and water are poisoned, it still feels like regular, old unpoisoned grass, like grass from wherever you grew up, before you knew what pollution was or what poison was. And whenever you do realize it, you realize the poisoned grass feels the same as all the other grass you've ever felt—how could you tell the difference if someone hadn't told you? And then you're not sure if every blade of grass you've ever seen has always been poisoned and you just couldn't tell—or if the poison doesn't do anything you can see, or if it doesn't do anything at all.

Sara knelt in the dirt. She had made a V for "Victory Garden," like women had done during World War II. We were in two wars now, Iraq and Afghanistan, but people didn't talk about it much. Sara wanted to acknowledge that we were at war. She called her garden her "other church," and for this church she wore a big, brimmed hat and sweated underneath it, wiping her face with dirty hands and gloves, so that she always came inside with dirt on her red, perspiring face. She always looked more alive when she came back from the garden, no matter that the dirt was poisoned, or the water. I was telling her my story of Dr. Madison, picking up pieces of grass and splitting them in two.

"Well," Sara said, wiping sweat from her forehead with a handkerchief, "she must be gay. If she wasn't gay, why would she respond like that?"

I laughed out loud and said, "No, she's not gay, she's pissed!"

Sara sat up and looked at me incredulously. "Sure," she said, "maybe she's got zero control over her emotions, generally. But one thing I've observed in my time is that there are only a few things that make rational, level-headed people act irrationally. Like, you and me, we don't fit into this category, a lot of stuff can get our emotions going and make us act irrationally... ! But Alexandra is like Kirk. It takes a lot for that man to change or deviate from his norms in any way. Like love. Or sex, at least."

Now I looked at her incredulously.

"You don't think she loved you a little bit?" she asked.

"If that was love, it's definitely not what they said it would be like," I said.

Sara laughed. "Well, another thing we know is that a lot of people who are gay don't have the ability to admit it even to themselves. But if she were straight, if she were a straight teacher and a male student had a crush on her, would she react that way?"

"A student she went on spring break with?"

"Well, that's another thing. That's just... You know, we have students over for dinner and to babysit, obviously... but actually, they're not usually Kirk's students, and it's not like Kirk is spending one-on-one time with them ever. So, it sounds like you two had a lot of one-on-one time, right?"

"Yeah," I said.

"Yeah," Sara said, standing and stretching toward the setting sun. "She's gay." She laughed, then said, "But I'm sorry she hurt you, my dearest. Someday you'll be somewhere where there are actual lesbians! I promise!"

"Your lips to God's ears!" I said raising a blade of grass as a toast.

She giggled heartily. "You. Are. My. Favorite. Person," she said. "And I fully support your being a lesbian. Although I have to say... I hope you don't become the super butch kind! That aesthetic is so... I dunno... it's just not *beautiful*."

I smiled, because I knew how to smile through that pierced-balloon feeling. I was always falling in love with people who thought they knew everything. But that was part of what I liked about them: confidence. And at least with older people, I could be sure I wasn't doing what had been done to me; I wasn't taking advantage of their innocence. I'd never felt innocent.

Sara didn't notice the sharp intake of breath I took.

"Do you know that Bruce Springsteen song 'I'm on Fire'?"

I didn't know it. She started singing it, and I felt that feeling like when Dr. Madison called me, like I wasn't sure what was happening was really happening. I blushed, and my mouth went dry, and I had trouble looking her in the eye or away from her. Her eyes danced, then she looked away and laughed in the sad way of laughing, like God had made a joke out of both of us. I fiddled with the grass. There was a little something wrong with everything.

Kirk turned out to be a nicer professor than he was a husband or father. One day, he snapped so harshly at Sara in front of me that she cried. He marched off, and she told me about the times she had almost left him. She had threatened to move away with the girls, and he always persuaded her to take him back. He'd resolve to be better and be better for a while, and then he'd get mean again. I asked her if she loved him.

"I love my children, and I think they deserve their father in their life," she said firmly.

When Kirk got mean, my mouth went dry, my palms sweated, I looked at my shoes, I turned red—until it would get so obviously embarrassing that he would stop. It started to feel like a cloud lifted whenever he left the house, that then we were free. For a while, we all pretended that it wasn't like that, but when Sara cried in front of me, we couldn't pretend anymore, and that felt like a cloud lifting, too.

The girls accepted that much of their world depended on keeping from their father that which their mother said he did not need to know. Keeping him happy was a priority of everyone in the house, because when he wasn't happy, he was mean. Sara's responses were theatrical and creative. One night while he raged about how messy the house was, she started singing, "Put a Little Love in Your Heart."

In a moment he was laughing, but no one else was.

Sara turned to me and said, "Wanna go out for dinner?" We piled the kids in the car and played the music loud. We sang along to "Diamonds on the Soles of Her Shoes" and I thought about what it meant to be a poor boy or a rich girl. We'd never had babysitters, except our grandparents and each other. I felt a pang that for some reason it was seen as industrious for me to be here getting paid to help Sara parent, while it would've felt like a defeat to be at home helping Mom.

Sara sang low, mostly to herself, but Zoe and Faith really sang. The music was so loud I knew no one would notice if I sang too, so I did, for the first time really letting go of my voice in front of other people. Charlie peered up from his book and looked embarrassed and delighted by everyone. Sara pressed "repeat" on the iPod, and we sang along to it together three or four times on the way home, the one wondering what it was like if everyone knew what you were talking about.

"I love you so much I might burst, Rebecca," Sara said, when we pulled up to the house and the kids had gotten out of the van.

"Do you love him?" I asked, surprised at my own boldness.

"I love him," she said. "And Christ is love. That is the point of the Gospel! Christ is the word through which all things came into being, he is God's act of love, creating the world, us, everything. That's why I think it's possible for everything to come back to love... even my husband." She smiled wryly. "I know it's not as bleak as all that, but sometimes it seems that way."

I never knew what to say, so I just listened. Later that night, Sara appeared at my bedroom door with a book by someone named James Baldwin.

"If you're going to keep living in my house," she said, "I hereby make it a requirement for you to read this book. If you don't finish it, out with you! He was raised deep in a church, he was even a child preacher... and he was gay! Black in America *and* gay!" She was the only other white person I knew who actually talked about racism.

I wasn't sure what being queer had to do with being Black, but when I read Black writers, I recognized a truth I hardly found anywhere else, about how it felt to be made into someone else's bad guy. I opened the front cover and read the first epigraph, attributed simply to "Traditional":

Work:
for the night is coming.

38 Feeling Good

2006–2007. Sara said I had to stop listening to so many show-tunes. She liked introducing me to new music: Sophie B. Hawkins, Suzanne Vega, Ferron, Nina Simone. She was still unpacking things from their move, and we made a project out of listening to all her CDs and records—a sizable collection—as I helped her organize the house while the kids were at school. We spent hours, days, weeks together, listening to her albums and unpacking their lives.

"You've never heard Nina Simone?" she asked me, aghast.

"Homeschooled," I said wryly.

She was already putting the record on the player, and Nina Simone's voice interrupted my joke. I'd never heard her voice before. I had been ready to make another joke, to say more, as usual, but Sara reached out her hand to shush me. Her finger paused right in front of my lips, just as the orchestra started vamping.

We sat there like we were in church, just listening. Nina Simone was singing that poem about feeling good and having a new life. Sitting there with Sara, I felt like she felt: that thing you know when you feel it.

"That's a show tune," I said, smiling, when the song was over.

"*No!*" Sara was genuinely shocked. "It's *not.*"

"Showtunes are *everywhere*," I said, and we both laughed, always on the same wavelength.

That December, I went home for two weeks and took the kids to the movies. Sara and I wrote long emails, chatted on Gmail, and told each other we missed each other five times a day.

I'd stopped taking the kids to church. Church wasn't a place I was sure I wanted them to know as well as I did, not anymore. Movies might be a better religion, the light of all the worlds we couldn't be protected from, no matter how hard anyone tried. Popcorn was Communion, too, a thing people were doing for some reason nobody could remember, in basically the same way all over the world, looking up at our priests and listening to stories of saints and martyrs and devils and angels, then going out to eat afterward.

Movies were the ritual where somebody told us the truth about ourselves. Even when everyone on-screen was trying to hide it, and everyone off-screen, too, a movie could still tell the truth like a cry in the wilderness, wedded to tension and the inevitable casualties of making people uncomfortable, just like God.

Even the stories that weren't true had taught us homeschooled kids about the worlds we couldn't see from our bedroom or living room windows, no matter how many telescopes we could get hold of or magazines we kept under our beds. We sat in the dark, bound together like the pages of things we didn't have a vocabulary for, printed on paper made from trees somebody cut down because they were so beautiful.

Christmas Day—the presents had been opened, the grownups were napping, and the kids were all quiet and happy, reading new books or playing new video games. I wandered away and sat down at the computer to find an email from Sara, the kind of email that breaks apart in your stomach.

The words "leading you on" beat neon inside my skull like one of the kids' infuriating sonic toys stuck repeating the same word on a loop. She went on to say she hadn't meant to lead me down any rose-brimmed paths. I couldn't figure out that metaphor. I kept imagining the yellow brick road and how yellow was the color of cowardliness or fear—and friendship, too. I imagined a road made of roses, yellow roses; a dreamy road extending forever, a blooming infinity of whatever I didn't exactly want. Something brimmed in my brain, telling me I'd done it again. Neon signs of all my failures flooded past, blinking, and blinking, and blinking. Neon Jesuses and Marys and neon angels and saints, all covering their mouths, shaking their heads at me.

I left the computer and returned to my family. There was a bottle of whiskey on the dining room table, which my grandfather had given my mother for Christmas. I sat down and started drinking it, staring at my mother.

"Would you love me no matter what?" I asked.

She laughed, "Are you about to tell me you're a serial killer, or a lesbian?"

She laughed, and I laughed, too, and said, "No, no," like it was so funny. My mouth was full of hay. I felt heavy, like I was sinking into the part of the ocean nobody ever comes back from or tries to get to. Some stone had fallen down my throat, and my throat was a well deep in the ground nobody knew about anymore. A long emptiness stretched out in front of me. I poured a glass of whiskey and went into the bathroom.

I locked the door, turned the water on loud, and cried as much as I wanted. I waited for Mom to knock, to ask me what was going on. I wanted her to come find me. When I came out of the bathroom hours later, she asked, not looking up, "Are you feeling better?"

"Yeah," I said, taking my seat in front of the TV, where she sat with her drink and her cigarette, and Evangeline lay asleep on her lap. No matter what flashed by on the TV that night, it didn't matter: there was no one like me on it.

I asked Sara if she wanted me to move out, and she squeezed my hand and said she couldn't bear it. We went back to watching movies and driving the kids to piano and avoiding Kirk. I applied to MFA programs, since I couldn't imagine doing anything except school. I applied for poetry, because in dramatic writing, you had to talk to too many other people. In fiction, you had to be too clear about what you were writing about. When I'd written a story about a girl and her teacher, everyone had figured out that it was about me, even though I'd disguised Hitchcock and myself and changed it as much as I could. Nobody knew what poetry was about. Poetry would buy me a few more years. The only artists I knew of who were lesbians were poets. I got into a program at the University of Pittsburgh.

"I know you should move to the city and have your own life," Sara said sadly, "but I just want you to know you can stay, if you want. You're still my favorite person."

I tried to stop thinking about that rose-brimmed path, like rose-headed lettuce, rose trees, rose planets, roses blooming out of cages and eye sockets, palms, belly buttons, mouths, and pubes, like saints' bodies miraculously not rotting, smelling of roses, people said.

Was it true, or did they just say it?

39 You Can't Get to Heaven

2007. A few months later, I had my own apartment in Pittsburgh, in a neighborhood called Friendship. The kitchen was so narrow I couldn't open the oven or refrigerator door all the way, but there was a balcony the size of a whole room. I liked being able to be outside and unobserved by anyone. For my birthday before my move to Pittsburgh, Dr. Reid smugly gave me a check for $1,000. It felt like an expression of his happiness that I was leaving, or a retainer for my silence about what had gone on inside his house. I bought furniture at thrift stores and spent as much time as I could on the balcony, looking out into "the world."

The new MFA students were "strongly encouraged" to participate in reading series during the first week of school, and even though my throat froze up at the prospect, I decided to do it. Luckily the reading was in a bar, and the bar was just down Fifth Avenue from the Cathedral of Learning, where all my classes were.

My hands shook as I unfolded the three pieces of paper I'd had stapled and folded up in my back pocket. I knew I was supposed to say something amusing before I started reading, maybe even share some witty banter with the audience.

"I'm Becca Mertz," I said, waving to the audience like I wasn't sure they'd wave back, "and this poem is about growing up gay and Catholic."

The room got noticeably quieter, and even the cool kids cast their eyes over to hear what I was about to say. This shocked me, because it wasn't supposed to shock them, but it did. I was the same age my mom had been when she had gotten inconveniently pregnant with me, in this same snowy mountain valley.

I read a long poem about Joan of Arc, and everyone clapped, and I felt like they could see me. A pretty woman who was too old for me came up to me after I read and asked me if I'd seen the Joan of Arc statue at Saint Paul Cathedral, up the street. I'd been to the cathedral many times on trips from Steubenville but hadn't seen the statue.

"She looks all cool and butch in it," the woman said a little shyly.

I wasn't sure I'd ever heard "butch" used as a positive before, and I did a little double take. She thought I was just surprised.

"You've got to see it," she said, and then she patted me on the shoulder and told me I'd done a good job.

The next day I got off the bus a few stops before Pitt and walked by the cathedral. I felt defiant going in, but it was my church, too, I decided. I blessed myself with holy water, genuflected in front of the big crucifix hanging above the altar, and glanced around the big dark sanctuary for a statue of Joan, probably wearing armor and waving a flag and looking triumphant. She was nowhere to be seen.

I wandered around for a few minutes and finally came to an entrance that went out to the street, figuring I'd make my way to school, and that's when I saw her. She wasn't wearing armor or looking triumphant. She was kneeling, leaning back with her chest out and opened up to God like an offering. Her hands were folded in her lap, and she looked up, straight up, at God, not like she was begging, but like she was talking to him. Her hair was short, and she wore the clothes knights wore under their armor. She absolutely looked like a boy.

I couldn't stop staring at her. I knelt down on the kneeler in front of the statue so I could look at her with more concentration, without worrying about holding my body up. There was a bird inside my heart, and it started flapping its wings like crazy, trying to get out.

"It seems like she's writing about God... or Jesus or whatever..." a third-year MFA poet named Kate said, during my graduate poetry workshop. Everyone leaned in when she spoke. "But, like, why? What's the point of writing about God anymore? Aren't we beyond that at this point? And what is this stuff about eating Jesus? Is it sexual? I just don't get it."

My professor was queer—a masculine of center lesbian who I always wanted to impress. She nodded thoughtfully, looking like she was reluctant to hurt my feelings but that Kate had an important point. "Yes, it might be more interesting to sort of allude to God as an absence, to deal with a disappeared God, rather than engaging in this sort of struggle over whether or not some god loves you."

I shifted in my seat. Everyone else nodded thoughtfully, too.

"Yeah," Kate said. "Like, if this was fifty years ago, it might push some buttons, but at this point, what's the point of fighting over religion with all these Neanderthals who think women shouldn't even be opening our mouths in the first place?"

With this one sentence, third-year MFA poet Kate made my whole life seem ridiculous. I felt my cheeks and ears go red. Everyone else laughed thoughtfully, and I smiled stiffly and tried to make it seem like I didn't care.

Kate invited me for drinks with her friends after class. After a few beers, she shouted to me over the jukebox music that I was a really great poet and gorgeous. I noticed how long her eyes lingered on mine and how my heart sped up. She asked me to a party and said she could pick me up.

That weekend, Kate drove me through neighborhoods in Pittsburgh I'd never been to, switching the radio station rapidly.

"You never know what might be on the next station," she said. "I used to play this game with my friend in college called 'radio gods,' where we'd sort of ask the radio a question and then whatever played, that was a message from the radio gods."

For some reason this seemed a lot more reasonable than the game I'd been playing my whole life, looking for messages from the real God. The radio gods seemed just as plausible. Songs were just as meaningful as psalms. I still stung from the accusation that my poems were so fifty years ago, so I said, "Now I know why you don't think people should write about Jesus. Because you're a radio god believer."

Kate looked over at me wryly. "I don't *believe* in anything."

"Oh yeah? Nothing? Poetry?"

"I mean, do I *believe* in it? I dunno."

"You think it's irrelevant to write about God? Or boring?"

"Well..."

I felt like, if I could change the subject, I might be able to kiss her, to be kissed—but I wanted answers, and I'd waited my whole adolescence to have this conversation.

I knew I had to start explaining myself. "I just... I grew up... I mean, my mom... my dad... my family... well, there was a lot of religion. Catholicism, mainly. Then I went to this school, and it was so intense, and everyone was like, 'You're a pervert and you're going to Hell!' and I was, like, suicidal—"

"Jesus," Kate said, drawing in her breath. "What the fuck? Why did you believe them?"

Later I would read in that essay by Kristin Dombek that there are sentences that tear a hole in the universe and ask you to walk through. That was the sentence for me. Nobody had ever asked me that before. I didn't know what to say.

Why did I believe them?

"I mean, you're delightful! What's wrong with you?!" Kate was indignant.

"That's not the point—the point is, like, why is it *interesting* to write about whatever else but not God?"

"It's not *not* interesting, it's just... like, you're thinking about if God loves you or not, and like, again, why wouldn't *she*? But also, it just feels like that's already been *solved*, like you're engaging on this life-or-death level in this debate that nobody's having. And like, why does it matter, you know? It's not political. It's not like the Church is gonna come knock on your door and throw you in jail for not going to church. Anymore."

"Yes, yes, yes!" I said. "It *is* political, it's still how people are getting other people to *vote* and to do all kinds of shit they don't wanna do and not do shit they do wanna do. People are having these conversations all the time, maybe just not people you know."

"But *why*?" she growled, annoyed. "Why are they still talking about this shit? These people have been fucking little kids and murdering Jewish people and Native people and colonizing and raping and pillaging alongside all the worst of everybody in the last thousand years! Why would anyone believe anything they say?"

I felt the blood rising into my face and my heart beating fast. I felt like she was talking about things I had heard of but for some reason hadn't read anything about. I would look it all up later, on the internet I was stealing from a neighbor, and realize how right she was about things I hadn't ever been allowed to know. I knew she was saying true things, and I hated how it felt to hear them. I'd been so stupid—I'd been so consumed with what the Catholic

Church said about me that I'd never bothered to have a crisis about how it treated anyone else.

"But they don't actually teach that those things are good; the actual teachings of *Jesus* and the real Catholic teachings *are* against those things." This was the best I could do.

"They don't teach that it's okay to kill non-Christian people?"

"Not in, like, a *long* time," I said. I wasn't sure why we were fighting—wasn't I out in the big world now, where nobody judged anybody and everything was okay?

"Well, did you ever think Jewish people were going to Hell?"

"No." I laughed. "The Church doesn't teach that Jewish people are going to Hell. Anymore. The idea is that everything is one, so if you're basically doing what you can with what you've got, you're alright."

"Well, they did a pretty good job of making you think you weren't alright."

"That's different," I said.

"Why?"

I felt exasperated, and I knew I could answer why for myself, but I wasn't sure if I could answer why for Kate. And nothing I could say would erase all the things the Catholic Church had done to everyone else besides me.

"I don't know," I said, and I felt, again, like the Catholic Church was right, that there really was something wrong with me, that I really didn't fit in anywhere. But I knew it couldn't be as simple as just doing the thing I'd been taught to do because everything else seemed too hard. I was starting to think that everyone just had the most sympathy, the most connection, with the first version of a thing they came across—religion, sex, art—but I knew the spirit of what she was saying was right, even if the words and the particular arguments she was making were answerable by all the priests and bishops and whoever else. Why hadn't I ever been outraged at all those other children they'd hurt to the point of no return, to the point of death, and convinced by their assailants that they were bad? Why hadn't that outraged me before?

I closed my eyes, my brain swarming with arguments. We had parked outside the apartment building where the party was. Then Kate saved me again from my own thoughts, kissing me on the mouth.

"I'll tell you a secret," she said, smiling, her lips touching mine as she spoke. "I just couldn't think of anything else to say. I couldn't find anything wrong with your poem, except God."

I kissed her back.

40 We Do Not Belong Together

2007. That night when I got home, I told Sara that I wanted to come out. "I think it's time for me to stop lying," I emailed. "I know Kate and I aren't really dating, but if I was dating someone, I'd want to be able to bring her around, and I really don't want to lie anymore. What do you think?"

I felt good when I went to bed and woke up relieved. Now I wanted to ask her about what Kate said, about why I'd believed there was something wrong with me. I made coffee in the tiny kitchen, looked out the window to the balcony, the table, the chairs. When I could hear the espresso bubbling, I turned the flame off, as I'd learned from Frank and Kirk. My dad had never made his own coffee.

But my coffee went cold as I sat at the computer, stunned by Sara's email. She was saying that I wasn't welcome to bring any girlfriends around. "In fact," she wrote, "I have to confide in you now that I've come to agree with the Church about homosexuality." I shook my head, not sure I had read that right. "And I need to ask you a favor, and I know it's going to be hard for you. I need you to do me this favor, as long as you feel the need to pursue this call of your conscience, as you put it. I need you to keep your distance from me and my family."

All of this, she insisted, hurt her more than I could possibly know, to have to ask this of me. I looked at the screen, reading the words over and over again. The thing that I had always known would happen had happened, but not at all the way I thought it would.

For the next two weeks, Sara and I exchanged emails. She seemed like a different person. I sat up at night smoking on my balcony, wondering if Kirk had hijacked her account, or if she had secretly been taking some medication that she was now off of, or a dozen other theories that could explain her total change of heart from one day to the next. She was saying things that I knew she didn't believe, or, at least, things she hadn't thought last week or last month. "I haven't wanted to tell you this, because I didn't want to cause you pain, but watching you and loving you has been part of what's led me to agree more with the Church."

I lived out my gayness like an alcoholic lived out their drinking, she said. I was going to rob my children of their right to a father, as I had been robbed of my father. Did I really want that for my children? My new friends might accept my gayness, but who were they, really? What I had in common with them was nothing compared to the ultimate connection of Christianity. "Watch, as friendships without Christ at the center of them just fall apart." She was drawing a line with her and Jesus on one side, and me on the other.

"I take some responsibility," she said. "I should have known better—if you were a young handsome guy, I wouldn't move you into the house to work with me or babysit my children, and I definitely wouldn't spend hours alone with you watching movies or becoming best friends. That was unfair of me, but you continued to tell me about your feelings even when I told you that I didn't reciprocate them."

Then she said that I had put the idea of leaving Kirk into her head. "And if I left him, if I were to run off with the babysitter," she wrote, "where would that leave my children? You were basically asking me to leave my husband and leave my children, even when I told you that I never had feelings for you! How could we ever remain friends under these circumstances?"

As we typed back and forth, the bridges I had built back to Steubenville burned.

Nothing about loving me could make Sara's life easier—unless I was just the world's best babysitter, kept in a set of boxes, "Babysitter" and "Friend," though we always seemed to spill over the lines. My coming out was irreconcilable with all of it, like a flower blooming in her living room all of a sudden that she'd have to say she hadn't tended. So she took me outside and let me go—I wasn't sure in the metaphor if she'd set me on the curb with the garbage or transplanted me somewhere friendlier—but she'd put me out. I felt that expression differently all of a sudden.

There were times when holding your breath was the best thing to do to be able to keep breathing later. Maybe all of Steubenville was underwater, and we were all just doing the best we could in such a strange place—maybe nothing made sense. I wondered what Sara would've thought of me or wanted from me if I were a man and older. But I realized, if I had been those things, we'd never have spent so much time together, and we might never have known how much we loved each other.

Love insists, I learned, on being reckoned with, somehow—Love was reckless, not dwelling on worldly consequences, and blind, in the sense that it lacked foresight, and like water, in that it would fill any shape we brought to the river. And maybe it was the same with me and Jesus—if I hadn't gotten so close, maybe I never would've known all the evidence and all the arguments from Jesus and the mystics and the saints, and everyone who said I was lovable in spite of whatever latest treatise the Church had put out. All that studying of theology had taught me that the works of men were temporary and that God's love was deep and mysterious—and that prophets were never recognized in their own houses.

I kept going to the corner store for cigarettes. Every cigarette felt like it burned away the taste of Sara, and Franciscan, and Steubenville, like I'd heard of burning forests, setting fire to the trees' bodies away to make better ground for new trees, new bodies. Jesus stood on the fresh burnt ground across the river from me. I objected, quoted Scripture, protested all of Sara's false narratives. I argued with her about every line she wrote. But as the days passed I realized that there was no point to arguing. There was no witness except God and God's body, the Church, which stood very clearly on the other side of a line from me.

God and Jesus were silent, as they always had been. Eventually I stopped writing back. Sara said I'd put a spell on her, and now she was burning me like you were supposed to do with witches, and heretics, and queers, and sacrificial lambs. Sara always said that Jesus was inside all of us, that we *were* him, and I never felt that I was him more than then.

I knew deep down in my gut that everyone in Steubenville would say she had done the right thing. They wouldn't need to hear about my "spells" or whatever I'd supposedly done to threaten Sara's family; they'd just need to hear that I was gay, and then the homeschooler, the homeschooling moms, and the Catechism of the Catholic Church would all agree that Sara should cut me out, that I'd be a dangerous influence on the family. I never got to ask her what she thought again. Across the Ohio River, Jesus sat propped up on a throne, watching me get burned away from Steubenville like I'd never been there, watching my execution like I'd been watching his all those years.

All day, I lay wrapped in a blanket, wishing every part of my body were paralyzed, anything if it meant I didn't have to get up. When six, then six fifteen, then six thirty, came and went, when it was impossible for me to go to class, I got up. I made a Cup Noodles and opened a can of Coke.

I watched a movie. I wrote to Heather and stared at the computer screen for forty minutes until she wrote back. She told me to get out of the house. I ordered Chinese food and put in another DVD. After a few weeks of this, Heather convinced me to go to Pitt's counseling center, where I started actual therapy with a woman named Becky.

She didn't care at all that I was gay, but she was alarmed by how frequently I had suicidal thoughts, which I had to measure out several different times on the intake form. Becky asked me if I knew how my suicide would impact my siblings.

"They'd be more than sad," she said forcefully, stronger than she appeared in her slight frame. "They'd be fifty percent more likely to do it to themselves."

This shocked me, and I bit my lip to keep from crying. Within seconds, I swallowed the lump in my throat, preventing any tears from appearing. Becky looked at me kindly.

"I'm not telling you that to make you feel shame," she said. "I'm telling you to keep you from doing something that you would regret—except that it would literally be better for you to do anything else, anything, because at least you could live to regret it. If you're not here, you're not here *forever*."

I stared at a glass turtle on her bookshelf for enough time that when she said something, it was that it was time to decide if we wanted to see each other again, and if so, how soon. I said that once a week was fine by me and made another appointment.

When I got back, Heather and I sat on my balcony. We looked so different than we used to. She'd cut her hair to an almost punk bob, and she'd started wearing more stylish clothes. I was still in ripped jeans and t-shirts, but my hair was getting shorter and shorter, now barely to my chin. Our lives felt better.

"What do you want to do?" she asked, smiling. "We can do anything we want now."

41 Defying Gravity

2008. It was Easter, so I decided to go ahead and tell my mother the truth—that I smoked. People think that Christmas is the most important Christian feast day, but according to the Catholic Church, it's Easter. God becoming a human baby is cool, for sure. But Easter is about conquering death. The Easter vigil Mass is the longest Mass of the year because there are so many readings, from all the prophets. There's a line that Dr. Tenerfort used to quote all the time and make sound so beautiful: *O felix culpa!* "Oh, happy fault!" Here the priest points out that without sin, without human fault, there would be no need for redemption, and even if we lived in a perfect world, without sin, without fault, we'd be missing out, because the redemption itself is beautiful, maybe even more beautiful than perfection. In other words, *it's the journey, not the destination.*

The priest says, "Oh, happy fault! Oh, necessary sin of Adam, which gained for us so great a Redeemer!... Of this night Scripture says, 'The night will be as clear as day: it will become my light, my joy.'" The resurrection of the dead meant that the dead could become the living just as the living could become the dead, and that it would go on like this, in gardens and graveyards and memories, everywhere. The miracle wasn't any particular outcome, but the fact that change was possible at all, that transformation was possible.

Mom sat in the spring afternoon sunlight, smoking her long, skinny menthols. Marianne and Jimmy sat at the table, playing a card game. The cleaning had been completed for the day, and daylight savings meant another hour of evening.

The littler kids played in the yard, on the huge swing set and playhouse Bob had been adding to and adding to over the years. I took one of Mom's cigarettes and lit it. She looked up at me, shocked. Marianne and Jimmy looked up from their card game, also shocked. I sat at the table and smiled like a cat.

"You're... a smoker?" Mom asked. She smiled in spite of herself. I knew how she felt, whether I wanted to or not, like, *Okay, yes, you can't hold this thing against me.*

I held the smoke inside for too long, imagining that I could go on forever without coming out, without saying it out loud, without ever having to do this hard thing, like I was looking down a long road through a sped-up telescope. I exhaled.

"Yeah," I said, "and I'm gay."

Marianne and Jimmy looked at each other with immediate understanding and then looked back and forth between Mom and me. Mom smiled, then we all smiled.

"You're gay," Mom said, not as a question but as a statement. She was still smiling.

"Yeah," I said, giggling. Marianne and Jimmy started laughing.

"I knew," Mom said. "Since you were, like, five."

"Now we have even *more* in common!" Jimmy said brightly. Marianne laughed even harder.

"Did you know already?" Mom asked them. They both said they knew and didn't know. Bob walked into the room, and everyone started laughing hard.

"What?" he asked. "Do I have something on my pants? On my head?"

"No, no," Mom said, "Becca just told us she's gay!"

"Well," he said seriously, "I'm glad you're *happy*." Then he laughed like a little kid.

He crossed the room to hug me as Mom teased him about making a pun. He didn't put much into words, but he kissed my forehead, and that said enough. We ordered ribs, which was the food we ordered when we really wanted to celebrate.

And we invited Nanny and Papa, though Mom and I both agreed that we didn't need to tell them yet.

For the first time in my life, I didn't want to change a thing. And for one night, I got to be with my family, where Mom and Bob and Marianne and Jimmy were keeping the same secret I was. I was not alone.

"You're perfect," Bob kept saying. Later he said, "You know, I always thought that the Church was wrong about gay people. Now I'm definitely sure."

I had been terrified of the worst possible outcome, and what had happened was happier than anything I had imagined. I had a flickering of understanding about why I was so angry at Mom all the time. Not for what she lacked but for what she had—and didn't have enough time or space or energy to give me. What I had been seeing so long as an absence was actually a presence: I wanted more of what she had, because it was good.

I realized my brothers and sisters were the only ones who would also always remember the house in the woods, who would know where the holes in the walls were, and the best hiding places, and the parts that had been torn down and built up again in new ways, and the way the kids toddled down the hallway in the morning, past all the old pictures of everyone—never the kind from the mall that some families had, but pictures of us wearing bathing suits and rubber boots and pirate costumes, our arms wrapped around cows or dogs or stingrays or each other, in our everyday best; together we could remember the way it felt to run in the grass, or sled down the hill of the field when it snowed, or curl up in the big living room that Bob had torn down a wall for, so everyone could fit. We knew the way it felt to come in heavy from playing at dusk, and the way dusk smelled there.

Mom got me away from Dad, out of Dry Creek, and into the world. Mom said that if I was a boy, she might not have left, but she knew she couldn't raise a girl there. She asked me if I was going to tell him, and I shook my head.

When I drove back to Pittsburgh the next day, I felt that old pain of wishing I could stay longer, instead of needing to escape, but now the pain felt like a gift.

The next night, I got my hair cut short. I closed my eyes and thought of Samson, and how hair was dead skin growing out of you, like memories, and how, in my case, it might give me more strength to shed myself of the past, the dead cells, the broken chargers, the burned bridges. I watched it all fall to the floor around me.

When she was finished, I looked like a boy and a girl. I smiled hello to myself.

"You look good," the stylist said, playing with the wave of reddish-blonde hair she'd left sticking up in the front. "It looks like a little flame."

I thought of Pentecost, when the Holy Spirit came down to the first twelve apostles, after Jesus was dead. There were tongues of fire on their foreheads, to show that God was talking through them now, too, not just Jesus. How now, everyone could be a Christ, like every human body was the ears and eyes and lips of God. That was the whole point of it.

She asked if I wanted my neck done like a boy or a girl.

"Boy," I said.

I walked out of the salon into gray spring. I pulled my green blazer a little tighter, lifted the collar to cover the newly shaved back of my neck. Walking into the Panera for coffee, I caught a glimpse of myself in the window and thought I was someone else. Would Jesus still recognize me? Would he ever come out to defend me, or the idea of me?

When I got to the coffee shop that afternoon to meet Matilda for our first in a lifetime series of off-campus coffees, she exclaimed when she saw me, touching my hair. She kept smiling, kept saying my name over and over again.

The next time I went home, I brought a car packed full of skirts, dresses, tights, shoes, and anything else that had come from the women's section, belts and bathing suits and hats with flowers attached to them. I didn't want to dress up like a girl anymore. I packed everything female of center into boxes, as well as the clothes from people I didn't talk to anymore: a hoodie of Jenny's, a t-shirt of Brad's, the scarf from Dr. Madison. I had so much from Sara, it took years to get it all out.

Evangeline rushed out of the house wearing her bathing suit, no matter that it wasn't summer yet, refusing to wear anything else. She and Todd jumped up and down, saying my name over and over again like a contest of who could say it fastest. At this commotion, Lily and Jimmy looked up from the tire swing where they sat with their heads tilted together in a private, infinite conversation. Marianne and Beatrice sat nearby, looking up from books. Everyone smiled big and jumped up from where they were to run and greet me. Bob came out of his workshop, his face red with sweat, still holding a hammer in one hand, a dripping cold beer in the other.

"Becca!" he said, grinning and handing me the beer, giving me a sweaty hug.

I was swarmed with hugs from the little ones, each one slightly bigger than they had been last time I was there, everyone saying my name at the same time.

"Cool hair!" Bob said.

"You look like a boy!" Todd said enthusiastically.

"Thank you!" I said, and laughed.

Mom appeared, smiling and reaching out for me. She took my face in her hands and touched the newly shaved back of my head. She pulled me in to stand beside her, leaning her head against mine. She exhaled like she'd been holding her breath. Evangeline jumped into my arms.

"Me, too!" said Todd, and I tried to pick him up, but I couldn't hold both of them at the same time anymore.

"One at a time now," I said, tossing the keys of my car to Marianne. "There's tons of clothes in there I don't want anymore, probably something for everybody."

Marianne, Jimmy, and Lily raced to the car, and Todd and Evangeline trotted behind them. Bob followed to supervise the impromptu swap meet. Beatrice put her arm around me and leaned her head on my shoulder.

"I'm so glad you're home," Mom said.

I wished I could say so many things to her, and all that came out was "Me, too."

All those years, people had told me I was bad, that even Mom would reject me. They filled my head with all the things that might happen, the stories of parents casting their children out. I'll never know what would've happened if I'd told my mom sooner, if I'd told her about my dad or Brad or Leslie or Jenny—if I hadn't kept all those secrets and lived with two faces for so long.

It was easy to blame Mom for the things I couldn't tell her. She never got to take me by the shoulders and tell me they were wrong, that there wasn't anything wrong with me that wasn't wrong with everyone else. I didn't give her the chance to—I didn't have enough faith in her. My dad, the Church, Franciscan, and the big outside world had all made me feel so small; they'd made sure I wouldn't tell the truth to anyone who loved me. My father was the one who was supposed to tell me who I was, where I came from, about my name. The name he gave me I couldn't tell anyone else. The history he gave me was a secret history. The language he taught me, he taught me to lie in. I didn't want to lie anymore.

If God was everywhere and everything, then God was what was real, and what was real was good.

Beatrice stood close to me, examining the two green stud earrings I'd left in one ear, like a colon hanging in the air between my before and after, the closeted and uncloseted versions of me. There was too much meaning on either side for any language to contain, and I knew it was that way for everybody.

Beatrice's eyes got wide like she'd just remembered something.

"Did Mom tell you?" she asked. "I'm bisexual! Do you think people will be allowed to marry a girl *and* a boy, ever?"

Mom laughed and raised her eyebrows. I laughed, too. Beatrice was only eleven.

"I don't know," I said. "Anything's possible."

I put my headphones on and walked down to Centre Avenue and up to North Craig Street into Oakland, where the cathedral was. I wanted to see Joan. Now we both had short hair. I knelt down in front of her, with my ass on my feet, not even thinking about the fact that we were mirror images of each other.

"I know my voices come from God," she had said. Matilda Ritter Blake had given me the transcripts of her trial, where the bishops examined her genitals to "make sure" she was a woman, which was their only theological problem with her. They were British and she was French, and she had led an army against them—but unlike a man who'd done that, who'd be killed or allowed to live depending on politics, she was handed over to the Church as a witch, and they put her through a humiliating trial, during which she, a twenty-two-year-old woman from the country, schooled the British bishops in theology. They called this witchcraft and heresy, and demanded that she be denied Communion if she didn't put on women's clothes. They also wanted her to admit that she couldn't hear God's voice. She refused, insisting on her own maleness and that it had nothing to do with God. She said the voices that told her she was okay came from God, which was another way of saying that her conscience came from God; that her own reasoning and thinking were enough, even if no one else heard or understood it; and that to oppose her, to oppose what she said, was to *oppose* God. She didn't waste her time trying to explain what was really going on to them, and what was really going on is still a mystery: she told them that God wanted it all to happen, that God was in on it, too.

Impossible, they said, and killed her.

They burned her to death as a witch, even though she was a soldier. But now the same Church venerates her as a saint. Joan, like Saint Francis and countless others, had pissed off the Church so royally during her lifetime that she'd been killed as a heretic—only to have her face printed on medals, hundreds of years later, and her body made into statues. In that moment, I realized that the point of the story was how Joan had defied *even* the Church. She wasn't just a Catholic mascot, and she wasn't just a heretical, witchy gender enemy—she was both.

I bowed my head and thought of all the times I'd tried to be one thing or another, my body tugged between places, people, ideas—Pennsylvania or Maryland, Mom or Dad, gay or straight, Church or world, God or self, girl or boy, good or bad? I'd heard something about there being a right wing and a left wing, and one bird. The two sides I'd been pulled between were just two of infinite points on a circle. I had to stop trying to choose.

Joan knew the secret, somehow, too: that by letting herself be the Church's enemy, she was actually being its hero.

I thought of the American bishops and how, for my whole life, they'd written that I was disordered and perverted and shouldn't be able to get married or have kids—all the while, we knew now, passing sex offenders around like candy to children, passing evil off as good. How could they condemn me? Joan had become a saint, and the Church, by accenting and venerating her, was celebrating some timeless, insistent queerness, even if it didn't know it, even if that was the very thing they'd been trying to burn away.

I realized I'd been asking God to change everything for me, to let me be who I was without the inevitable results, like if Joan had asked to lead an army and have it all work out okay. I had to let go of the idea that I could avoid the inevitable pain of being myself.

Years later, I'd read about Saint Wilgefortis, who prayed that God would make her "grotesque" to avoid an arranged marriage. God made hair grow from her chin, a full beard in some versions of the story. When the would-be husband saw her, he refused her immediately. When the father found out what had happened, he had his daughter crucified. Maybe I believed I was bad because my father tried to crucify me. Like Marshall had said about Abraham and Isaac: How was that supposed to make me feel? And why had it taken me so long to even think about feeling it?

Things might've been different if I had heard about Wilgefortis, if I had heard more about Joan, and less about what the homeschoolers thought about birth control, less about what my dad thought about gay people, less about what Hitchcock thought about Woody Allen and what Woody Allen thought about everything. Stories were important, and I was just beginning to hear the right ones. In Wilgefortis's story, the father was the villain and the bearded lady was the saint. The Church removed her feast day from the calendar in 1969, the same year as Stonewall.

If anyone came upon this statue, they wouldn't if Joan was a boy or a girl without the name plaque. Maybe in the future, without a plaque or anything, they would just know that Joan transcended, that Joan was trans.

I looked at the statue for a long time, for as long as I could; then I got up and left the Church.

42 The Flesh Failures (Let the Sun Shine In)

2015. I had started to introduce Matilda Ritter Blake as "my friend, who was once my professor." When she was finally able to quit her job at Franciscan, and get out, too, she asked me to go back one more time. She just had to get the last few things from her office and return a book to the library. She was going to become a therapist—one of those people who saved people's lives by listening.

We were going back together for the ritual of it. It felt less like going back to a college campus than going back to a battlefield we'd only very nearly survived. All for a "higher purpose," for God and Jesus and the Catholic Church, and all the saints, steeping our lives in compromise and denial, sacrificing ourselves up for somebody else's culture wars. The war wasn't a metaphor.

I hadn't been back in almost ten years, but I decided to go, just to see what it would feel like.

For the first time in a long time, I didn't know how to get dressed. I was everything I always wanted to be, finally proud of myself when I looked in the mirror. But in Steubenville, a visible queer might as well be wearing big, feathery angel wings and not expecting anyone to react to them. I put on a jacket and tie, rethought it, undid the tie, unbuttoned the shirt, put them back in the closet. In a tank top and jeans, I looked just as queer, but at least I wasn't overdressed.

Matilda and I did mindfulness exercises as she drives us through the tunnels out of Pittsburgh and west. I didn't know all her stories, but she knew most of mine; she was the one listening when they were new and fresh and bloody, and I thought I was going to Hell and I didn't have anyone else to talk to. Years later, we talked about *The Canterbury Tales* and how we're doing a reverse pilgrimage. I vaped out the car window. I rolled a cigarette, the wheels rolled over the bridge, and we made jokes about how we never could've imagined this day and how we'd both always imagined it.

Driving up the big hill going from the main road into the campus, I still had the feeling that I was leaving "the world," that I was going from the outside to the inside, behind the theater curtain or behind the projection of the Wizard of Oz. The windy road is steep, too, and it's a miracle that fifty years of drunken students coming and going haven't killed anyone, though I knew the school had a way of pretending things hadn't happened when they had. Up the hill, you could go one of three ways that all eventually turned out to be the same road through campus, branches jutting in different directions that all bled back into the same vein, the same deadly road back out to the world.

Some people came and never left, it seemed, or the turnover of people who came and went prevented anyone from really knowing how long anyone else had been there. I thought about the night in graduate school when I'd googled "cult" and seen the list of qualifications, and how, without fail, Franciscan University had checked each box. In the 1970s, Father Michael Scanlan and other members of the so-called "Charismatic Movement" had been corrected by the archdiocese for doing things like arranging marriages between members and other cultish activities that concerned the Church at large. It was everything except funny to look back on the things the Catholic Church condemned, compared to what they weren't condemning. They were still condemning me and my friends.

According to *The Atlantic*, in 2016 the number of students in the United States who were being homeschooled hovered around two million, almost double the number of homeschoolers than when I graduated high school. About two-thirds of North American homeschoolers identify religion, primarily

Christianity, as a main motivator in their decision to keep their kids home. This places rough estimates of Catholic homeschoolers between eight and one hundred thousand, depending on who's doing the math. The *Catholic Herald* wrote in 2018 that one in ten men "in formation for the priesthood in the United States" had been homeschooled.

Franciscan ranks highly on lists like "25 Most Conservative Colleges in the U.S." (no. 6), "Best Conservative Colleges in the U.S." (no. 13), and "Top Conservative Catholic Colleges" (no. 5). It's hard to believe there's anywhere *more* conservative than FUS, but I believe it because of the number of people I knew who transferred to Franciscan from more conservative Catholic colleges and breathed sighs of relief about how they didn't have to fold their underwear anymore (Magdalen College, New Hampshire), or hide their nose rings (Thomas Aquinas College, California), or wear skirts to church (Christendom College, Virginia). At Franciscan, they said, they could "be themselves."

The big names that float in and out of Steubenville and the list of affiliations, honorary degree recipients, and major donors include names like Newt Gingrich, Rick Santorum, and Alan Keyes, as well as such infamous clergy as Cardinals O'Connor, Wuerl, and Law. I marveled at the hypocrisy of it all, that Jesus was always about people at the bottom, that we were supposed to love and love and love, that love was supposed to conquer all—but maybe love wasn't about conquering.

I found out years after my last visit there that Father David Morrier, a priest I'd gone to confession to, had been indicted for the rape of a student who confessed to him. The Franciscan TORs who ran FUS sent him to Saint Maria Goretti Catholic School—Maria Goretti, who had died fighting off her rapist. "It wasn't an accident that he got sent there," a friend told me when the news became public, "It was them making a joke."

Father Sam Tiesi, one of Father Scanlan's two right-hand men in the revival of Franciscan and the Charismatic Movement, was also accused of assault and harassment by a female student who confessed to him. The year I graduated, Franciscan University settled with the former student, whose only demands were that they pay for her therapy (roughly $30,000) and that they implement some changes in how they handed sexual assault and harassment allegations. That year, they dedicated the chapel on campus to her rapist. One article covering these cases included the revelation that there was a support group for women on campus who had been sexually harassed by priests and male students, where women spoke openly about several priests on campus. At least three of my male friends from college told me in later years that they'd been sexually assaulted by priests as children, teenagers, and adults.

I didn't go to church anymore. Sometimes I prayed. I prayed every time a child got killed by the police, a trans woman got beaten to death—I marched, and made signs, and prayed with my feet, like Frederick Douglass talked about. I sang and chanted in the choirs of people rising up. I knew that's where Jesus was, anyway, not boxed up inside of what some white men said about him. I marched with strangers, saying the same simple words over and over again: "No justice, no peace."

There are people who say that life isn't a musical, but there's music everywhere; sometimes we choose it, sometimes we don't. When Gotye's "Somebody That I Used to Know" was a hit, it was a hit on every continent, topping charts all over the world, and it wasn't impossible that most people in the world might be singing the same song, and some people were singing the boy part and some people were singing the girl part, and I was singing both parts.

I remembered the Leonard Cohen song that Sara had become obsessed with, how the light got into us all through our broken, open places—which was one of those lines that sounded like it'd been around for a million years, like a line of music that people kept putting together, in different times and places, because our bodies were all basically the same shape and made the same beats and echoes. The notes were all around us, waiting to be combined, just like language, just like cells and ingredients. Like the stars in the sky appeared to kids before they'd noticed or been warned about their patterns.

It turned out my mom was right all along. People are people. The Catholic Church was hiding sex offenders and child abusers, and so was Hollywood, and so was the music industry, and so was politics, and so was every other kind of place, everywhere—we were hiding it from ourselves, the terrifying light that we couldn't bear to look at, of how powerful we *all* are, the levels of devastation we can wreak, and how terribly and completely we can wring the peace from each other, how we can clip each other's wings, pin each other to walls, tear each other apart completely.

Terrifying, too, were those words I identified with now, "non-binary": how could Woody Allen, J. D. Salinger, Harvey Weinstein, Michael Jackson—how could they have done so many beautiful things, made things that lifted people's humanity—and then do the terrible things they did, too? How could Bob Fosse have created so many things I loved and have raped one of his dancers in the alley behind a theater?

The problem was that it was all true: those we'd loved were gloriously good *and* were terrible; they held power over people's destinies as much as any gods. My dad, too. My dad, naked in the shower, giving me instruction on what to do to him. My dad singing along to "Leader of the Pack" in the car; my dad getting into bed with me and pulling off his underwear; my dad making everybody laugh at the beach; my dad asking me how I could be so stupid, undermining my authority to me and everyone else, for years; my dad signing someone's loan papers at the bank where he worked, giving someone a home, then coming home from work and changing the whole energy of the house with his mood; my dad singing "American Pie" in the car, with the windows down, with a fresh bag of McDonald's fries, forever.

Eventually, I'd write down what he did to me that I couldn't say out loud to anyone, not even my therapist. I folded up the paper and felt better. Relieved. It was out, done. I had heard Dylan Farrow describe over and over and over again for years, what Woody Allen did to her, and I thought, *So that's what it would've been like if I'd told someone.* Even if there had been video of me talking about it the very next day, and I'd had a movie star mother doing battle and a whole legal team, and talked to a series of child abuse "experts" and the whole world, I would still not be believed, and, worse, I'd believed and told I was making too much of a fuss about it, too. Against that, I might still choose my silence. Of course, the most obvious and insidious part of child sexual abuse is how little evidence there can be and how children, still developing and having less language than adults, have less language to advocate for themselves. By the time we are adults, with our wits finally about us, we are told that too much time has passed, that we must be remembering wrong, that memory is a funny, tricky thing.

I know how old I was when my father did certain things to me because of the size of the furniture that happened to be nearby: the bathroom sink, for instance, which was as tall as I was, when he pressed his erection into me as I brushed my teeth. The top of my head reached his waist when we were in the shower together, both naked. When I was in the bed, I could've been any age, any size; I only know that the little twin bed that he barely fit into still seemed to swallow me when he'd get into it with me.

I didn't question other memories from my childhood; if, all of a sudden, I remembered being in the grocery store in that little town where he lived, standing at the meat counter with my grandmother as she explained what "ham salad" was, I wouldn't question that that memory was true, even though I don't remember the story around it, or how it all played out, or what day that was when we stood there. I don't associate much feeling with that memory, except the general tension of being in that town, in that world, in that role that wasn't me. Some memories provoke more or less feeling, more or less reflection.

If you can't explain what the reasonable story could be, it must be impossible: Why would I be in the shower with my dad, naked and alone? Why would he be saying what he said to me? What story could explain that? The feelings I remember are confusion, discomfort, and fear, especially fear of anyone else seeing what we were doing. But as an older child remembering this, with no words for what was happening, I could think nothing but: *I guess I'll understand that when I'm older.*

When I was older and remembered the same things—the shower, the bathroom sink, the bed—I was also old enough to have been gaslit in a million other ways into doubting myself, my judgments, my characterizations of people, and my memory. How many times throughout my childhood had my dad acted one way in private and another way in front of people? How many times had he lied to people about what had just transpired between us in order to make himself look better? He had sown doubt all through me, carefully, like a tapestry. He had all the tools of patriarchy to ensure that by the time I could think for myself, I knew that his version of things would trump mine every time, even if I did somehow have it all on tape.

When I was older and I remembered the shower, the bed, the bathroom sink, I thought, *Well, that couldn't be right.* In what story did those things make sense? I must have imagined it. But as an adult, I know the difference between remembering and imagining. In my notes for this book, there is a scrap of paper that says, *Sexual abuse is almost impossible to integrate into the narrative.*

We were creators and destroyers of worlds long before the atomic bomb. Humans create and destroy in an infinite multitude of ways. What had kept my story inside me so long was the same thing that protected everyone else—all the artists, the coaches, the teachers; all the priests. It was the mindfuck of the contrast.

Who could contain it all without "going crazy"? And who believes "crazy" people?

At the end of *Annie Hall*, Alvy says that people keep falling in love because they need the eggs. The joke is a man's brother is insane and thinks he's a chicken, and when asked why he keeps his brother around, the man says, "I need the eggs." Woody Allen didn't make that joke up; it's an old joke. He's just the first one who said it in front of me. And it isn't just about falling in love: we keep looking for friendship, for understanding, for goodness; we keep hoping, amid all the perils of being alive, because we need the eggs.

The problem was that it was all true—it wasn't even a matter of both, because, as I always found myself saying in class, there weren't two sides, there was a circle, and it and we were all *always* moving.

Caring for outcasts, defending the defenseless or working for righteousness or justice or loving, or letting yourself be loved was the best thing a person could do, whether or not they were praying while they did it. I'd learned in school that language was all a symbol anyway, and the theologians said Jesus was "the word made flesh" –that God was all of us, connected, the connection itself, and the mystery of how any of that could be true, which is just what poets and singers and psalmists called Love.

My theology and philosophy professors in Steubenville and my poetry professors in Pittsburgh had all complained about the same thing: that somehow, we'd watered down language, especially the important words like "love." Love was now about your favorite pizza; you loved a chair, a pair of socks, a sandwich—it wasn't about the creation of the universe or the generation of life, the firing up of cells, Shakespeare's sonnets or The Crucifixion. And now there was no word for that, versus how you felt about pizza.

Everyone's life was just as hard-won and complicated as the cathedrals in Europe my professors would go on and on about—how they were built by thousands of people over generations, but the people who made these incredible structures wouldn't even see them completed, nor their children. I knew I'd spend my life pushing my culture just a tiny step forward, hopefully, like building a part of one of those cathedrals. Eventually some queer kid would be able to just walk in if they wanted to and not be afraid.

I thought about Heather and Mark Angelo talking about Athanasius: "so that man might become God." Not like God. Not gods. Not *like* gods. God.

My heart raced as Matilda pulled into a parking space behind the building where I spent years coming and going and hiding and shaking and lying and thinking about ending my life.

I clutched a perspiring iced tea, cold enough it floods my senses, a trick I learned in IOP: *Hold ice when you're stressed out.* But also: get a full night's sleep, tell the truth when it helps you, not just when it gets you into trouble or pisses people off.

I walked through the bookstore knowing that if I publish my book about this place, it would never get stocked here. Someone might put it on a list of some kind—"Authors to Pray For," at the very best. Assortment titles were proudly displayed: books by people I used to know, my old professors, most of whom were always kind to me. The theology professors—the ones who were underwriting the idea that I was a pervert, that I was insane or confused about my gender, that me and my love were vampires tearing into the neck of Western culture—were some of the sweetest men I'd known there. I had fond memories of friendly conversations in their classrooms and offices about women's ordination and feminism—homosexuality wasn't up for debate. Occasionally, it was suggested by a radical leftist that homosexuals might not be destined for eternal damnation, if we played our cards right.

"Can I help you find anything?" a young student wearing a bookstore polo and a nametag with an obscure saint name on it was there to help me find my way. She smiled brightly, like she didn't care what kind of sinner I was. Her hair was short in a *Sound of Music* kind of way, in the girls-who-say-they-want-to-be-nuns way.

"No, thank you," I told her, remembering what made it all so complicated: that this girl and many others here weren't mean-spirited or hateful, that if this were an Old Testament story, there'd be ten good people in the city who, someone like Abraham could argue, should prevent the whole town from being burned up. The other thing was, she might not want to be a nun; she might be like I was, hiding in plain sight. I knew it was different now, that she could watch *Glee* and google things—or maybe, somehow, she couldn't. How could I forget how easily people had persuaded me I was wrong about everything, just because I didn't trust myself?

I wondered if there were other people who looked like me on campus now, gender nonbinary queers or butch dykes who were trying to push the limits of the Catholic Church. I knew that the administration had recently forbade a woman from speaking on campus who promoted herself as a "chaste" homosexual—she followed the Church's teachings that people should refrain from same-sex sexual activities but still identified as a person with "same-sex attraction disorder" (and was willing to talk about it). The president of the university had said she couldn't speak on campus, and a group of students had hosted her at a local bookstore. I still couldn't decide if this episode represented any kind of progress, or if this was just another example that the world was the same as it always was.

After a half hour on campus, with Matilda's books collected and running into no one, I think I might be over it. We take selfies against the backdrop of the new construction, the pro-life rally advertisement on the kiosk, the flyer for a meeting to discuss "Christian Masculinity": this is the evidence that even though things have changed in us, they haven't changed here, and the university is still expanding. A new crop of students had arrived that semester the same way I did almost fifteen years ago, ready to surrender and submit themselves to Jesus.

I felt strong going back there and not having to ever go back again. But when I get to my apartment in Pittsburgh, I spent two hours throwing up.

I couldn't tell if I needed to expel something from within my body or if the problem *was* my body.

I vomit until I'm vomiting nothing, rendered into a prayer posture against my will, my body crouching over the bowl, begging for someone to take this pain away, to convert it, to change it into something else, to redeem it, like a promise or a coupon.

The last time I saw my dad was at my first wedding. I was the same age he was when he married my mom. It was one of the best days of my life, even though he was there. That day I felt like I could tell between the people who were genuinely happy for me and the people who were faking it. I'd been taught to think any negative reading of anyone else was a judgment of them, but finally I was learning that acknowledging someone's sins against me wasn't a sin against them. I started letting myself see people as they were, rather than how they could be.

I had been avoiding him since graduating from college, and he'd started avoiding me, too. We were in a game of chicken with each other to see who would call first, and we were both winning. I hadn't planned on inviting him to my wedding, except that now that I was getting married, everyone was asking questions about him and where he was and whether he was coming. I'd been trying to live my life, to not live in the past, and to be who I wanted to be. I didn't want to think about him, but it wasn't just him, it was his sister, my coolest aunt, and her kids; it was my stepmom, my brother, and my sister—I wanted the rest of them there, and he came with them. "Incest," I said to Alexis. "The gift that keeps on giving!"

I swallowed something I didn't want to swallow—that old taste of keeping in a secret that's killing you—and sent them all invitations. He called me. I hadn't heard his voice in at least a year, but it made me feel like I was small again.

We fought about problems that weren't the real problems between us, and he told me they could attend the wedding and had planned a vacation to Ocean City around it. After we screamed at each other on the phone about whether he'd been supportive about me being gay (which didn't matter), we picked up and pretended everything was fine, our old show.

But Nanny, the most gracious, hospitable woman I ever knew, who'd let you do a line of coke at her dining room table if that's what you wanted to do, couldn't help herself. After the ceremony, she saw my dad put his hand on my shoulder, and instantly she appeared next to us, eyeing him and his hand suspiciously. He was frail, ravaged with diabetes and chronic health problems and, I imagine, guilt and rage. As soon as he touched me, I started dissociating.

"Isn't she amazing?" Nanny was saying to my dad about me. "Aren't you so proud of her?" He wasn't, of course, but she wanted to see him squirm, she wanted to see the shit rise up his throat and come through his teeth. When she was dying and delirious, she said to me, "I wish we'd never let you go there." But on my wedding day she said, "Isn't she just more wonderful than you ever could've imagined?" She was beaming.

"Yeah," he managed to say, his voice shaking, which he was trying to pass off as emotion.

By the time he was digging his fingers into my shoulder bones, I was fully separate from my body, watching everything from above. Later, Alexis told me she'd been trying to cross the room to get to me, and my stepmother had kept stepping in front of her.

They left the party soon afterward, and the next day he asked to be my Facebook friend, convinced that our father-daughter dog and pony show had been revived. When I got back from my honeymoon, I emailed him and told him that the way he'd touched me at the wedding had made me uncomfortable, and that it reminded me of times when I was a child and his touch made me feel uncomfortable. I said I didn't want to be Facebook friends, that I wasn't sure how I felt about having a relationship at all.

This was the tip of the iceberg, cresting the ocean's glass ceiling. I held my breath for a day and a half waiting for his reply, though I knew he obsessively checked his email. Finally, an email from him arrived in my inbox, bold and new and ready to be opened.

"I didn't mean anything by the hug," he wrote back. "Take as much time as you need."

So I did. I took all the time for myself. I wouldn't spend any more minutes or hours unsure if I would be disappointed by him—I was disappointed by him. I stopped waiting for it to be one of those times he—but what was I even referring back to? *Were* there good times? There were times when he said yes to ice cream, when he made a joke instead of yelling at me unexpectedly. The moments of positivity were just relief from torment, only good in comparison to pain.

Now that I knew the words for what had happened when there was no one there but us, when I was three, four, five years old—now that I knew that there could be such a difference between what one person told you was okay and what was okay—now it didn't matter to me what he'd meant to do or didn't mean to do, or how he saw it, or whether he remembered it or had pretended even inside himself that it hadn't happened. None of that would alter the years I'd spent with that static in the back of my mind all the time, with those broken parts that no one else could see that I'd had to heal myself.

When he told me he was dying of cancer, the thing he thought killed only stupid smokers like my mom, I wrote to his other two kids and tried to explain that I would not, could not, come to see him. I knew this would make me a monster in their eyes. My other option was to interfere with their vision of their father—good or ill—right before he died. I didn't want to complicate it, to be the whisper of doubt in their ears, just in case he had changed into a better parent to them, a good father. I didn't understand how this might be possible, but I knew that abusive parents didn't necessarily abuse their children the same or equally. Something made me feel like it was just me, though later I'd learn that most victims of child sex abuse feel this way, like they were the only one.

"You think you're so special," he would say to me, and I wouldn't know what he meant, what he was talking about, or how it applied to what had just come before it in the conversation.

"No," I'd reassure him, "I'm not special. I know I'm not special."

What if he had been able to keep up the performance of the good dad for my brother and sister, his second-draft children? I didn't want to sow anything that wasn't there on its own, not the year he was dying. We'd arrived at a point that told us, in countless different ways, that we weren't really family, that the family unit we operated as when I visited them was animation, an illustration of life as it was supposed to be, as everyone wanted it to be: a good dad; a smart, thoughtful divorce; a blended family; happy kids. But for the kids, we knew: that wasn't real. I showed up, spoke my lines, played my role, and went back home. It didn't make sense to them, either; I knew because when they were little they'd cried, asking why I couldn't come for Christmas or why I couldn't live there. In the end, I don't know what he told them, of why I wasn't around more, and in the end they didn't write me back, unfriended me on Facebook.

I had to let go of what they thought of me, because I wasn't ready yet to tell them the truth. He was a dying man in a hospital bed, but he was the storyteller, and there was no contradicting him now. According to the story, we were supposed to be at his bedside, laughing and remembering the good times. I knew that if I went there and didn't tell the truth, I would burst into flames. I would lose my mind. I would want to kill myself again. And if I went there and told the truth, what would that do? For whom? I knew that even from his deathbed, he'd act like he didn't know what I was talking about.

I imagined going to his bedside and losing it, like Jesus in the Temple. Would that tear open the world for them in a way that would help them step through to somewhere better? But there was no amount of language that could encapsulate it to them, if they didn't know it already for themselves. And if they did, *would* it help them? And if they didn't, would it help them?

He'd caught me in a trap, and I had to leave part of myself behind to get out. The wolf always gets the credit for this in the metaphor, but in reality, all kinds of animals will do this, especially humans. It depends less on the species of the animal and more on the trap, and what documenters of this phenomenon will refer to as the "spirit" or the "character" of the animal who has done it.

What usually goes unromanticized is the animal's likelihood of survival after such a trauma. We don't get metaphors about what it's like to be a wolf who's chewed off its own foot to escape the jaws of a spring trap. Although that might be what art is. Some animals, according to the internet, have gone on to live full lives. Others bleed to death after their escape, or, once they realize what they've done, their hearts stop with shock.

When I was a teenager, my dad lost his job at the town bank. He'd explained it to me one day in the car, trying to make it sound innocent.

"There's all this money just sitting in the bank, doing nothing," he said. "So I thought I would just take some of it and use it to try to make more money, and then put the original amount back."

There was a little scandal, but the VP of the bank decided not to press charges against him, since he'd only done it once (that they knew of) and since he was otherwise such a nice white guy. That's when my dad stopped paying child support. He stopped coming to pick me up in the car, because he was too ashamed to see my mom and too tired of performing interest in me. When my grandparents, his parents, picked me up one day, my mom remarked, sincerely, that it was a shame, what was happening to him.

"You reap what you sow," my grandfather said.

43 You Can't Stop the Beat

2019. I woke up, and sure enough Cece had texted me, try-ing to get me to join her at the Lesbian Festival, where she'd already been camping for the past three days with her friends. She offered to pay for my ticket, if I could find someone to watch Scrappy. I could put off that weekend's grading and join her if I wanted to, but I wasn't sure if I wanted to.

We kept breaking up and getting back together, and it was starting to feel silly. I looked at Scrappy, the long-haired Jack Russell terrier curled up in a little brown-and-white ball at my feet, gazing up at me like it was just another day. I had about $100 in my bank account to last me the next week, which was a lot for me—of course I couldn't take a spon-taneous trip to Ohio. Then I thought about her mouth and the shape of it when I was on top of her, how she opened it for me.

I texted back my thanks and said I would try. This was when I most hated being broke, having to decide between borrowing money or just not having an experience. I texted my friend to ask if she could watch Scrappy for a night so that I could go to the Ohio Lesbian Festival and pursue romantic adventure. She replied immediately, in all caps, saying I must go. Scrappy looked annoyed.

Ohio was an endless stretch of straight, flat roads I hadn't chosen in years. Every mile I drove I felt like I was getting deeper into the Midwest, that place where folks mostly voted red, where Jenny was a social worker and still lived in the closet (but texted me about her girlfriends), where folks argued about which bathroom I should use and people looked at me more and more like I was an apparition, the kind of person they'd only seen on television. Heather had come out as a lesbian, too, and fled to the West Coast.

For some reason my car only picked up radio stations in Pittsburgh. Once I left the city limits, it was all static. I'd rigged a shitty speaker to the rearview mirror of my aging Ford Focus, because the CD player in the car had stopped working the month before. I wondered if my clothes smelled like weed, or if I'd packed my stash inside enough coffee, deep enough in my backpack, or if a dog would be able to smell through all of that anyway. I ate a hash truffle, took a hit off my vape pen, and pressed "play" on "All the Young Girls Love Alice."

Roadtrips made the years a palimpsest, a montage in my head of people and places I'd left behind or was maybe getting closer to. I thought about being a kid, wanting so much to be a dyke and not thinking I'd ever be brave enough. When I thought about the Christians now, I knew some people I used to know had changed, like me, and some people were still the same. I met new people all the time, but none stayed seared in my imagination like them, the chorus who acted out my particular odyssey.

It was one of the last weekends of summer. The nights would get a little cold, but the afternoons were still hot. I wore shorts and a tank top, hairy and tattooed and not wearing deodorant because Cece hated the smell of anything unnatural and she liked the smell of my sweat. She hated that I smoked, and it had been the source of a few heated arguments. But she liked the taste of it in my mouth.

I thought about the women I'd loved when I was a Christian. They'd taught me that my love was something to be had on the side—like an adjunct—how could any two women build anything together that wouldn't be eclipsed by a man, like a shadow in the doorway? Everything in that world had been about what God had destined us to: obedience to his Church, to those rule-making men who said that they were necessary in every sphere of life and we were not.

As I got closer to her, I felt all the blood rush to my cunt. I remembered reading Luce Irigaray, hidden behind a shelf in Barnes & Noble where no one could see me. She told me that my pussy was a thing with two walls that moved closer and farther apart from each other, like a dialogue. I drove faster, singing loud and hard to what came up through the shuffle of my playlist—the one about whether or not God had a face or a name.

I was hesitant about the whole Lesbian Festival thing. I knew about Michigan, the original women-only lesbian festival, but only through the testimonials of others. Cece had gone every summer for years, the years when I was in Steubenville. She talked about it as this beautiful, liberating part of her life where she got to be naked in the woods in a matriarchy. I'd read all the articles about the original festival dying because the cis women who ran it didn't want to let trans women on "the Land," as they called it. They'd decided to end it rather than let trans women participate.

I shifted in my seat thinking about the dykes who'd let that beautiful thing die because they didn't want to affirm that trans women were women, too. I felt like it was my body they were breaking in half, into acceptable and unacceptable parts, like straight culture had always been trying to do. The lesbians seemed to be mostly worried about *seeing* penises. "What if she'd had her penis removed?" I asked, but Cece was talking about all the women who'd had violent memories of penises.

"I don't love my memories of penises, either," I said, "but nor am I under the impression that people without penises won't cause me violence or harm. Which, by the way, is a pretty dangerous assumption, since lots of people without penises *do* cause all kinds of violence and harm to people with *and* without penises."

Cece and I fought in circles, but I'd had to reckon with the fact that not everyone who'd participated in Michigan *hated* trans women. Still, the whole subject made me realize that even within the safe harbor of queerness, there was sectarianism, prejudice, power-mongering, silencing, and the kicking to the curb of whoever ranked beneath the ones allowed to kick.

This festival in Ohio was supposed to be all inclusive. I tried to remember that that meant I was included, too. The farther out into the country I got, the more Trump stickers I saw. Google Maps said that the park hosting the festival was just ten miles off the highway. My chest tightened as I lit another cigarette, knowing that soon I'd be with her, and I'd have to see her look disappointed whenever I smoked.

I drove through a country neighborhood; the houses were all far apart and already had little fall decorations out front. One house was surrounded by pickup trucks and families eating off paper plates, standing in little groups and smiling. A family reunion or a birthday party, I thought, or someone's going to college. I thought about Bennington again and imagined what my life would've been like if I'd gone there. Looking at the kids running around in the grass and the old people in their lawn chairs, I wondered if the families without queers were more soluble than mine, if the gatherings went off without a hitch, or if everyone felt the years like an accumulation of absences and silences echoing against their bodies like the past was the clapper of a bell tolling between them.

I turned off past the family reunion, down a windy country road that made me sweat more than the sun did—and then I saw a long fence with a few RV rooftops and rainbow flags visible in the distance, if I strained to look.

The Christians had always said that life was so much easier out in the world, for gays and drug addicts and sinners—we were all just living it up, without a care in the world, screwing little screws into Jesus's wrists. I tried not to think about the seventy dollars left in my bank account after filling up my car with gas, and I tried not to think of the $250 a month that the government garnished from every paycheck, for the now illegal type of student loans I'd taken out when I was eighteen, for Jesus.

I could never shake the feeling that God and Jesus and Mary and all the saints were watching me all the time, and everybody else, too, like *The Truman Show*. It was hard to believe nobody was watching.

There was no big sign that said LESBIAN FESTIVAL! Maybe so we'd be safe from people who might want to hurt us. There was a sign with the name of the park on it, and I turned onto a dusty dirt road. A woman wearing a cowboy hat, cutoff jean shorts, an unbuttoned vest, and a scarf that just barely covered her breasts bent down toward my car. I noticed her tits droop downward toward me, and she smiled a wide grin.

"You know where you're going?" she asked.

Then I saw Cece, in a yellow sundress, approaching my car. She smiled bigger than the fights we'd had, and I smiled back bigger than how angry we'd been and all the ways we were so different.

Cowboy Hat Tits grinned at me like she knew something. She pointed wordlessly toward a temporary white awning set up over two long folding tables and slapped the roof of my car as though it were a horse's ass, and I gave the gas a tap. I parked by the ticket table and got out of the car. Cece came up and laid her head on my shoulder, and I wrapped my arms around her.

"Kiss her! Kiss her!" someone was saying. We looked up and laughed, and a golf cart whizzed by, driven by an old-school butch in her fifties. The woman shouting at us to kiss was her passenger, a luxurious Latina woman wearing a turquoise dress. They both cackled joyfully.

I kissed Cece, her fingers resting on my hips, and she pressed into me.

"Let's get your ticket sorted and I can show you around," she said.

I felt a little pang of suspicion as I picked up my ticket. Were trans women really welcome here?

I'd never been to Michigan, but it had become a ghost of another thing I could never do—maybe because I was more trans than not, or maybe because the older generation of dykes had done what all the male institutions I'd ever known had done: they'd rejected their chance at evolving in favor of keeping things the same. Lisa Vogel, feminist hero and founder of Michigan, and the AFABs in charge of the festival couldn't wrap their minds around trans woman-hood. They got bogged down in hypotheticals that made no sense. Instead of rising to the challenge, they killed the thing they'd created, the harbor where Cece and many others had found refuge and found themselves.

There was no escaping this conversation about who was what, and who was using their for power right or wrong, and when to stand up against it or not. Sometimes I felt just as scared to say the wrong thing in a posse of liberal queers as I had back with the Christians, except that Christians called "canceling" "excommunication," and they were *much* better at it than liberals were.

When Trump got elected, we—the four eldest siblings—sequestered ourselves at Thanks-Taking, to sit in my grand-mother's bedroom. We had all just looked at each other and shuffled upstairs, through the old colonial house we'd all thought was a mansion when we were kids. Our grandmother's bedroom was decorated in light oceanic colors, reminiscent of a room in the Cayman house. Marianne and I sat on her bed, Lily on the floor, and Jimmy in the rocking chair, holding his three-month-old baby.

"This is fucking scary," he said, tapping the baby's back lightly.

"What the fuck? I didn't know it was so hateful out there," Marianne said.

"They've always wanted to kill us," Lily said. She was nonbinary, too, and looked like me. "Every period of history," she said to me, her eyes clear and sober and deep blue, "they've always wanted to kill us. Nothing's different."

We were all quiet for a few seconds, till the baby started fussing. Jimmy bounced her, and I held my arms out.

"Here, Uncle Becca," he said, handing me the little one, who didn't know anything was wrong yet, whose gender and heart and destiny were still a mystery. She smiled up at me.

"Look," I said to Lily. "She's happy. Her world will be better than ours, I think."

Lily looked back at me like kids on TV looked at their parents when they were saying something ridiculous.

"Okayyyy, Uncle Becca," she said sarcastically, "I'll try to have faith in humanity or whatever."

"Just a little," I said, and sang a few lines from "Put a Little Love in Your Heart." Lily rolled her eyes, but she smiled.

Cece walked, swinging her hips playfully, twenty feet in front of my car as I drove at a snail's pace toward the parking area. She looked at me flirtatiously. I'd had to stop caring how I looked in order to look like myself, and now it amazed me that anyone thought I was desirable, but she made me feel like I was on the cover of the "Most Beautiful People" magazine.

When we'd broken up the week before the festival, I'd missed her and the way she looked at me, even through the phone, from all the way in New York City. I'd decided that I wanted what I wanted, and that what I wanted was her. I'd tried to use the language that she initiated—"I care about you," I said, "and I... I like caring about you, and..."—but we were on Google Hangouts instead of WhatsApp, and the audio was shaky, and she hadn't heard me.

"What? I'm sorry, I didn't hear you," she said, looking apologetic, because she knew how much it sucked to try to say these things over video.

"I said I love you!" I half yelled, and she knew I hadn't said that, but she smiled, and I continued: "And I like loving you, and I want to keep loving you!" I said it loud, so she wouldn't mistake the emotion that made my voice waver for hesitancy.

She had just looked surprised and smiled, with her eyelashes somehow deep and part of the smile like a wave is part of the shore, coming and going all the time. She liked to talk about things more than most people, except the things she didn't want to talk about, which she didn't want to talk about more than most people. I knew she wasn't going to say she loved me back, but I was still trying to figure out if it was because she didn't love me or because she just couldn't say it.

After I parked, we walked toward the edge of the woods, and an opening became visible in the line of trees that I hadn't noticed until we were a few feet away from it. Small wooden signs hung in the trees declaring this LESBIAN SPACE, ALL WOMXN WELCOME, and made some use of the word "Amazon" that made me wrinkle my nose and want to explain racism to someone. Already I had seen women of all colors, which had surprised me. I tried to let go of my political vigilance, the familiar taste of my privilege lingering in my mouth.

Cece led me along a dirt path, and we passed all manner of lesbians in various states of dress and undress. A naked woman wearing a tool belt tended a George Foreman Grill, while a butch spread peanut butter or jelly on a sandwich for a small child waiting nearby, wearing rainbow fairy wings and red cowboy boots, flexing and unflexing her knee back and forth in a sign of universal childhood impatience. Another child tugged at the butch's arm, and the butch just kept making the sandwich—no patience like a butch's patience.

Cece held my hand, and I felt like I didn't need to be anywhere else. She had a little two-person tent, where I put my bags and got out my pot. We'd fought about how much I smoked, though she was never bothered by my behavior or ability to listen or pay attention to her, just the fact that I was smoking pot while I was doing it. But this time she didn't make a face when I got it out.

Amid a little circle of tents, there was a canopy set up with a living room underneath, complete with outdoor rugs, a coffee table of some sort covered in fabric, an air mattress set up as a sofa, and an assemblage of other furniture. A series of tables set up nearby served as a kitchen area. There was a topless soft butch cooking something with her back to us.

"Amy," Cece said, "this is Becca. She came!"

"Hey, man!" Amy said, turning and waving. She was nerdy, with big glasses like mine, and I said hi nervously back, a little like I was on the playground at some weird new school where there were other kids like me and our genders weren't hidden.

I sat on the "love seat," a double fold-up chair, hoping Cece would sit next to me. I tried to look relaxed. A short-haired femme appeared from a tent in mechanic coveralls open to her belly button, with a red scarf tied around her neck. She moved fast and cornered Cece in the "kitchen," where they talked quietly, and I could see Cece's face telling the other woman to stop asking whatever she was asking. I figured it was about me, the way Cece kept trying to shush her and the way she blushed a little and smiled about something, too. All of a sudden the new woman turned around sharply to look at me, playing with a long, feathery earring she wore in one ear.

"What do *you* think?" she said, walking through the kitchen and around the air mattress sofa, extending her hand to me. "I'm Rae."

"I've been documenting Rae's ass," Cece said, sitting down next to me and swinging her legs onto my lap. "Lemme see," she said to Rae.

Rae turned around and stuck her ass out. It wasn't particularly pronounced in the coveralls, but Cece took a picture for her series. Cece started stroking the back of my neck with her fingers, and I put my hand on her thigh, as Rae talked about her wardrobe choices for the night. Amy was sitting, too, now, loading a pipe.

"Baby," Rae said to Amy, "you've gotta get dressed."

"I know, I just wanna smoke a little first. Are you sure you won't have any?"

Rae said something in Hebrew that I didn't understand, but I recognized a thing I was very familiar with: Rae wasn't smoking for religious reasons. I knew Rosh Hashanah was coming, and I knew Judaism included as much fasting as Catholicism, and that Catholicism was just some weird bastard kid of Judaism who'd grown up homicidal and full of empire.

"I want to," Rae said longingly, in a way I also recognized: the playful tease of the faster, who didn't want to be good but who was being good anyway. There was something in that old book about not letting people know you were fasting, or not telling your left hand what your right hand was doing, but I wasn't sure which part of the book it was from, mine or hers.

"You're a good person," Amy said consolingly, as she lit the bowl.

I gestured toward the two little jars of weed I'd brought. "I brought these," I said, embarrassed that it wasn't more. "That little one is good weed. The one with more in it is shitty weed, for mixing or whatever."

Amy nodded appreciatively, trying to hold her toke. She offered Cece the pipe, but Cece shook her head and pointed to me, and Amy extended it, smiling as she released a puff of thick smoke in my face. Rae sniffed it dramatically, then looked over at me, zeroing in on my chest.

"I like your 'Holy,'" she said, pointing to me. "Is that 'Holy, Holy, Holy,' three times?"

I nodded, holding smoke in my lungs like I used to hold words there.

"What's that from?" she asked, more like she was quizzing me than asking me.

"A lot of stuff," I said, exhaling. "Allen Ginsberg..."

"'Holy,' three times?" Rae said, like she was surprised. "Three times?"

"Well, he says it a lot more than that in the poem... in 'Howl'..."

"It's from the Kedushah," she said. "The holy of Heaven, of earth, and of God's work, between the worlds. Or the holiness of Heaven, where the angels are, and space, where the stars are, and the holiness of earth, where we are."

"Wow," I said, knowing I'd go over what she said in my mind later. "It's also from Catholic Mass, too. Which, I mean, is all from Judaism... We also say 'Holy' three times."

Rae nodded, looking me up and down. "Catholicism, huh? Are you still religious?" she asked.

I never knew how to answer this question. "It's complicated," I said.

"I guess so." She laughed.

"It's not perfect," I said, "but it's mine." She looked like she wanted to hear more, so I kept talking even though it was hard. "I think of it like a language—for the universe, for the mysteries. It's the one I speak most fluently, anyway. But I don't *attend*. I mean, they don't acknowledge my moral authority, and I don't acknowledge theirs. So, we're at an impasse." I laughed, getting self-conscious; I might've said more than she'd wanted to hear. I got out my cigarettes.

"You sound a little Jewish," she said.

"Well, I'm nonbinary," I said, and everyone laughed.

Rae turned toward the periphery of our little circle and grinned. A golf cart sped up next to the minivan and stopped suddenly with a little lurch. I spotted the fifty-something butch who'd been driving around the Latina goddess in the turquoise dress. The butch wore denim cargo shorts, a black t-shirt, and what seemed to be a fishing vest with sundry patches and pins instead of lures or war medals. She was medium height and chubby, and she disembarked from the golf cart with a mischievous grin and a bag of weed in her hand.

"Ziggy!" Cece said cheerfully. "Are you done with your shift?"

Everyone laughed.

"Are you done with your shift, Daddy?" Rae asked, and Ziggy shook her finger playfully.

"I got Angelita's weed, but it's only for good lesbians."

"Oh, I'm a good lesbian," I said, raising my hand.

"Yes, you are," Cece confirmed, and everyone whistled or made those other sounds men usually made, which usually sounded scary but not now. Two more women in their fifties or sixties appeared. One wore her hair in a short, military-style buzz cut and had on a pink bra with fur fringe and capri cargo pants, and the other was a near-miss for Steven Tyler, never without an aura of dazed confusion, wearing black jeans and a black denim jacket and with a mop of fried salt-and-pepper curly hair held up by a tired scarf.

"Jill! Myra!"

People were calling out and greeting each other like they'd all been to the same slumber party for several nights in a row (which, I realized, they had).

Cece kissed my neck, behind my ear. Her thigh was still in my lap, under my fingers. Ziggy handed me a big glass bowl full of fresh, sappy, expensive weed; the little crystals on the bud were visible, I didn't need a magnifying glass to see them. With one hand gripping Cece's thigh, I thanked Ziggy, lit the bowl I held with my mouth, and inhaled my tangible good fortune. Maybe I was in Wonderland.

Cece traced the hairline on the back of my neck with her fingers, and I watched the women passing the pipe around the semicircle. She hated pot smoking, but not here, not today. I offered my two kinds of weed again. Jill smiled down at me from the air mattress, like the Cheshire cat. She reminded me of an elementary school teacher, whose secret out-of-school life I was witnessing.

"Take this," she said of my weed, "and put it back in your little bag, baby. We do not need any shitty weed this week. We don't have to live like that anymore. You help yourself to whatever's on the table, that's the communal pot." Here she guffawed and slapped Myra on the chest. "Get it, the communal pot?"

"There's nothing to get, honey," Myra groaned, straight-faced.

"Get me a light or you're not getting *any*," Jill said, passing the pipe back to Ziggy, who smirked and whistled through her teeth gleefully, as her smirk waterfalled into a chuckle. Jill lit a cigarette. "It's almost time for Lisa!" she said, grinning now like a schoolgirl.

Everyone talked excitedly about how Lisa Vogel was going to be on the stage that evening before the music. They called the feminist legend LV, like they knew her, and I realized that maybe they did. I hadn't known she'd be here this weekend—Cece had left that part out of her invite. Where did all my new friends stand in the conversation? Had they been at Michigan and kept trans women out? Did it matter, here and now, as I smoked with them and drank a beer? Cece knew I was getting worried about it, and she squeezed my hand.

"What time's LV go on?" Myra asked.

"Six," Ziggy answered, packing her bowl again. "We have twenty-five minutes."

"Wanna walk around a little?" Cece asked. I did. When we were a few steps away from the "living room," she said, "I'd like to hear Lisa Vogel... I wonder if she's gonna bring up why Michigan ended... I mean, this festival is supposed to include everyone, and yet they have her as a speaker... People keep calling this 'the Land,' like Michigan could just be anywhere. I dunno if I like it or not."

The festival was set up like any other, with tents and booths full of merch to buy and people happily milling. Queers everywhere, their kids running amok. Tits everywhere. Hair of every shape and size. The freaks outnumbered the normies, but even the normies were getting their freak on a little. There were so many rainbows, it was like we were one big rainbow, hidden off in that little park in Ohio. I thought about how I couldn't see any of it from the road. I thought about that poem Dr. Madison and I loved:

So be it when I shall grow old,
Or let me die!
The Child is father of the Man…"

Whatever Mom had tried to protect me from, and whatever my dad tried to do to me, and whatever everyone else had done, too—none of it could match the volume of my voice inside myself, for better or worse, and the voice inside me was made up as much of our whole culture as it was of the particular people I was made of.

In 2000, a news show did an episode on Brandon Teena. I forgot it for years, until I stumbled across it one day on YouTube and remembered watching it for the first time at sixteen, sitting in the living room. When Mom turned the TV on, I started to get up to read elsewhere, but stopped when I heard the words: *"The woman, Teena Brandon, who had been living as a man…"*

I looked over at the TV and saw Brandon's face smiling back at me from one of those school pictures that had the weird neon background Mom would never let me get. A boy wearing a turtleneck and a big poofy winter sweater, grinning and young and still soft. There was a second picture of him in the hallway with another boy his age. *What did they mean*, I thought, *"posed as a boy"*?

I'd read about women who dressed or lived as men in "the olden days," who wanted to be soldiers or doctors or rabbis, like Yentl. But this wasn't hundreds of years ago, it was now. This wasn't about being allowed to go to college to be a doctor or something. My hand shook, and I lost my place in the book. If I kept standing there, would Mom realize why I was watching this show so intently? But I looked over, and she was watching intently, too, and glanced at me with the same worried expression I had. We both turned back to the TV, hoping the other didn't know what we were thinking, when we did.

They kept saying "he," "he," "he," the people who knew him. If they said "he," then wasn't he a boy? I was confused.

"Is that a boy or a girl?" I asked my mom.

"She was born a girl, but she lived as a boy," Mom said, bouncing Todd on her lap.

"Why, though?" I asked, confused.

"I don't know," Mom said. "You have to watch."

A bunch of women talked on the screen. They said "he" mostly—"*He* was such a great kisser." I wondered if my mom could tell what I was thinking. A few of the girls seemed disgusted that they'd kissed Brandon, and I felt my blood turn a little, the turn of a wonderful kiss into something else, just like that. They kept saying "sex change," and I really wasn't sure what that meant.

"What's a sex change?" I asked my mom. She was burping the baby.

"I'll tell you at the commercial," she said, but Todd started fussing, and she never told me.

The women on TV were saying "faggot," "dyke," "lesbo," "freak." I blushed and looked over at my mom, but she was smiling at the baby, then back at me, like nothing was happening.

"Falls City is a white community," a harsh-sounding woman was saying, and I wondered what being white had to do with it. "We may have had one or two families up here who were Black," she continued, "but as far as having gay people come in, Falls City would, I'm sure, escort 'em outta town."

I knew exactly why Brandon left home as a boy. To kiss girls. I was the only lesbian I knew, so I thought all lesbians must be butch or pretending not to be. How did you get to kiss femmes if they didn't think you were a boy? It always made me think of the Chelsea Hotel song, about making an exception.

Soon enough a man was saying that everyone who loved Brandon was brainwashed, lied to by this twenty-year-old genius manipulator. The lilt of his voice and his tone of ignorant arrogance reminded me of my dad.

"Them kinda people have AIDS," a woman said. "It was evil... knowing somebody could get into your mind like that and manipulate you like that, making you think a totally different thing than what was true."

Christmas music played while the voice-over described the beating and the rape Brandon survived a week before his murder. "O Holy Night" played as somebody said that the rapists' friends had made fun of them for raping Brandon, that people had called them faggots. That's why they had to kill him. He'd turned them into faggots, and they hated how it felt, to be a faggot. A week later, they killed him and his friends, an interracial couple, Phillip DeVine and Lisa Lambert, who were sheltering Brandon, who also fit into the category of sexual transgressors—people who, it was written somewhere, should be killed for doing what we did.

A man in a rural backyard drinking a Pepsi—the sheriff, who spoke with a voice like my dad's—not an accent, but a voice—explained that if we locked up everyone who had raped and killed people like Brandon, who had done what Brandon had done, "We'd have a lot more people locked up."

Now I was safe, though, supposedly, surrounded by people like me. If there were enough of us, were we safe? To move through the world, hardly ever seeing yourself reflected back anywhere, and then to be in a place where it happens so many times you stop noticing—I felt like I had been wearing armor and had taken it off. I wasn't used to a circle this big around me of people who didn't think I was weird or who I didn't have to be a little afraid of. I hadn't realized how much I felt it in my body.

When we sat down to listen to LV, I got nervous. There were chairs and a blanket all set up, and Myra and Jill were already there, passing around a joint. I wasn't sure what the laws about marijuana in Ohio were, but it felt like it didn't matter.

On the stage, there were two living room chairs, and a butch lesbian was introducing LV. LV was full of platitudes and anecdotes, and the crowd of dykes stretched out in the field, on lawn chairs and on quilts, holding babies and each other, and smoking weed but not cigarettes, laughed and clapped and reacted like a gymnasium of Franciscan students hearing about Jesus.

My heart got a little tight. This was supposed to be the place I fit in, but did I? LV talked about a controversy she'd faced in Michigan—not the one we'd all heard of. She wanted to tell us about the negotiations between the BDSM lesbians and the Wonder Bread family lesbians, who'd brought their kids to the Land and didn't want to walk up on a three-way spank fest with their toddlers in tow. It felt like Jesus was up there, but he was talking about the time John and Lazarus couldn't agree on a hymn, not why he'd decided to turn over the tables in the temple.

LV didn't mention why the festival didn't exist anymore; she just accepted the accolades and smiled big, waving as everyone cheered. Later, I found out there was a small group of protesters in the front row, who I couldn't see from my blanket. They'd held up signs that the audience couldn't see but LV could. She'd ignored them the whole time, smiled and laughed through it.

All our mothers had laughed through what they could, because maybe after a certain point, people just couldn't hold any more contradictions and gave up trying. Everyone loved LV for creating this thing, but she'd rather see it die than stand up for trans women, trans dykes, and nonbinary people to exist in it—not like my mother.

There was nothing about her children's identities, and nothing we could say or do, that would prevent my mom from welcoming us back into her house. Not like a church or a queer festival. Real God and Love, too, I knew, must be more like the mother who stretches her mind around queerness and polyamory and all the limits of gender, and keeps inviting the children back who've hurt her or done what she never would have—a mom who believes in Love.

My mom had made our family, and my family was my church. That's where I pilgrimaged for the high holidays. I weighed my heart and mind against theirs, and returned to them again and again for rituals, for remembering, for watching movies together like other people read psalms. There we weren't having a conversation, we *were* the conversation, we were a text about the world, and right and wrong, and what love is. I am limited, I know, because they showed me with their faces, looking back at me as I broke down over years and years, until I figured out how to heal myself.

I'd texted my mom where I was, because we texted every day. I knew she'd never be in a place like this—nor any of my siblings, probably—but she sent me back a bunch of high-five emojis and hearts.

As we walked around the festival and I thought about how everyone had cheered for LV, I couldn't shake the memory of the homeschooler and the zealots at Franciscan. Absent the tits on display, the rainbows, and the sex toys, and absent the absence of men, this could very well be a convergence of homeschooling families. The mood was the same. Everyone smiled like they were only among friends, like we all thought the same thing, like we were free. I didn't like the idea that the freedom depended on sameness.

That night, everyone walked around with wide, flirtatious grins or linked in arms like high schoolers away from their parents for the first time. Cece and I never stopped touching.

Cece was calmer here, with no work and no dog and no people in the street to worry about. The world was somewhere else, and we were here, set apart, and here everything was easier for some reason. I wished we could stay here forever, like the homeschoolers, and I thought if I had kids, I'd want to take them away and try to protect them from everything I was scared of, too. Only I would know, from watching my mom, that it was impossible—there was no place far enough or wall or subculture tightly built enough to withstand the ocean of everybody else. There was no controlling seeds or wind or water, or anybody's hearts. I wouldn't make the same mistakes she did; I'd make new, different ones.

At the end of the night, Cece took her clothes off and got into the tent. She'd developed a love for walking around naked on the Land in Michigan, and I loved that she could do that, like she could fly. I stripped down to my underwear and took off my sports bra as nonchalantly as I could and got into the tent fast.

When I laid down, I thought of all those times I laid next to a girl in college, not knowing what might happen. Cece leaned over to whisper something in my ear, and I kissed her, as softly as I could at first, and then hard, when she pulled me on top of her, and for a little while it felt like we could lift off, away from the hard journeys we'd each traveled to get to this little tent outside Cincinnati, in this field full of lesbians.

That night when I had to pee, I got out of the tent naked and walked to the line of blue portable toilets in just my flip-flops. People were still awake, though now that it was the middle of the night, they were mostly sitting around fires or walking fast toward somewhere in twos or threes. Still, I passed people naked.

I didn't know why I wasn't afraid anymore, but I thought I might have absorbed something from her skin or from the ground. Was the idea really poetic, or was that some residue of religious thinking that I should shake off?

The next day, we walked around the festival smiling sweetly at each other like we'd never fought. The things that came between us were all outside and far away. During breakfast, everyone talked about Ferron and how she was going on that afternoon. I was the only one of my generation who knew who she was. As we meandered around the festival, Ferron did her soundcheck and played the old song I used to listen to when I first moved away from Steubenville, the one about life being a brook, the first song of Ferron's Sara had ever played for me. I wondered why Sara knew about Ferron, the butch folk singer, when hardly any lesbians I knew had heard of her. But now here was the real Ferron, just twenty feet away from me, singing about how the brook kept going, kept changing, and kept changing you. I stood still to listen.

Maybe that's one of the things that helped people like us survive and be out—it didn't feel like bravery, which some people said it was. Most of the time it felt like blind faith—faith that today the better angels would win, and if someone did hate me, they wouldn't hurt me. Every day I had to believe it wouldn't be *that* day, and that maybe the hate was draining out of people, a little at a time. Maybe if I kept waking up and getting dressed, eventually I'd be old and die some very normal, boring way.

I knew Cece probably wasn't "the one" I'd end up with, if I was lucky enough for such a thing, but I didn't want to let go of her yet. I kissed her whenever I could. At the same time, I knew I'd fought so long and so hard to be able to love like Ferron was singing about, like these kids were dancing inside of—the love that created life and art and transition. That's what I believed in, I realized, or I'd never have sacrificed so much just for the chance of it.

Love was always singing that song by Abba about waiting for us to change our minds, and take a chance.

44 Don't Rain On My Parade

2020. Last night I dreamed of Steubenville, as I often do. I'm wandering around campus, trying to find a parking spot, then trying to find a classroom. There's swarming students everywhere. In my dream, the buildings are different, and I don't recognize anyone or know where I'm going, but something about the dream is so much like being there that I wake up relieved.

My apartment smells like grilled beef and a man's after-shave, even at five in the morning, even though I don't use after shave and I don't eat meat. The scent is the ghost of the man who used to be here, the last tenant trying to get their life together in this tiny studio. I grind coffee beans, boil water, and stretch my back using the forty-five-degree slant in my kitchen-area ceiling. My back holds my trauma like a vault, but I've learned how to relax it every morning by stretching, how to comfort the parts of me that hang on to the past.

I remember that I wasn't supposed to get out at all, that my adulthood was purchased and won by whatever resilience I managed to clutch on to—the stubbornness that insisted that everyone else should change, that the world should change, not me. And it did.

On the shelf there's a stack of ten or eleven manuscripts, very-nearly-published: books of poetry, most of the poems in them published in literary journals. I tell my mom I'm not the Tom Cruise of contemporary poetry, but maybe I'm a Sam Rockwell or a Steve Buscemi.

I sit back in the chair Leslie left with me when she moved back to California. On Instagram I see a picture of her and her wife and their kids, and I smile triumphantly: we survived, and Leslie made people, people who would grow up with queer parents and think people like us were perfectly normal—or at least as not-normal as anyone else.

The coffee is thick and strong, and I am thick, and strong, and alive.

To look like a teacher, I stand at my tiny bathroom sink for a half hour, brushing and flossing, shaving the hair that grows naturally all over my chin like I'm a thirteen-year-old boy. Sometimes I leave a five-o'clock shadow, but only if I'm in a good mood and I know it won't bug me if someone insults me, or if I'm sleeping with someone who asks me not to shave. I put eye drops in my eyes, to hydrate the red lines that come from pot, lack of sleep, and too much coffee.

I run hot water over my hair, bent over the bathtub like I'm bowing down to an old god. When we started dating and Cece asked me if I believed in God, I said, "I believe in metaphors." I believe in stories and the power they have over us, how they change our lives and how we choose our roles and change the narratives and break open languages to include more people. You can do the opposite, too, with silence and gaslit language that erases what's true, what really happened.

The hot water runs through my swath of auburn hair and over the buzzed, prickly parts. I scrub myself clean, a baptism I can do myself. I clean my hairy armpits, wash my face, and arrange my hair in the mirror with my hand. I put on a sports bra, and since I'm poor and skinny and my tits are small, I look more like I have big pecs once I put on a black or gray "wifebeater" tank top. I try to remember what else it's called, but I can only remember "wifebeater."

I close my eyes for a second, like I let myself do sometimes, and imagine getting top surgery. Someday I would figure it out. It would become more available, and I would sell my book or get a better job. I remember reading about the woman warriors in Herodotus, the ones the colonizers named the Amazon River after because the Indigenous warriors who attacked them were either women or men who had no beards, who looked like women to them. When I read about the women in Herodotus, the Greek warriors who chopped off one breast, I thought, as a kid, *Just one?* But it settled deep in my imagination, something to be dug up later and remembered like an artifact, evidence that I have always been who I am.

I should put that in the book, I think, trying to remember where my list of things to put in the book is, and knowing there is always too much.

I find a pair of dark jeans with a brown leather belt already strung through them, and Scrappy wakes up and shakes his tail back and forth like a hummingbird's wings. He stretches, and I scrape the last of some wet food from a can for him.

After grabbing a plaid button-down shirt, a tie and a vest that don't entirely *not* match each other, I collect my phone, wallet, keys, cigarettes, vape pen, dog, leash, book bag, and, finally, myself.

Leaving my building, I put on my headphones, turn on the Bluetooth, and I can hear the last thing I was watching on my phone: an Instagram video of people in a subway station singing "My Heart Will Go On" after a Celine Dion concert. I couldn't stop watching it. Strangers singing loud, in full voices, all together. The song was impossible not to know when I was a young teenager and too embarrassed to sing it. Some people in the background of the video were a little unnerved; others were bewitched, charmed. But a whole crowd of people were singing their hearts out, just like the words said, with stubborn, ship-nosed hearts, built to plow through oceans. It was impossible that they were just naive, that they hadn't been heartbroken, that none of them had suffered something that would've made plenty of people cynical.

When they sang that song we all know the words to, their love showed. They kept falling in love, in spite of all the reasons not to. It meant something about the capacity of hearts to keep beating, to keep running, to keep falling into each other. Their hearts *were* going on and on. Everybody's does. The "you" in all the love songs, good and bad, wasn't a person, it was Love, returning when you least expected it. Nobody could shake it, and sometimes there was nothing to do but sing about it.

A lot of people say that life isn't a musical, but they just aren't listening.

As I walk through a hall of the school where I've taught for almost ten years, I see a picture of one of my first students, under a banner that says MEET OUR NEW ADJUNCT FACULTY. A pang goes through my heart and stomach, and I hope he has enough gigs to get by and wish he'd done anything but follow in my footsteps—until I think of him teaching and know it's right. I remember when he said, "I thought gay people were bad until I took your class." It was James Baldwin, not me, who'd changed his mind. I think of him, a football star, a poet, a strikingly tall, beautiful Black man, now another safe harbor for the students who will need one, like Matilda was for me, and somebody I don't know the name of might've been for her.

In the fall, students are randomly assigned to my class, and I have to worry about winning them over. But it's the first day of spring semester, and I know that the majority of my students this semester will be students who took my

class in the fall and chose to take me again in the spring—
they already like me. I don't have to wonder if I make them
uncomfortable, or if they grew up in houses where people
like me were erased, or belittled, or worse. If they did, it
didn't work. As I get closer to the door, I stand up a little
straighter and prepare myself to be the teacher, to be serious,
to scare them a little into listening to me.

As I enter the classroom, they burst into spontaneous
applause and cheers and call out my name.

Musical Numbers

1. "Hurricane" from *Hamilton*
2. "Tradition" from *Fiddler on the Roof*
3. "You're Never Fully Dressed Without A Smile" from *Annie*
4. "There's No Business Like Show Business" from *Annie Get Your Gun*
5. "Ya Got Trouble" from *The Music Man*
6. "Every Day a Little Death" from *A Little Night Music*
7. "Giants in the Sky" from *Into the Woods*
8. "Wicked Little Town" from *Hedwig and the Angry Inch*
9. "Unworthy of Your Love" from *Assassins*
10. "Sixteen Going on Seventeen" from *The Sound of Music*
11. "I Cain't Say No" from *Oklahoma!*
12. "Sit Down, You're Rocking the Boat" from *Guys and Dolls*
13. "I Know Things Now" from *Into the Woods*
14. "For Forever" from *Dear Evan Hansen*
15. "Willkomen" from *Cabaret*
16. "One" from *A Chorus Line*
17. "If I Were a Bell" from *Guys and Dolls*
18. "Stars" from *Les Misérables*
19. "Somewhere" from *West Side Story*
20. "Could We Start Again, Please?" from *Jesus Christ Superstar*
21. "There's Always a Woman" from *Anyone Can Whistle*
22. "Razzle Dazzle" from *Chicago*
23. "I Had Myself a True Love" from *St. Louis Woman*
24. "Truly Scrumptious" from *Chitty Chitty Bang Bang*
25. "My Favorite Things" from *The Sound of Music*
26. "I've Got Your Number" from *Little Me*
27. "Pick-A-Little-Talk-A-Little / Goodnight Ladies" from *The Music Man*
28. "I Know About Love" from *Do Re Mi*

29. "Smoke Gets in Your Eyes" from *Roberta*
30. "I Hid My Love" by John Clare, set to music by Steve Marzullo
31. "Too Darn Hot" from *Kiss Me, Kate*
32. "People Will Say We're in Love" from *Oklahoma!*
33. "Nothing" from *A Chorus Line*
34. "There's Gotta Be Something Better Than This" from *Sweet Charity*
35. "It's Hot Up Here" from *Sunday in the Park with George*
36. "What Would I Do if I Could Feel?" from *The Wiz*
37. "Skid Row (Downtown)" from *Little Shop of Horrors*
38. "Feeling Good" from *The Roar of the Greasepaint—the Smell of the Crowd*
39. "You Can't Get to Heaven" from *The Life*
40. "We Do Not Belong Together" from *Sunday in the Park with George*
41. "Defying Gravity" from *Wicked*
42. "The Flesh Failures/Let the Sun Shine In" from *Hair*
43. "You Can't Stop the Beat" from *Hairspray*
44. "Don't Rain on My Parade" from *Funny Girl*

Credits

THANK YOU to everyone who kept me alive throughout what seemed like the endless writing of this book. Whenever I try to write these thank yous, I get overwhelmed and know that no words can really do justice to the complexity of survival and change and relationship. I am grateful to everyone living who was in this book who was kind to me, even if they weren't kind, too. I have of course not portrayed myself in the worst light I could have, and for this I ask everyone's understanding.

Thank you specifically, particularly, to my Mom and Bob for loving me, nurturing me, being weird, and making my favorite people. Thanks forever to each of my siblings, who have kept me wanting to stay alive throughout the events of this book. Watching you become yourselves has been the best movie of my life, and you're all my heroes.

Thank you to Mary Elizabeth Bourke for being yourself, for marrying me, for the stars and the moon. I would not trade one second of this life that ends up with us together.

Thank you to my grandparents, Jim and Peggy, who were my playmates, actors in plays I directed, and summer camp counselors on the best of days. I am besotted with both of you, all days.

Thank you to Holly, who never made me feel wrong. I would not have made it through without you. Thank you, too, to Eric, Juliana, Andrew, and Sage Mohr, who love Holly as much as I do and who will be my friends forever.

Thank you to Ruth and Nihon, who will always be my neighbors and best friends.

Thank you to Marshall Botvinick for that thing it took me twenty years to learn: that God wouldn't want anyone to kill me. And thank you for endlessly making me laugh.

Thank you to Daniel Forsythe for writing to me, for teaching me about priesthood, for coming out with me.

Thank you to Kari for making me feel like I finally had a friend like the people in books did. Thank you to Kate, Eleanor, Deanna, Tim, Walker, Cheryl, Loretta, & Pete for being my friends.

Thank you to Matt O'Brien for teaching me history and kindness, to Matt and Gina for trusting me with the most important work, and to Thomas for letting me read to him and to Julia for making me laugh with the truth.

Thank you to Patricia, for forever. I cannot imagine how I could've found myself without you there. I cannot write enough books to explain how you reached back for me. You could've answered my questions, but instead you taught me how to get answers myself, how to answer for myself, to myself.

Thank you to Lindsey Ingram for her incredible insights and reading. Thank you to Sarah Bowlin and Danielle Bukowski for their encouragement and formative work on this book. Thank you to Anna and Karen Knutson and Mishel Brown for loving this book.

Thank you to Alexis Gannon for believing in me, for feeding me, for sitting with me, for hours and years.

Thank you to Teekie Smith for betting on me and for being my best man.

Thank you to Kit Ford for the prophecy.

Thank you to every student I've ever had, especially Brandon, Ray, Shaniqkua, Destiny, Randall, Lauren, Austin, Jessica, Mariana, Caitlyn, Ethan, Sam, James, Tamika, Stormie Brice, Henry Yates, and Cisco—and so many others: yes, you.

Thank you to my therapist for reminding me about musicals and myself. You're the superhero in my imagination, wearing a cape and flying into my brain like Superman just in time to block me from the cliff.

Thank you to my therapists in the IOP program, who made me laugh even while I (literally) wanted to kill myself.

Thank you to my writing teachers: Cheryl Shoots, who always encouraged me, and Toi Derricotte, for teaching me that writing is like driving at night and being able to see only a few feet in front of you, but knowing the road is there. Thank you to Dawn Lundy Martin for being tough on me and so generous. Thank you forever to Stephanie K. Hopkins for reading this book and for telling me to keep going. You are an amazing writing teacher, and I am forever in your debt. Thank you to Kristin Dombek for her essay "The Two Cultures of Life." Thank you to Eileen Myles for their poems, especially the one about the leash and the movies, and for writing me back. My first favorite poet was Stephen Sondheim, and I thank him for all his work, forever. Plenty of us still wear hats.

Thank you to Kelsey, Chris, and Olivia at Unnamed Press for giving this book the hope/home it desperately needed. I am so grateful to you, Chris/"Max" for your understanding, enthusiasm, giggles, insights and hard work on this book. As my grandpa would say: "God damn. Jesus Christ."

About the Author

R/B Mertz (thee/thou) is a genderqueer non-binary butch poet and artist. They wrote the essay, "How Whiteness Kills God & Sprinkles Crack on the Body," the forward for John J. McNeill's *Freedom, Glorious Freedom: The Spiritual Journey for Gays, Lesbians, and Everyone Else*, and poems, including "*(We all end up in) the CAN*" published by American Journal of Poetry. Mertz taught writing in Pittsburgh for eleven years and was honored to be a finalist for City of Asylum's 2020-21 Emerging Poet Laureate of Pittsburgh. On January 1, 2021, Mertz left the US for love, and they now reside in Toronto, Ontario, traditionally the territory of many nations including the Mississaugas of the Credit, the Anishnabeg, the Chippewa, the Haudenosaunee, and the Wendat peoples.